*f*P

....For Rabbit,

..............................and

with Love.....
Squalor...........

An American Read

Anne Roiphe

The Free Press

New York   London   Toronto   Sydney   Singapore

ƒP
THE FREE PRESS
A Division of Simon & Schuster, Inc.
1230 Avenue of the Americas
New York, NY 10020

THE FREE PRESS and colophon are trademarks
of Simon & Schuster, Inc.

Designed by Karolina Harris

Manufactured in the United States of America

10 9 8 7 6 5 4 3 2 1

Library of Congress Cataloging-in-Publication Data

Roiphe, Anne Richardson.
    For Rabbit, with love and squalor : an American read / Anne Roiphe.
        p. cm.
    1. Roiphe, Anne Richardson—Books and reading. 2. American
    fiction—20th century—History and criticism. 3. Novelists,
    American—20th century—Biography. 4. Men in literature. I. Title.

PS3568.O53 Z47 2000
813'.54—dc21
[B]   00-060977

ISBN 0-7432-0505-7

Acknowledgments

I want to thank Lore and Morris Dickstein for their friendship and advice, Lisa Bankoff for her support way beyond the usual or the required, Elizabeth Maguire for her good eye, her work on this work's behalf. I want to thank Katie Roiphe my closest reader and valued critic, Becky Roiphe whose clarity of mind encourages always, and Herman Roiphe who makes it possible for me to write by keeping all things in proper proportion.

To Daniel Herz Roiphe
and Zachary Herz Roiphe
Tomorrow's men

Contents

*For Rabbit,
with Love
and Squalor*

R*e a d i n g* is the water that flows over the rocks. The running water brings out the depths of color, the greens, the marble streaks of rose or rust, the moss that clings, the white chips at the far edge, the smoothness of texture, the realness of the thing. The force of the river over the years brings dents, bends, curves into the hardness of granite, the geology of self. Of course, the sunlight, the snow melting, the reflection of this or that bough, the tail flash of fish and insect, these too are part of the rocks' condition. But the water is the words we read, and the water is the home of the rock.

This book is the description of a small part of the river—how it flowed over me and into me and around me. I am grateful for the words I have read, the stories that have covered my spirit, imbued it with its most personal sheen, connected it to the place in the river that is mine.

Here are Holden Caulfield, Robert Jordan, Dick Diver, Rabbit, Nathan Zuckerman, Frank Bascombe, and Max. These are males I have known well—not the only ones, of course, but important ones, ones who left their mark, ones I loved until I moved on. My love is not uncritical, my involvement with one did not preclude the clinging to another, and none of them prevented real life from its usual bulldozing activities. These men, characters only, were not actual participants in my fate but they were real participants nevertheless. They served as my friends, my counterspies in the gender wars, my distraction.

I thank them for what they taught me, for the pleasure they gave me, for the raising of my sights and the warning of catastrophe. Even when I couldn't take the warning I appreciated the intention.

1

Holden
...... Caulfield ......

Holden Caulfield

J. D. Salinger's
The Catcher in the Rye

No matter who I french kissed, the one I really loved was Holden.

O*n e* snowy night when I was sixteen years old I went with my date to Jimmy Ryan's on 52nd Street. As we waited in line, I calculated and recalculated the year of my birth. What would it have been if my actual age had been eighteen? You needed to be eighteen to get through the door, and as we approached the threshold, the bouncer stared each of us in the eye. You were required to give him your year of entrance into this world, quickly, with confidence, without looking away, without stumbling. A stutter would exclude you. My date was the equally underage editor of the Andover yearbook. I remember his pale face and his wide jaw. I remember the clean smell of him and the pink skin at the back of his neck. I remember the dissolving flakes of snow on the shoulders of his blue overcoat and his Brooks Brothers thin blue-and-red-striped tie. I remember his holding my white-angora-mittened hand as we approached the door. His last name, of course, I have forgotten. Maybe it was Kaufman. His first name was Bill, or perhaps that was someone else.

It was Christmas vacation 1951, and our class dance at the Plaza Hotel had already been held. Lester Lanin's orchestra had played, and I had kissed a boy behind the potted palms just outside the chaperon's sight line, leaving crayon-red blurs of lipstick on his mouth, which he wiped away with the back of his hand. The boy had invited me to Jimmy Ryan's. He had come to my house and promised my mother that he would bring me home before midnight. Jazz was inside, floating down the street every time the door opened to let someone in. Jazz and smoke, drink and smoke, jazz carried a kind of pain, a pull in the inner organs, a weight of desire and regret. I didn't yet understand any of it, but wanted to. How badly I wanted to. I had on my camel's hair coat and a Harvard maroon-and-white-striped wool scarf another boy had given me. I was wearing a girdle and stockings, and my waist was pulled tight with a wide patent leather belt. There was a black felt poodle on my skirt with a shining rhinestone in its collar. I carried my mother's small velvet pocketbook in which I had a quarter for the woman in the ladies' room, and a few dollars for a cab in case my date got drunk and I had to get myself home. Mad money, we called it then—money to escape a date you were mad at, or money to escape a date who had turned mad? I carried a pack of Chesterfields in my pocketbook and a book of matches from El Morocco that I had found in my mother's purse.

Holden was J. D. Salinger's alter ego character from his newly published, sweeping-the-world book, *The Catcher in the Rye*. Jimmy Ryan's was a bar like the bars Holden went to alone in New York on the edge of his crack-up, thrown out of three schools, a lost child afflicted by disdain for others and a sure nose for hypocrisy—or at any rate a nose dedicated to uncovering what again and again he called phoniness. *Phoniness* was his favorite word. I hated phoniness too. But what exactly was it? Or rather what exactly was real, honest, true, not phony? I was worried about the nuclear bomb and the third world war that would end my just beginning life. I was worried about the strange sad world of the drunk or lonely or bitter or broke or cheating adults I was reading about each week in the short stories of the *New Yorker.* How to avoid desolation, isolation, the endless sorrows of Dorothy Parker or Jean Stafford? How to avoid becoming James Thurber's cartoon wife who waited for him with a frown? I was worried about what I might catch from a public toilet seat. I knew for a fact that you could go blind or crazy from a germ on the toilet seat. I worried about the newly founded state of Israel. So many enemies, so few friends— once again David against Goliath under the indifferent sky. I worried whether the tree I had planted, actually sent money for someone else to plant (phoniness) in the Galilee, was getting sufficient water. Sometimes while falling off to sleep I could see my tree, third from the end of a long line of infant pines, shriveled, bare branched.

I had seen a play by Carson McCullers on Broadway called *The Member of the Wedding* and like the heroine, Frankie, I too worried, "Who is the we of me?" I repeated this line each night as I brushed my teeth, a mantra of both expectation and failure.

Above all I was worried. Was I too a phony? I smoked without inhaling. I coughed if I drew the smoke into my lungs, so I had perfected a technique of a quick short drag and a long, slow exhale that mimicked inhaling, or so I hoped. That was phony and I knew it. I pretended interest in boys I didn't like so I could get invited to boarding school weekends, to college football games. I allowed kisses that I didn't desire. I desired things I didn't allow. I was deeply fond of a woman English teacher who strode through the halls like a man and wore no makeup or nail polish and stared out the window at the boats in the river that flowed by the school building with a ferocity I found breathtaking. I wrote her a poem that I never showed her. Was that phoniness? What was fake, what was the genuine me?

Holden had posed the question, and of all the boys who had taken me to dances, kissed me in the lobby of my building, invited me to have tea with their prep school masters, the only one I wanted to spend the rest of my life with was Holden, and he wasn't even real. Certainly my love for Holden was a big phony.

Everyone believed that communism was the implacable enemy. The father of my best friend told me that we were being sabotaged by hidden spies and fellow travelers. Some people thought radicals were stirring up race trouble. Some people thought that the unions were the source of all evil. I had been to see *Death of a Salesman* on Broadway. In the silence at the end of the play, I blew my nose as tears streamed down. Ah, the cold cruelty of American prosperity. Did I notice the phoniness of my sympathy, born as I was of management not labor, fed and clothed by the hard sweat of other peoples' hands threading the sewing machines? Probably not.

Some people (I had read Howard Fast) thought it was stockbrokers and John D. Rockefeller and the snooty swells who went to the opera who were at fault. To them this was the explanation for the low but constant moan of unhappiness, the undercurrents of dissatisfaction and anxiety, that rose from the towns and the villages and the farms of America.

We, however, knew, because we had read *The Catcher in the Rye*, that it wasn't the communists or the socialists or the Democrats or the Republicans who were causing ulcers and bad dreams. It was the phonies who were undermining the ground we walked on, turning everything into a hollow mockery of itself.

Everyone in line waiting to gain entrance to Jimmy Ryan's had read *The Catcher in the Rye*. It was our book, our story, our photograph of ourselves.

Bill and I sat at a table up front. The musicians were loud. Jazz was not background noise; it was the subject, the purpose, the bearer of tidings of the heart. Sophisticated people knew that jazz was the truth, nonverbal truth, transporting truth, unifying truth. I liked words, however, and conversation at Jimmy Ryan's was difficult at best. The musicians were sweaty from stage lights, from the sheer strain of it, from the pleasure or pretended pleasure of it. They were, except for the drummer, Negro—browns of all shades with shining bald scalps or hats with small brims, and their cigarettes dangled from their lips, shoulders hunched, feet waved and stomped, and the light shone on the gleaming yellow brass of the horns and the white keys of the piano, hard and sure. Nicotine-rich smoke floated under the blue stage lights, hung over our heads, a soupy fog rising and sinking as burning ashes glowed red like distant lighthouses from darkly silhouetted rocky shores. I ordered a rye and ginger ale. Bill ordered a manhattan. At the bottom of his glass was a maraschino cherry. That was my favorite part of drinking, the delicious inviting blood-red cherry. I resisted the temptation to put my fingers down into his glass and grab it. That would not be sophisticated. I puffed on my cigarette. I let the smoke drift out my mouth as if I were a dragon in the Chinese New Year parade. The horn blasted. The clarinet chimed in. The melody rose and fell between us, a promise: "Someone to Watch Over Me." "When the Saints Come Marching In."

There was some pounding on the drums. Bill reached into his jacket pocket and pulled out a letter. "I wrote to Salinger," he shouted across the table. "I asked him to do the introduction to our yearbook. He wrote to me." I felt dizzy. He had actually written to Salinger and Salinger himself had actually answered his letter, and here was the answer. A sacred object was pushed across the table toward me. I unfolded the letter, which smelled of peanut butter. I couldn't see the words. I pushed the letter to the middle of the table and brought my head down near the small flickering table candle. The letter was handwritten. The ink had smudged the last words on the page, the way ink did when pens needed to be filled and inkwells rested in little round holes at the edge of each school desk. I can only paraphrase the letter because of the time elapsed since then, but I remember that the author declined the request for an introduction to the Andover yearbook. He said that because he had never attended Andover he felt unqualified. He offered a substitute: On the way home at Christmas vacation walk through the cars of the train until you see a small thin boy struggling to get his suitcase on the upper rack. No one will help him. He will be alone. No one chooses to sit with him. He will have a cold and his nose will be red and there will be perspiration drops on his forehead and acne on his chin, and his wet handkerchief will be falling out of his pocket. He is the one to write the introduction. He is the expert on Andover.

I folded the letter and handed it back to Bill. Of course Salinger would say that. That's what Holden would say. The editor of the yearbook must be a big fat phony. Bill wanted to know what I thought. I thought Bill should publish the letter as is. That itself could be the introduction. (We didn't know in those days that letters were the writer's property, and someday Salinger would sue somebody to make the point clear.) The smoke made my eyes tear, or maybe it wasn't the smoke. I was thinking of the small boy on the train whom no one wanted to sit next to. The sadness in my heart was delicious. Just delicious. I felt superior, exactly how I couldn't tell you, but a glorious sense of my own sensitivity, my own humane nonphony soul, filled me with gratitude. I decided I would let Bill kiss me at the door, let him lift up my sweater and unhook the back of my bra and feel around. After all he and his Salinger letter had earned it.

Neither of us was cruel or cold like the others. We knew the secret: everyone suffers, only honesty matters. The system, the school, the grades, the ambition of parents, the hardness of the world: it was nothing, it was phony. We were real. Our hearts were still on fire and had not yet turned to ash. I ordered another rye and ginger ale but then I couldn't drink it. Those drinks tasted really awful.

Holden Caulfield failed everything at Pencey and the other three boarding schools he had attended except English. He had a writing gift. As he leaves for an evening with his date, Holden's smug and successful roommate asks him to do an English assignment for him due the next day. We know that Holden is a writer and a reader. Me too, I hope. Holden reads not in an ass-licking please-the-teacher kind of way but in a real, genuine, words-matter, stories-matter, truth-is-in-the-story way. The boy of better character writes; the other one puffs and postures and stares at himself in the mirror and boasts about how girls love him. I don't love him at all. If only Holden were a real boy I would let him read my last story.

Holden is a portrait of the artist as an endangered bud, the first frail sign of intellectual spring in the long, cold, dead winter of the fifties. "Me too, me too," my soul shouted. But of course so did the entire generation chorus back.

Not meaning it most of them, not really meaning it, but nevertheless, for a moment, anything seemed possible, as if a submarine had risen out of the depths of the sea, water spilling over the iron sides, the sun striking the metal and the air bursting against the glass of the periscope as the sound of a gull over the next crest of wave seems to lift the boat higher and higher. In that television-commercial way for a split second everyone in my generation was Holden—even the future stockbrokers, corporate lawyers, accountants, even the Smith and Wellesley girls who would soon enough turn into matrons with little hats on their heads attending art shows or concerts in flocks, cooing like pigeons after years of spending their afternoons carrying children to dancing lessons and orthodontist appointments. All of us looked out and gasped.

In *Catcher in the Rye* it is the young hero who possesses the wise and honest eye. No wonder the young have, for half a century, taken this book as their personal, private bible. How could they not respond to the antiauthority, hypocrites-all portrait of the adults that populate this tale? The sixties slogan, "Don't trust anybody over thirty," was a distillation of Holden's finger-pointing. Generations of budding, pimply, hormone-flooded, underage souls have loved Holden's awkwardness, his bravado, his bluster, his sweetness, and the way that he's still a child, but a child with moral vision, a truth teller.

But they can't love Holden the way we children of the forties and fifties did. Because for us he was the waking trumpet. For us, our hero Holden pierced the high walls of conformity that so marked our homes, our childhoods. *Phony*, he yelled at us. *Phony*, we whispered to each other. This was the light under the crack in the still-closed door. If you could name the malaise, you might beat it.

Ours was truly an age of conformity. This country that had just sacrificed so much for its principles of freedom and individuality was slipping into a cold, icy, frozen landscape. We were waging a new war of bluster and bluff, of insurgency, spying, and Voice of America radio programs. Under the shadow of total annihilation, we were slinging arrows at the tyranny of the Stalin-blackened turf. We were the knights in shining armor protecting free thought, free religion, free markets, individualism against the dark expanse of gulags run by inefficient, murderous, Godless paranoids stumbling over their five-year plans. Nevertheless, we on our side of the divide were strangely enough not particularly fond of those who deviated from the norm.

But right behind *Leave It to Beaver* and the *Mickey Mouse Club* a countertheme was emerging, a defiance was brewing. It had always been there, of course, but now as it strummed louder than ever, it seemed needed more than ever. The lawyer and the banker, the insurance agent and the informer, the Rotarian and the Elk and all the folks of Sinclair Lewis's Main Street, the ones who threw the schoolteacher out of Sherwood Anderson's Winesburg, Ohio, who nailed up Jim Crow signs on water fountains were more and more often confronted by writers and artists and contrarians who moved in small groups and wore odd clothes and spoke of Paris as the center of the world.

Art and the artist, the outlaw artist, were at the tip-top point of this counterculture, anti–state pyramid, standing up there and laughing at those with more ordinary aims in life, more mundane concerns. The practical job keepers kept the wheels of society greased, but artists, like the writer Holden would surely become, drove the chariot. Artists told us what really mattered. They saw through the phoniness: they were our salvation. Art was not phony. It was the one true thing, or so some of us believed.

It was not simply an accident or a mere economy measure that so many houses in the spreading suburbs were built alike. It had to do with our communal desire to be alike, to smooth out the differences. Normal was like everyone else. Everyone was afraid of being abnormal. To be a spinster or an old maid was a social catastrophe. To be an unmarried man made you the object of whispers. Faggots and dykes were not yet loved by the conservatives; they were hated by all alike and most lived secret lives, double lives. Women's magazines did not discuss orgasms, yeast infections, money, breast exams, or menopause. It wasn't just homosexuals who were in the closet. It was all of us. We were presumed safer if we stayed in the closet even if there wasn't quite enough air to go around.

We didn't want to be talked about. I would have done anything to avoid a reputation as a fast or easy girl. For most of us in this generation our social well-being demanded that true desire, lust, and fantasy be pushed under the table or into the dark alleys of the wrong side of town. It demanded that we be polite to our elders and hide what they would disapprove of. The consequence of this cowardice was, at the very least, audible. We had no music of our very own. We were a generation that danced to the songs of previous eras. To have our own would have made our voices conspicuous. As a generation it seems we wanted to tip-toe through this vale of tears unnoticed. So we Charlestoned, so we waltzed, so we did the Mexican hat dance, so we sambaed and foxtrotted cheek to cheek as had our parents before us.

We didn't have wild dancing in which the hips were pushed provocatively rhythmically forward or the dangerous, nasty taste of forbidden drugs that might loosen the tongue or break down the carefully constructed, defensively valued barriers of reason. No one but musicians from the wrong side of the tracks smoked dope, and nice girls and boys obeyed the parietal rules of their schools: slippers in the hallways, one foot on the floor if a boy was in the room, out by ten. If the rules were not followed, a girl could be tossed out of the game and her life ruined, completely ruined, before it had started.

My mother told me again and again, If you're not a virgin, no man will want you. Personally I thought that Holden would have me, virgin or not. I went on a prep school weekend and the handsome boy, brother of a friend, who had invited me put his tongue in my ear while we held hands under the blanket on the hayride in the moonlight through the snow-covered fields in northern Massachusetts. I wanted him to invite me back. I wanted him to lick my neck. I wanted to smell hay and boy, horse and wet-snow-soaked glove forever more, but I didn't want him to think I was not a nice girl. What did he think? What did I think? I worried that in chapel on Sunday morning he would notice that I didn't know the words to any hymns. I was a pretender. I had let him take my hand and place it over his organ. Since I couldn't breathe and keep my hand there, I soon pulled away. On the train back to New York City that Sunday afternoon after our tea with the headmaster, I picked at my cuticles until they bled. I wrote in my diary that I was in love and then I scratched out my words. He never invited me back but that was all right.

Girls were profoundly ashamed of menstrual blood and profoundly humiliated by breasts too little or too large. Parents wanted to be just like the other parents and expected their children to blend, to be popular, to obey the unwritten as well as the written rules. No one wanted to stick out or stick their neck out. It might well be placed on the block. If you expressed sympathy for the poor or the Negro, if you thought that perhaps the state might do more to help the elderly, if you said these thoughts aloud in the wrong place, you could lose your job or your friends. If you signed a petition to help the disabled or open a public golf course, you could end up on a list, and your former friends would pretend not to know you. If a person admitted mental illness, he might be shunned. If you said the word *cancer*, you whispered it. If you said the word *debt* aloud, you kept your face averted. If you said *pregnancy out of wedlock*, you fled your town, your home. If you said the word *Jew*, you dropped your voice to a scant whisper.

Holden was not as cowed as most of his peers. On the way to an intramural match, Holden left the fencing equipment for his school's team on the New York subway. It didn't bother him much. Holden wore his baseball cap backward. Holden was not cruel to outsiders. Holden was not touched by what others told him he should care about. Holden was not as ashamed of being thrown out of his third prep school as he should have been. This was another large reason to love Holden.

When Holden called everyone phonies, his accusation rang true to us. It made us laugh. It tore open the low ceiling over our heads and proclaimed a new day. I didn't know that Holden was an American version of Stephen Dedalus because I hadn't read *Portrait of the Artist* yet. I didn't know that *Catcher in the Rye* was just another in a long line of initiation novels because it wasn't taught in English curriculum yet, and so I didn't know that men were always writing about boys' passing out of boyhood into manhood. I didn't know that running around calling other people phony offered its own not very pretty possibilities of moral disfigurement. Most important of all I probably missed the real center of *Catcher in the Rye*.

So did the *New York Times*. The reviewer was one James Stern, author of *The Man Who Was Loved*, a book of short stories long ago turned to compost in the cold damp dark warehouses where the no-longer-read are laid to an undignified rest. Stern's review appeared on July 15, 1951. He writes in a fake Holden voice as if he were speaking about a girl named Helga. He parodies and pokes fun and with his mocking tone makes it sound as if Holden's conversation is no more than a sneak preview of Valley Girls on the way to the mall and as if Holden is just another self-absorbed (thinking he's superior) nutty kid in need of a spanking. Now that I too am a weary worldly-wise adult, I can see that Stern's parody isn't all that bad. Holden could easily rub you the wrong way and strike you as ridiculous in his johnny-one-note unvaried "I'm honest but everyone else is fake" worldview. But Stern-the-Never-Went-on-to-Fulfill-His-Promise missed the powerful message contained in Salinger's book and in so doing pinned himself down for immortal ignominy as one of those unfortunate reviewers hoisted by their own archived microfilmed words on the gallows of error and condemned to eternities of embarrassed remorse.

Stern did not see that Salinger's Holden was the beloved fairy-tale hero: the little boy who saw that the emperor had no clothes. He didn't understand that Holden had called the soul disorder of the times for what it was. Holden said aloud what the rest of us suspected but dared not think: those who do best, those who are quiet and just like everyone else and are rewarded most lavishly, are not necessarily the remarkable of mind, the purest of heart, the most loving of friends. What Holden, a.k.a. Salinger, saw was the underlying cruelty, the exploitation of the sexes, each of each, that made up our peculiarly fraught adolescent rites of passage. What he saw was the meanness of it all, the brutality to the weaker or the different, the dark skinned or the thin skinned or the smaller or the lonelier, that simmered just under the surface of all the butter-is-melting-in-my-mouth brotherhood talk, the freedom talk, the one-nation-under-God talk. He saw that this America that had won the war against totalitarianism was steamrolling right over the variety and the beauty and the respect that nourish each individual person. The mass culture, the new suburbs, the ice in the veins of the successful, were stifling dissent, choking us all.

Holden saw that and it drove him to drink, or at least to want to drink, if anyone would serve him, which for the most part they wouldn't. Drink was his way to pretend to be an adult instead of a frightened child. Isn't that always so? Drinking was the way to join the grownup world, which he thought might be better than the one he inhabited. Also Holden really needed a drink to make his reality, the one he didn't want to think about, more bearable. This too is achingly familiar. Smoking was his way of pretending to be an adult. Smoke and drink—dear Holden I loved you for smoking and drinking in the small wee hours of the morning. I knew it was whistling in the dark. I knew you were frightened and just as gawky as you looked, but I felt you trying, crashing at the gates of some adult mystery where everyone who understood the pain of life smoked and drank, flirted, and went home sloshed just before dawn in a cab.

Holden threw the first stone that was to become the sixties. This is why in 1951 *The Catcher in the Rye* became a Book-of-the-Month Club selection. This is why Salinger, even if he hadn't disappeared into New Hampshire wrapping a blanket of Zen around his body, would remain an important figure, a bearer of Sinclair Lewis's torch and Sherwood Anderson's torch, and if there is some ongoing literary Olympics relay race, he was in it. He did his part heroically.

Mary McCarthy who debunked the Salinger cult in the pages of the *New Republic* also made a mistake. She, like Stern, like most other readers even the most appreciative ones, missed the center of *The Catcher in the Rye*, the part that was in the title, that was underlined through the entire piece, but went all unmentioned by critics at the time. This, Salinger's first and really only novel, was primarily a book of frustrated and unrecognized mourning. "Catcher in the rye" refers to Holden's fantasy of himself as the one who would stand at the edge of a cliff and save the children who were playing a game of hide and seek among the high stalks of rye and, coming to the edge, would plunge to their deaths if he didn't catch them and save them, one by one. Ask any adult you know what the phrase *catcher in the rye* means and you'll get a blank look. But the point of the book is carried in the title which is such a good title that everyone remembers it but has forgotten what it means.

What is bothering Holden is not simply the social inanities of his passing scene; in fact his irritation at schoolmates and masters is a mere cover for his high state of grief for his younger brother Allie who had died of leukemia some four years before the story begins. Allie, Holden tells us, is the real writer in the family. Allie had poems scrib-

bled across his baseball mitt. Allie is the younger brother whose funeral Holden was not allowed to attend. During the funeral Holden
locked himself in the garage and smashed his hands against the window panes, broke the bones in his hand, and was hospitalized. After
which he was sent off to boarding school. This scene is not heavily
dramatized or extended in the book. It is remembered, reported
briefly. It is only a paragraph or so long but it is the clue, the trigger,
the real subject of the novel: death and the way in which we are not allowed to mourn, to face, to see what is there.

The act of phoniness that begins Holden's obsession with phoniness is the one of pretending that what has happened has not happened, that death can be coated over and life goes on as if it hadn't
happened. This is the first silence that casts Holden into his state of
rebellion, into his outsider status, and haunts every moment of his
waking life.

The second death in this small book is the virtual murder of a boy
at Holden's first boarding school who jumps out the window to his
broken-boned end in an attempt to avoid the vicious bullies who are
attacking him in his room. This death too is coated over; the boys who
chased him are never punished or called to account for their actions.
The small boy, the misfit boy who died, is forgotten by all. Teams of
grief counselors were not brought into the school. If the other school
boys had any emotional reaction to the death, no one noticed, en-
couraged it, or cared. But Holden remembers. Holden thinks about
it. Here is the second death that no one allows him to mourn or to
mark. Here is the sign that man is as cruel as God and the pain that
Holden feels causes him to turn against, away, build for himself a
shell, one not really hard enough, not nearly strong enough.

Today everyone who has ever seen the Oprah show could tell you
why Holden needed to go to his brother's funeral. He needed to
mourn so he wouldn't feel guilty, so he could confront his grief and so
on—. But back then so many years before confessional TV, before
Princess Diana would discuss her bulimia with the press, all the cultural forces lockstepped together to conceal the vital and raw facts of
biology from children. These were days in which schools did not have
sex education classes. These were days in which a stork flew over with

a baby held in a diaper in his beak and children were assumed to be both dumber and more innocent than proved to be the case.

The Catcher in the Rye is above all a book about mourning prevented, mourning aborted. It was written in the immediate postwar era. While it points forward toward the sixties with equal force, it looks back toward the forties. The deaths of the soldiers, the boys of America buried in fields far across the Atlantic, lost at sea, abandoned in the Pacific, these deaths were somehow brushed aside by the shiny new victorious America intent on optimism, on suburban sprawl, on prosperity. Holden, child of the thirties, spoke of death obliquely, briefly, grief as a prod to the conscience, grief as a reason for a long drunk, a school failure, a hole in the heart.

Perhaps if he had been any more direct the book would not have been so popular, so accepted. But all across America the dead were hanging about, unbidden ghosts at our revels. The soldiers who had gone to war and not returned were just gone. Brothers, sons, fiancés had vanished. The grieving was private, too private. The pictures of Auschwitz, the piles of limbs, the bomb at Hiroshima all created a shadow of still-unacknowledged numbing death that Holden responded to.

Holden's fantasy of becoming the catcher in the rye, the savior of young children, tore a rip in the curtain of denial. The book appeared at a moment when the culture was absorbing the fact, not yet discussing it directly, that the children had not in fact been saved, not the Jewish children, not the wet-behind-the-ears not-more-than-boys soldiers on the bloody beaches. Among the things that no one was talking about, the unhealthy hush around us, were the piles of dead children.

Holden wonders at least twice where the ducks go in the winter. In New York's Central Park there is a small liver-shaped lake crossed by a walking stone bridge where in the summer months iridescent green, brown, and white-flecked mallards wait for passersby to toss them Crackerjacks and half-consumed hot dog rolls. The lake is often frozen in December and the ducks are gone. What Holden is asking about is his brother who was but isn't. He is also asking about the missing, the unspoken of (the Holocaust-destroyed, the on-everyone's-tongue unmourned for), the disappeared. And this before the Argentinian and the Chilean military took the word from the innocent magicians who performed hat tricks at children's birthday parties and gave it to the chill of torture machines in basements and bodies dropping out of airplanes.

I did not see this when I first fell in love with Holden. I was a scraped-knee, basketball-playing, math-indifferent, daydreaming girl at one of the private schools Holden mentions in his book. I wasn't worrying about dead soldiers or final solutions. Although I didn't know what, I knew that something was rotten. Holden knew it too. For this I loved him. We had a lot in common I believed. His jaundiced view made him an outsider and I was an outsider too. The odd thing is that so many of us loved Holden that we must have made a quorum of sorts, we might even have been a majority of outsiders. This may have been a somewhat phony pose, but it was also a legitimate response to the silences all around.

I walked along the East River boardwalk on my way to school, my blue uniform high up on my thighs, baggy across the chest, waistless like a child's, my white blouse stained with my morning's coffee. I stared at the dark waters and the tugboats and the red neon sign on the factory in the small island under the distant bridge, and loneliness rose in my throat, nauseous like the existentialist I had not yet read, exhausted as if I had lived a hundred years instead of sixteen. "Amo, amas, amat—Arma virumque cano." I was a Latin student. But would I, could I, would anybody come and save me from the skin I lived in? What was there to sing about if one was not a soldier in a heroic battle? Should I jump in the dark river? I wrote a poem instead, so dreadful even I knew it. I gravely considered a relationship with a river god who would consume me with his black lips. I saw my body bloated, floating off under the Triborough over to the warehouses in Queens, my saddle shoes still on my feet, my pencils still in my jumper pocket, and my dark too-curly hair limp like weeds in a swamp following behind.

The one good teacher at Holden's first prep school picks up the dead body of the boy who has fallen from the window and carries him tenderly to the infirmary. This teacher is visited by Holden at the end of a long, drunken, sleepless night in New York City in which he has pretended to be older than he is, is avoiding telling his parents that he has been again thrown out of school, has taxied from one end of Manhattan to the other. The married teacher seems kind and allows Holden to sleep on his couch, but Holden wakes to find the male teacher touching him with a little too much heat. Holden jumps up and runs away in disgust and feels betrayed by the teacher who had been the only adult he had trusted.

When I first read the book I'm sure I didn't understand that scene at all. That homosexuality existed I knew. Vaguely. We whispered about it. I couldn't get a clear picture from anyone. No one explained to me whatever it was that homosexuals actually did. I wasn't too clear about what heterosexuals actually did either. Facts were hard to come by. What I did understand were secrets. Terrible secrets. These I knew were everywhere. Holden's horror at being the object of a male touch while he appeared to be sleeping seemed so normal that I probably missed the fact that this teacher is the only adult in the book who encourages Holden, respects him, and has shown true compassion. In terms of the book, the teacher, the potential catcher in the rye, is too lame himself to prevent anyone from falling off the edge of a cliff. From our new-century perspective we can see that Holden himself committed an act of phoniness by fleeing the teacher's home, by his inability to see through the prejudice and unkindness of the common attitudes toward homosexuality.

But I'm asking too much of grief-struck Holden. I'm asking too much of myself. I'm fairly certain that the teacher seemed like a phony to me too. Being male in America in 1950 had no ambiguity about it. It was simple as apple pie, pointed as Jayne Mansfield's breasts.

For Holden the teacher's gesture had exposed another lie, uncovered another hypocrisy. But while I can respect the fact that the awkward, innocent, and virginal Holden, uncertain of his own masculinity, might easily have reacted to his teacher's touch with acute visceral panic, I myself should have recognized that the flaw was in Holden whose prickliness sent away many potential friends and allies and who couldn't hear the lyrics for the drumbeats of righteousness in his own head.

What did Holden know about homosexuality and when did he know it? Were the readers meant to see more than Holden could? Hard to say. But stories have resonances, they echo beyond themselves. Was Holden's creator indulging in irony by having the good teacher be secretly gay? Was he pulling the rug out from under Holden again or was he signaling that secrets, hidden lives, the need for repression were themselves the cruelty that sapped our energy, drove us mad, soured the day?

Hemingway in *For Whom the Bell Tolls* said that the writer must be a bullshit detector. That sounds right but it's another of those far-easier-to-say-than-do job requirements. Even heaven-blessed writers get the wool pulled over their eyes sometimes and miss the real shit around. Maybe that's what happened to would-be writer Holden. It certainly is what happened to this reader.

At least today the marginalized have a hot line to call, while back in the fifties only the French writers, Jean Genet, André Gide, Marcel Proust, might have understood the teacher's hand straying to the forehead of his troubled and multiple-times-expelled pupil. Most of us hadn't read or didn't understand those writers: not yet. Today a person in a Marilyn Monroe wig has a chance to dance in the streets at least on Halloween or wave a fist at a cathedral at least on St. Patrick's Day, but then the sexual terror of anything that wasn't straight missionary was ubiquitous. The need to lose one's virginity in a vagina was a clear imperative for a male. The need to preserve your vagina from intruders was equally clear for a female. Naturally the air was tense with the possibility of misstep.

Faggot and *fairy* are words that ring in high schools still. Secrets we have, taunts we have. Ah, Holden, if you knew that in the 1990s football teammates that set fire to a boy's tutu while he was pretending to be a cheerleader dancing on a table in a high school cafeteria in Arkansas were not even slapped on the wrist, what would you say?

What is the opposite of a phony? Have you ever seen one, or are they like unicorns—fantastical creatures that live only in the woods of

New Hampshire and never come out, especially if a journalist is knocking?

Even though the English class at Columbine likely read *Catcher in the Rye*, the words themselves formed no safety net. Sorry.

Holden was a sexual innocent, a sweetie pie one might almost call him. He says,

> —I've had quite a few opportunities to lose my virginity and all, but I've never got around to it yet. Something happens. For instance if you're at a girl's house, her parents always come home at the wrong time—or you're afraid they will——The thing is, most of the time when you're coming pretty close to doing it with a girl—a girl that isn't a prostitute or anything, I mean—she keeps telling you to stop. The trouble with me is, I stop. Most guys don't.——you never know whether they really want you to stop or whether they're just scared as hell———I get to feeling sorry for them.

A girl could love a guy who felt sorry for her in this tight spot. A girl could certainly love a guy who guessed she might be scared, all messed up, with her blouse open and her makeup running there in the back seat of the car.

But did she really? I know that a lot of Holden's fans would not have been so pleased if he had appeared at the actual door to take them out. If he had called them in the early hours of the morning they would have hung up in a nanosecond. They may have pretended to themselves that they wanted Holden the artist, the outsider, the troubled, and the perceptive to sweep them off to the dark northern mountains where they could live in innocent harmony ever after. But did they mean it? I did but that was my problem.

The harsh truth is that a girl, even a sensitive Emily-Dickinson-loving girl, couldn't help but see Holden's fright. His uncertainty would stink for miles around. Despite his good intentions and his sympathy for the female plight, many a girl might not have accepted a second date. Holden's own fear would have contaminated the mating space. Although they might have found Holden's sincerity, his basic human decency, his lack of big-shot bloat, his bravado, and his dislike of the prevailing team spirit charming, the vast majority of young girls would have been worried by him too. They would have been afraid that he wouldn't really manage, not as a half kid, not as an adult. They would have been right. Holden's vulnerability, his sympathy for the underdog, his clever artist mind could not have disguised his evident and constant pain. He really needed his psychiatrist.

His kind of wound would not have had universal appeal. Salinger may have tried to convince us that Holden was sane and the rest of the world in need of therapy, which was not entirely untrue, but he couldn't fool the eye of the wise girl who knew that when it came to a person's real future you were far better off with the jock roommate than Holden Caulfield. The macho myth, the invulnerable male, protector and provider, took two to tango as they say. It was a male and female co-constructed, co-endured folly. Most girls searched the face of every flower-carrying youth who came to their doors in hopes of seeing a trace of John Wayne, a shrug of Jimmy Stewart. Most were looking for a boy with a pugilist's training who could read if he had to.

Sally, in *The Catcher in the Rye*, is described as a cold cookie, a girl with her eye on the opportunistic ball, a realist, a sort of tease. You are not expected to like Sally but the truth is that more of us were like Sally than like Holden's perfect little sister Phoebe. This was not because so many girls were phonies but rather that so many girls grasped that with a guy like Holden, you could be in real trouble. This was not evil as much as sensible. Sleeping Beauty was not roused from her thousand-year snooze by a guy in need of Prozac and Rapunzel did not let her golden hair down for a cripple and Cinderella had not gone to the ball to capture the heart of the butler. It was not a sign of bad character in 1951 to get that point.

Biology or the common evolutionary rap gives the top primate the top female for good-sense species-survival reasons. From this point of view Holden is a primate far down on the list and no girl with a fighting chance for the top beast would pick him out of the pack.

On the other hand Holden had an advantage over his peers when it came to girls. The very aspect of his character that was a turn-off was also an attraction. A paradox yes. Holden needed healing. He was a wounded pup. He was in trouble. He required a nurse. Some few women for reasons that remain between them and their therapists are attracted to men who require propping up, sewing back together, not just standing behind but holding up. I was one of those girls. Holden won me with his neediness. This was not necessarily good news for the rest of my life but it was so. Not to admit that would make me these long years afterwards a very big phony.

Holden tells his psychiatrist about Sally. Like me Sally went to dances and movies and the theater. Like me she went out on dates with boys from prep schools up and down the east coast. Like me she flirted. But unlike me she wouldn't even entertain the idea of running away with Holden when he asked her. She was practical, cold, clear about the agenda of her life. She was more like one of Jane Austen's practical characters, charted, directed, moving ahead toward an inevitable destiny, a chess game of marriage, fortune, and social place. Sally saw what I could not: Holden is a bird whose already lusterless feathers are dropping off, resting dingy on the brown-stained newspaper that lines the floor of the cage.

Here is Holden weary from lack of sleep, afraid to go home, running out of money on a date with Sally. They've been to see a Broadway play. They've gone ice skating at Rockefeller Center. They are having a Coke; the waiter wouldn't bring Holden the scotch he desires. He is aimlessly burning matches. He says,

"I have about a hundred and eighty bucks in the bank. I can take it out when it opens in the morning, and then I could go down and get this guy's car. No kidding. We'll stay in these cabin camps and stuff like that till the dough runs out. Then . . . we could live somewhere with a brook and all and, later on, we could get married or something. I could chop all our own wood in the wintertime and all. Honest to God, we could have a terrific time! Wuddaya say? C'mon, Wuddaya say? Will you do it with me? Please!"

Sally responds, "You can't just *do* something like that."

Of course I didn't know then that in a decade a million children would go off to Woodstock and then settle in the little villages of northern states. I didn't know that herbal tea and organic bread were coming. Here is the sixties dream not yet dreamt. Holden without knowing it speaks in the voice of the hippies, the tie-dye dropouts, the chopping-their-own-wood types who later streamed through America like over-age under-financed Hansels and Gretels. In 1952 I felt like Holden was talking just to me.

> "Take cars . . . Take most people, they're crazy about cars. They worry if they get a little scratch on them, and they're always talking about how many miles they get to a gallon, and if they get a brand-new car already they start thinking about trading it in for one that's even newer. I don't even like *old* cars. . . . I'd rather have a goddam horse. A horse is at least *human*, for God's sake."

Holden rails against consumerism, materialism, accumulation. Holden was my man. I knew exactly what he was talking about. I felt it too. Of course I couldn't imagine a world in which flowered skirts and no bras and bare makeup-free faces were in style. I couldn't imagine a place where boys dropped out of law school and rode the highways in painted vans, but I felt squeezed into my corset, my garter belt, my future. So did almost everybody else. I would never have left Holden hanging out there. I would have held his hand, been his companion, or so I thought. So I think.

I would have emptied my piggy bank and followed Holden because he needed me, because I would have served as his buffer, as his practical arm, as his servant and his friend and his secret sharer of dark and wonderful thoughts. I would not have let him go alone to bars at night. I would have stolen out after my mother thought I was asleep in my bed and accompanied him on his journey to the edges of adulthood. Unlike the ultimately disappointing and obviously shallow Sally, I would have revived him with my love and returned him whole to the reading world. Or so my version of the story went.

I think of the American frontier stretching out along miles of sand or mountains, purple in its majesty. I think of herds of sheep or the pounding hooves of horses or the high grain towers guarding the rail tracks lined with wildflowers and I want to go away, somewhere, anywhere. If I (instead of Sally) were sitting with Holden having hot chocolate at the Rockefeller Center skating rink and he asked me to go away with him I would not have stalled him, reminded him he was coming to help decorate my Christmas tree, poked practical holes in his plan. I would simply have said yes. I would have gone home and packed my things. Holden needed me. Holden and I could find in the woods a way to live. We would talk and read and write and escape the eyes of disapproving adults, of unhappy adults who couldn't figure out their own lives, who drank and wept and seemed to suffer all the time, to bully others, to betray trust, even though everything looked as if it was in order.

I knew it wasn't. Holden knew it too.

I might have had some second thoughts. What would we do when our money ran out? But I would have kept them to myself. I couldn't have caused Holden pain. I just knew that Holden was right. It was a good idea to get out of here. Never mind that I liked a warm bath as much as anyone. Never mind that I didn't know how to cook or drive or plant a flower. I wanted Holden to choose me. I intended to be his muse, his protector, his editor when he wrote his stories, his love, and in return he could save me from where I was. So I thought. So did a lot of girls.

Holden was a natural-born writer. That was his ace in the hole. It gave him more shine than a trust fund, more shine than an athletic letter, at least to some. At the end of the fifties in the shadow of the bomb, in the face of our disillusion with political schemes to save mankind, our knowledge of God's silence in the recent holocaust, we were left holding the bag, and only art, only witnessing, only testifying to what was happening, making shape of the shapeless, seemed respectable, a potential way out. Some of us glorified the role of art in human life way beyond what it could bear.

It follows logically then that artists are superior beings, that art will provide salvation, that writing will made you better, that the real world will disappoint. After reading *The Catcher in the Rye*, after Holden became the first man I really loved, I determined that my flesh-and-blood loves should all be like Holden: an eye, a looking eye, a careful observer, a man who would not take it lying down but would protest in words or paint or revolutions or something. I, like thousands of my generation, was hooked on the romance of the wild man, the true seer, the artist.

I believed a little madness was a good thing because like Holden, the mad could see further than the sane. I thought that the emotionally troubled heart was superior to the collected one. I thought that only the dumb would be mentally healthy in a world so daft as ours. This was a romantic idea—as silly as believing that killing bulls made you a man or that communism would lead to an end of privileged elites.

Yes, I also identified with Holden. Was I a kind of girl version of him? At the same time at least in fantasy I wanted to heal him, save him, love him back to health. I was Echo to his Narcissus or more exactly he was Echo to my Narcissus. Either way there was a genuine danger of somebody drowning. A high school friend of mine went to a Frank Sinatra concert at Radio City Music Hall and waited for the star after the performance by the stage door and somehow managed to get her program autographed by the singer. He touched her sweater in the process. She slept with that sweater under her pillow. I put my copy of *The Catcher in the Rye* under my bed so it would be hidden from sight. It was not illegal to own the book. It just seemed as if it ought to be.

Having read *The Catcher in the Rye* I arrived at the Smith campus in 1953 at the age of seventeen, and before the October break I told the boy who had loved me all through my high school years that I would never see him again. The reason: he had joined an Amherst fraternity, ZBT. I was committed to artists and artists were by definition outsiders and did not join fraternities. I looked him in his heartbroken eyes and thought I was striking a blow for equality, justice, for Holden. In fact I was a phony. Cruel and stupid. If only I could take it back and have loved where love was due.

It took me a long while to see that dressing like a beatnik in my black leotard and jeans and despising girls who were pinned to fellows from Harvard and Yale was its own kind of conformity. We had a pack too. We were hoist as they say with our own petard.

When in high school I read Salinger's story "Uncle Wiggily in Connecticut." Holden was not in the story but Holden's slightly puritan and very satiric eye vis-à-vis his alter ego creator most certainly was. Two women, former college roommates, meet in the Darien home of one of them and drink the afternoon away. The hostess has lost her true love in the war and is now married to the father of her awkward child, a man she has no fondness for. She neglects and mistreats both husband and child as well as her maid, whose husband she won't let stay in the house despite a storm raging outside. At the end of the story she weeps with recognition of the kind of nasty woman she has certainly become. Today we read this story and see the germ of the Feminine Mystique. Normal women with nothing to do, lolling the suburban afternoon away, stew in their own despair and grow bitchy in the thick of their disappointments. No big news. But there is something else here: the innocent child is once again harmed. Holden the would-be catcher in the rye has let another one slip off the cliff.

The two harsh, shrill, indifferent women are suffering too; alcohol is bathing everything. The little girl is drastically nearsighted; so too the adults have lost their moral sight. Everyone is damaged. The story made me miserable. What is he saying, I wondered? Would I grow up to be a woman like this? Why was love lost and male and female life like a Punch and Judy show, violent in its small cruelties? I believed in Holden's vision. I believed "Uncle Wiggily in Connecticut" was an accurate forecast of how I would be in years to come. Why else would such a tale be in the most reputable *New Yorker*?

Today of course we read the same story differently. We can see a splash of misogyny in the portrait of the women. We can grieve for the loss of soldiers in the war and the victims of the war who stayed at home stripped of the affections of the now dead. Today we can see the entire story as an invitation to avoid the prison of American suburbs or conventional marriage or loveless family relationships. But when I go back to "Uncle Wiggily in Connecticut" I see the same thing I saw when in my sweat-reeking gym uniform having a chocolate soda at Schraffts I first read the story and despaired for the rest of my life.

The story takes place in a frightening emptiness, a long boring day to be endured, a martini-requiring afternoon, and a weepy remorseful bitter evening stretching out ahead. This is really a horror tale, more terrible than anything Stephen King could put before us. Oh God. How to escape?

Domestic America must be the most dangerous place in the world. When I read this again over the next decades, in only slightly altered forms, in Marquand, O'Hara, Cheever, in Updike, in Rick Moody's *The Ice Storm*, in John Updike's Rabbit series, in Richard Ford's *Sportswriter*, I am no longer shocked. The original imprint was made in Holden's voice. He well enough described this level of American hell—well enough to last a lifetime through.

The sixties truly did begin with Holden and if you hate the sixties you would most likely find all Salinger's writing exceedingly subversive. The epigraph to *Nine Stories* is a Zen koan that now reads like a tired cliché but when I first read it on the opening page I was most astounded. Its words were fresh but they baffled. "We know the sound of two hands clapping. But what is the sound of one hand clapping?"

What indeed? I pretended to know. I still don't know. One hand clapping is the avoidance of human sound, two bodies thrashing, etc. I didn't want to avoid human sound. I wanted every human slurp, burp, bang, bubble, twang, and cry I could find. Is the sound of one hand clapping the lowering of the coffin lid, the shovel's thwack against the dirt? When I was a freshman at Smith College in the fall of 1953, I read Aldous Huxley's *Doors of Perception*, which was about a mescaline trip, a search for the inner light of God, that Huxley had taken by the rim of the Pacific Ocean. I was fascinated. I wanted to try mescaline. I went to the Smith infirmary to ask the nurse if she might obtain some of this interesting stuff so I could try it. My request was not granted.

Ah, how innocently the drug culture reared its ugly head, a little bud of curiosity, a green shoot of hedonism, a Heimlich maneuver performed to remove the sorrows that stuck in the soul. The rush to drugs, the sad journey to the washed-out, washed-up, beaten-up bodies of Haight-Ashbury began with a genuine sense that underlying this world was another, a place where the spirit could flourish in freedom and beauty and the mind could journey to places beyond reality, beyond what was known, and discover some truth, some saving truth. This alternative Mass, a kind of prelim to the main feature in the movie house, where your eyes run down tunnels and speed upward through golden circles, turned out to be a false lead, a dangerous path that led more often to destruction of mind than to a flowering of any kind but we didn't know that then. No one knew it then.

The interest in Eastern religions by girls who had been given tennis lessons and boys who were licensed to drive Fords and Chevys not yaks or llamas was in part rebellion against the establishment church, against the old-worn out pieties, against the image of church as authoritarian institution, part of a search to find something real, not phony, a charge led by Holden. A lot of people began to worship in their own living rooms with a little bit of weed when it became possible or socially acceptable and soon a pack of fellow travelers could be found to accompany a person down a road, an open road. There some found Buddhas and gurus and orange robes and vegetable diets, karma and one hand clapping and peace. Did they find peace?

The other message, the one that attracted Holden's creator in his subsequent tales, was that individualism, the quirky honest self which Holden was a fine example of, ego was itself the problem. I am not so sure Holden himself would have liked this development in his creator. Me, it left cold. I believe in ego, combined with its jailers, id and superego.

While Mary McCarthy missed the appeal in *The Catcher in the Rye*, her cool eye did notice the danger, the foolishness in all that sensitivity, all that soulful soul superiority. She wasn't the type to make excuses for homework not done. Holden was. Whatever one might want to say about McCarthy's slowness in admitting to the malignancy of communism, she did not often wear rose-colored glasses. Holden for all his bitter humor was always making generalizations. Like most other romantics the brakes on his emotions were loose. Over and over he called us like pigs to the trough of morality.

In the 1950s I could be found at the White Horse Bar in Greenwich Village where Dylan Thomas was destroying his liver and reciting odes to pretty girls who blew smoke into the eyes of young men who would stagger back to dorm rooms and apartments with bathtubs in the living room when the bar closed or sometimes fall asleep on the subway or in the doorway of the cleaners across the street. Many nights I could be found at the West End Bar up by Columbia University where I missed the physical presence of Allen Ginsberg and Jack Kerouac by a mere year or two, but their beatnik blackness, the dark eye of "Howl," the romance of rejection, hung around like a particularly strong after-shave. The lights were faded yellow, grimmer than the Automat, more menacing than the yellows of Lautrec's bordellos, the tables pock-marked, the sandwiches soggy, and the beer, the beer flowed, and the countercurrents, the antibourgeois currents, swelled and were swell.

I didn't think I was a phony in my black leotard and my black sweater with a large ragged hole above my left breast. I thought it was more honorable to be lost than found. I had become a writer's moll. At bottom I was still Holden's girl. And below the bottom I was still Holden. My mink-coated, clunky-gold-braceleted, high-cuban-heeled, red-lipsticked mother should have laughed at me. Instead she cried. "Are you a lesbian?" she wept into the phone. "Are you a virgin?" she shouted. "No," I lied for a while.

For Allen Ginsberg and Jack Kerouac and William Burroughs, Holden had become their totem character, the one they had eaten to become him. They took his themes and let them ring from all the seedy bars in all the great cities of the country. Beauty and truth, Keats had called it. Whatever name you gave it, it was missing from American life and if you didn't drop out and go crazy like Holden you were in for it. Of course you were in for it if you dropped out too but despite Holden's narrative position as patient talking to his psychiatrist, that wasn't so clear then, not clear at all.

• •

Holden is ultimately transformed into the character Seymour who has had a breakdown in the war from which he won't recover. Buddy is his brother who will lose a brother and Franny his sister who will try to merge with the universe and all are members of the Glass family who are clever but all too eager to disappear into internal mists or take long exiles of a more literal sort like the one their creator ultimately takes to New Hampshire.

But me, I couldn't care less about merging with the cycles of eternity. I didn't then and I don't now. More heroic I think to stick around and take it on the chin. The wisdom in the later Salinger stories seems less wisdom than balm for cowards who can't tolerate the burden of the human soul and want to dump it down the Milky Way like so much toxic waste. I know this is terribly First World, Western, and parochial of me but so be it. "Don't kill yourself," I wanted to scream at Seymour. "Divorce Muriel and marry someone with a shimmering heart, like me."

At the time when I read "Franny" in the *New Yorker* I thought that she was having so much trouble because she was pregnant, not that she was searching for a closeness to God. Rereading the book now I see that she was not pregnant. In 1956 I was the one obsessed with fear of unwed pregnancy, of dying on an abortionist's table, of hemorrhaging and ending my fertile life. Franny was really thinking about the godhead. I was the one thinking about sex. I misread. Franny was an early Shirley MacLaine, a premature seeker of a holy path. Later everyone would know what a mantra was. At the time I couldn't imagine what Franny was doing repeating prayers in a bathroom in a New Haven restaurant. I couldn't believe that Holden was serious about this vanishing-of-the-self religiophilosophy. I still think it's a copout, hemlock for weaklings. As Holden would have soon found, phoniness did not disappear in the ashram, it just took on other forms.

Now from the vantage point of the century's end we can see that Franny was not just young. She was a naif. The giving up of the self can become just as tacky as the obsessive boring materialistic cherishing of the self. The dirty robes, the shredded underwear, the inheritances handed over to frauds, the spiritual search that washed out their faces and put needles in their arms was just as much of an illusion of safety and beauty as the more common vision of becoming a partner in a law firm or owning a house by the beach. Phoniness did not disappear off the streets of Haight-Ashbury, it just led pretty young girls and boys to premature tooth loss, rashes, and grinding poverty. Holden, a.k.a. Buddy and Seymour, Franny and Zooey, and all the Glass family were original voices yes, but in the end they were pied pipers leading the children off to a sealed cave from which there was no escape.

Today at the millennium's cusp we are more of a mind to succeed in this very worldly world. Our children aren't protesting or dreaming of utopias, they aren't even most of them interested in their own salvation, eternal or temporal. They want to have down payments for mortgages and a web site of their own. We inhabit a nation that keeps ideals in their proper place, in politicians' platitudes and fringe groups' survivalist warnings. We go about our practical business with little talk of heaven's chimes. Thank God.

Most likely something strange is bubbling under the surface, the hippies and the orange robed, the reincarnated and the spaceship visitors and the barefoot children and the peyote smokers are waiting their turn and something will surely arise to crack the smooth surface of the status quo. Because when Holden gets frantic enough he goes AWOL from his life and the rest of us are touched, changed, altered at the core.

We don't know if the listening psychiatrist in *The Catcher in the Rye* was a phony too because he never gets to speak, for which I suppose we should be grateful. Maybe the psychiatrist was not a phony. Ultimately I married a psychiatrist on that supposition.

The girl Holden loved was his sister Phoebe. Phoebe is the archetype for characters like Franny and Esmé and Sybil who appear in other Salinger stories. In *The Catcher in the Rye* Holden's younger sister is an almost perfect alter ego, a fellow traveler, a no-pretense, all-giving spirit blessed with perfect sweetness and a quick intelligence. Phoebe is Holden's ally against his parents, his teachers, and the entire cruel world. Some critics found Phoebe cloying. I can see that. She is too good to be true.

In *For Esmé—with Love and Squalor*, Esmé is a young girl Seymour meets in a teashop in London before being shipped off to fight on the Continent. She writes him a letter which he receives while on a ward where he has been hospitalized for a nervous breakdown, a posttraumatic stress disorder that threatens his very life just as if it were a land mine left behind on the road by a retreating enemy. Esmé's letter brings Seymour back to the living for a while, just as Phoebe is able to console Holden for a brief respite. In the story "A Perfect Day for Bananafish," a little girl, Sybil, whom Seymour meets on the beach in Miami, talks to him with directness (without phoniness), with trust, she lets him float with her in the waves. When he kisses her foot with perhaps some mixture of emotion not quite proper, she bolts. Wise Sybil. Sad and damaged beyond repair, Seymour will soon kill himself. As we listen to Seymour's wife, Muriel, on the phone we feel overwhelmed with the flatness of consumerism, the boring pettiness of women's talk, the too bright light, the ugly sad physical striving for artificial beauty, the stupid and the daily vanities that destroy connection and feeling.

We the readers may be supposed to connect this crop of little girls with innocence and endow them with a purity that is absent in the adult women around them. But this idea is sentimental at best. Children are in fact sexual. Children have fantasies that make Aeschylus and Stephen King look like amateurs. If there is anything pure in this world it is not a child, and if there is anything slightly suspect, sexually suspect, it is probably Salinger's odd, slightly Humbert Humbert lust-tinged affection for such perfectly clever little girls. Maybe Seymour was kissing Sybil's foot out of an urge to touch his own childish feet, a time of his own innocence, but maybe it was more than that. Maybe one of the things that prompted Salinger to his self-imposed silence was a fear he would say too much, reveal too much of his own sexual imagination. Maybe, maybe not. It only matters because Holden and Phoebe, a boy who saw through the fake and the deceitful and his good sister, rose from the imagination of a man who was certainly playing with some kind of moral fire.

Little girls are not sugar and spice and you can get burned thinking so. Seymour is not Holden and neither character is identical with his creator. It's just that all of Salinger's little girls are creepy. We view them through the eyes of a seducer even when this is not apparent. Of course I'm not accusing Holden of child molestation in his affection for Phoebe, but in his use of her as his one true friend he brings us to the edge where Esmé will take over as angel and Sybil will ultimately fail to rescue the so badly in need of rescuing. Something odd is going on here. It sounds to me as if Holden's psychiatrist, like Seymour's, did not get to the root of the matter.

Salinger did write of one evil sister. She was not a Glass. She appears in the story "Teddy." She carries in her little female body the meanness, the unkindness of mankind. This family is sailing home on an ocean liner. Teddy is the brilliant religious child who spends his time being interviewed by religious experts the world over. He has had glimpses of his former existence and believes he may escape the human condition entirely after his death, which he senses is near. His sister Booper is first seen maltreating a very little boy at a shuffleboard game. "I hate you, I hate everybody in this ocean," Booper says to Teddy. Teddy has predicted the ambiguous final action of the story. Booper comes up behind him and pushes him into an empty swimming pool and his skull is crushed. Or he pushes Booper into the pool which would be an equally plausible explanation of the action. Booper is the agent of fate but she is also the live squirming selfish hateful human mind that Salinger is running from as fast as he can. No reader will identify with Booper. She embodies our worst instincts, the ones we pretend only others have. But here in this story the saint sister of *The Catcher in the Rye* may have turned into a murderess. At the very least if she was in fact the one murdered we won't spend too much time in mourning.

Does Salinger believe that it is women who destroy? If he does he is not alone of course. Besides, Teddy didn't mind dying. He called it illumination. Was Holden so afraid of death he had to deny its permanence?

I couldn't follow him there. I hated the story "Teddy" when I read it. I wanted to create life not transcend it.

Holden I did give the best years of my youth to you and you did not return the favor, not simply because you were only a literary character and had no power to jump from the page but because the way you were, the Holdenness you created in me, was not as innocent or as helpful in living a real life as one might have hoped.

Holden suffered from the self-righteousness of adolescence. So did I. His easy condemnation of others as phonies was not entirely attractive. But back then it was hard to know why the American dream seemed so bleak, why we were sad when we had so much. That we knew what was phony did not mean that we knew what was real.

When some years later I was in Paris living in a small apartment on the Left Bank with an American writer who drank all the time, I thought I had found my Holden. He had found a woman who was capable of editing a story. As the romance lost its flavor I often sat alone in cafés and tried to read Proust in French. This was hard going, requiring a dictionary and patience beyond my besieged attention span. There I met poets and painters, translators of Rilke, winners of awards in art and literature, and I looked into each of their eyes, watched them look at me. Whom could I run away with, whom could I save from poverty, madness, loneliness, and suicide? I looked for men who were in Gerard Manley Hopkins's words "counter, original, spare." I was interested in men who seemed contrary, too thin or too ugly, too sad or too angry, men with an angle on the day, men who needed to be given everything but did not need to give.

Unlike Holden who would indeed have near expired with gratitude had a woman put a soft and caring arm on his, these men, more like Seymour, were intent on going off to the beach and then placing a gun in their mouths, killing themselves at the seat of language, at the site of communication. The mouth is the point of the thing for the writer. Writing is speech on paper. Holding the attention of the other, making the listener fall in love, that is the goal of the writer. No wonder Seymour shot himself in the mouth. When Holden's creator moved to New Hampshire and refused to publish ever after, he metaphorically shot himself in the mouth. At a certain time in my life I would have tried to stop him.

Fame was very much on our minds as the fifties neared their end. I married a writer who intended to be famous before the age of twenty-six which was the magic year that Keats expired. My first husband frequently drowned his ego with enough alcohol to flood half of China. Watching this I noted the peculiar diametrically opposed desires, the one for wild recognition of self and the other for quick obliteration. Was the competitive pain of fame withheld or temporized so dreadful that one fled to its opposite, to die a drunk under a bridge, buried in a potter's field in an unmarked grave? In one sense this seems like an overly dramatic, perhaps unhealthy romantic worldview. "Give me fame or give me death." On the other hand it was a point of view that would soon be expanded and popularized in the coming sixties: *give me celebrity or give me God—worship me or let me disappear in the great omming of the galaxies.* From this distance this romantic gambit seems a little like blackmail. It seems as if Holden would call it phony. But it wasn't exactly phony. It was Dr. Doolittle's two-headed llama, pushmi-pullyu, of the times.

Certainly I accepted my writer spouse's binges and despairs as normal. I had spent a real long weekend with Holden as he avoided telling his father that he had been kicked out of school. I knew that artists were fragile souls on the edge of death and crackup and that alcohol was the heart pump of the whole package. There was something heroic in despair. The sensitivity of a Seymour or a Holden or a Franny picked them up above the rest of us and gave us something to strive toward, some soul quality we hoped we had.

Dearest Holden I might have been better off had I never loved you.

It seems a bare second between the time I had a drink in Jimmy Ryan's and was reading a letter from Holden's creator to the moments when my own children fell from the grace of childhood into the not so fun house of their own passage into adulthood. I watched as they averted their eyes, whispered into phones, stared with anger into mirrors, lied to me, stayed up until dawn, wept and laughed, ate too much or too little, threw up in the bathroom, glared and stared. They claimed they were terminally lonely or terminally bored or terminally uncertain because they believed nothing or too much or were planning on going off to South America to aid in a revolution and would go to college on their return or smoked stuff on the roof or slept in beds not their own. Like mad dogs running in a pack they moved about the subways of New York and I was always waiting, waiting for a key in the door, waiting for a phone to ring, waiting for someone to tell me what was going on, who was the boy I saw leaving? I saw purple hair and tattoos. I saw tie-dye dresses and dirty bare feet. I saw empty cartons of cigarettes and empty bottles of beer, enough to fill a New Jersey dump.

Why is the rite of passage so hard? Why don't we just arrange a short stay in the forest and let each child have a vision and come back and behave ever after like a responsible member of the community? Why are so many of our young sure they are ugly or weak or stupid or fat or doomed? Something is wrong that growing up should be such an ordeal, a test by fire.

I thought a lot about Holden then. What the hell was wrong with him? Why didn't he just stay in school and take his SATs and stop mewling about like a sick cat? I lost my patience with Holden. I'm sure you understand.

. . . .

East Hampton: I ride my bike on the road near the ocean. There are joggers and runners and skateboarders weaving between the cars. If you look toward the sea you can catch glimpses of the huge houses that lie on the top of the dunes. The gulls fly above. You can catch the shape of a fishing trawler, its insect-like arms spread with nets. I am thinking about real estate. In the Hamptons you think about real estate the way babies think about their pacifiers.

I didn't hear it coming. Then a crunching sound, followed by a shriek of brake. My bike is over on the asphalt. My leg is under the handlebars. My elbow is bleeding. I have all my teeth. I have ruined my shirt, my jeans are split in a way that affords me the least dignity possible. A man about my age is bending over me. He is tall, silver haired, dark eyed, and very concerned. I sit up. I see his Mercedes pulled over off the road. A gaggle of cyclists have stopped and are staring. A few cars pass, a Lexus, a Jaguar, a Porsche. "I'm fine," I say. "I insist you come back to my house with me," he says. I stand. I waver, the center line in the road seems to be dancing to some tune I can't keep. I take the man's offered hand and once in his car, the remains of my bike in his trunk, he introduces himself. "Holden Blakesfield," he says. I give him my name. I ask permission to call my husband who will come pick me up. He offers me his cell phone. We go up a long driveway lined with massive oaks.

From the living room of the house we see the waves crashing on the sand. I am still thinking about real estate. This is real real estate. I admire my surroundings while Mr. Blakesfield's housekeeper fixes me a glass of iced tea. "I was just off to the club, a round of golf," he tells me. "They can wait," he says. My ankle has swollen. My chin is bleeding. I don't want to bleed on the chair. He is looking at me with concern. I wonder if he is thinking I might sue. "I'm fine," I say, "Accidents happen, the road is crowded, I should have seen you coming." I smile. He smiles.

"Beautiful house," I say. I wonder if it was in his family for generations. "Just bought it," he says. "I always wanted an ocean view." There follows an awkward silence. I tell him that my husband who will arrive in a few minutes is a psychoanalyst. He looks at me with interest. "I know about those types," he says. "Actually helped me a lot at one point in my life." I see the Whiffenpoof photograph on the hall table. "Yale?" I ask. "Yes," he says. The phone rings. He answers it. He comes back "It's my sister Phoebe. She's coming over with her grandchildren this afternoon. We're going to the duck pond to feed the ducks. Ever do that?" he asks me.

"Are you a writer?" I ask him. Not many writers live in houses like this, but perhaps. He laughs. "No, no, my younger brother, he died a long time ago, he would have been a writer. I am in mergers and acquisitions, IPOs—that sort of thing. I'm a very ordinary investment banker." "You seem to have done well," I say. "Yes," he says. "I've always had an eye for the genuine."

"Is your last name genuine?" I ask. Holden doesn't say anything. I don't either.

· · · ·

2

.... Robert Jordan ......

Robert Jordan

Ernest Hemingway's
For Whom the Bell Tolls

It doesn't make you a jerk to get tear-jerked.

S*o m e* years ago we took nine girls from our daughter's all-female school out to a Chinese dinner. We were celebrating twelfth birthday of our youngest child. The girls were wearing dresses with lace collars and velvet ribbons in their hair. They had on shining black shoes with tiny heels and one or two wore lipstick, very pink. Most sported silver bands around their teeth. One or two were plump with rounded soft bodies. Some had breasts, tiny upward-turned cups, newly tender buds that promised milk one day, barely visible, embarrassing to their owners. The girls were horseback riders, basketball players, one had a passion for science fiction. Usually they wore their school uniforms, socks slipping over the ankles, sneakers, and white blouses under blue jumpers. At first they were stiff and formal with each other, awed perhaps by the paper dragons with tiny light bulbs for eyes that hung overhead, but by the time the meal arrived they were laughing and telling terrible stories about some of their uninvited classmates. Loudly they sang "Happy Birthday" after a waiter produced a slice of pineapple with a flaming candle. After the fortune cookies we left the restaurant to walk up Third Avenue.

The girls were straggling behind us as a woman passed on the right side of the street. She was slightly built, her blonde hair was tied back in a clip and I smelled her perfume as she passed. A few steps back a young man wearing jeans and a sweatshirt, with long legs and muscular chest, was moving up closer. He came up behind the woman and with a quick gesture, tongue of snake flickering in the open air, pulled at the gold chain around her neck and she screamed and the chain broke and the young man began to run. I looked back at my flock of girls. They were standing still as people do at accidents, seemingly frozen. My mate, a man then in his fifties, a gray-haired psychoanalyst whose only sport was fishing and who spent all his days in a black leather chair behind a couch, sprang forward after the chain snatcher. Lifted by the force of his anger he ran like a man chasing his own soul. In less than a quarter of a block he caught up to the object of his pursuit and he pushed him and he yelled as he tripped him and in the banging of bodies he himself went crashing down. The two of them, the older man and the far younger, limbs entangled, writhed on the sidewalk. The thief might have had a gun. He might have had a knife. He might have simply punched my spouse whose glasses had slipped off, whose boxing skills had never existed except perhaps in his dreams.

As tears ran down my face the younger man jumped up and ran across the street dodging oncoming cars. My mate was slower to rise than his opponent. He was limping. He had scraped the side of his face. Blood was staining his white shirt. Even so he tried to continue the chase. Across the street the thief disappeared. The gold chain had been left on the curb. My spouse picked it up and returned it to its grateful owner.

I was angry but the nubile girls, eyes bright, rushed over to the limping hero of this urban encounter. They stared at him. They giggled and touched his jacket arm. "You could have been killed over a gold chain. What came over you?" I demanded to know. He shrugged. Under my fury another feeling surged up like a blowing whale into my consciousness. Like the little girls, I was exhilarated. He would defend us. He would protect us.

Something primitive had happened on the street, and the man who had just shared our sesame noodles and orange prawns was now patrolling the dangerous wilds, averting threats to his women (a category which for better or worse included the passing lady). It was foolish. It was stupid. What if the sudden exertion had strained his back, broken his ankle? Ah yes, but there was a rightness in his act. For a moment standing there half a block down from the Chinese restaurant, as my spouse wiped the blood from his face with his tie, there was a balance in the world, and we were enfolded inside a magic circle—safe. The girls, who would soon be women themselves, daughters of women who were lawyers, doctors, professors, thought this was the best birthday party of them all. I thought of Robert Jordan in *For Whom the Bell Tolls*.

Robert Jordan is another of Hemingway's maler than male alter ego heros. He is a teacher of Spanish at a university in Montana, a would-be writer. When the Spanish Civil War breaks out he goes to fight against the fascists because he believes he must. He is a man who knows the forests, who knows how to survive by fishing and hunting. He knows guns and dynamite and he knows how to blow up a bridge. This dangerous blowing up of a bridge is his obligation, his task, the narrative thrust of the plot line in this novel by Hemingway published in America in 1940 at the edge of the world war that would involve some sixteen million American men before its end.

This novel is about fear and courage, bravery and cowardice, and how close they are one to another and how they arrive in our lives and tell us who we are. It is about politics of course. Fascism and communism fighting each other, and each side (this Hemingway knew and told us) was capable of cruelties that betray the entire cornucopia of the human heart. The Spanish Civil War was a small preview, a short brief prologue to the savagery that lay just ahead. But it was horrible enough and Hemingway saw it. Or rather his character, alter ego, Robert Jordan saw it and told us about it and in doing so became a hero for all time, a man of moral rectitude, strength, quiet wisdom, a man a woman would follow to the ends of the world if only he hadn't been killed in the last pages of the novel.

Yet I could accept that Robert Jordan had to die, that the integrity of the story would have been violated had he lived, that the tone of the novel, lyrical, fable-like, simple, pure as water from the mountain stream, tragic in intent, could not have supported his living happily ever after with his girl-woman Maria in America's Montana. If he had survived false notes would surely have cracked the lyric universe Hemingway had so carefully created. Maria would have betrayed Jordan with a younger fellow from the English department or their children would cheat on their math tests and the dishes would mount in the sink as the sound of the vacuum would replace the hum of the fascist airplanes scouting the hills. The ash-blue light of American television would in another decade have colored their dreams and Maria, once animated only by love, would in the decades to follow have begged for a bigger refrigerator. The everydayness of real life would erode the characters until they were no longer heart stopping, but transformed into rather plain, gray, undone souls, petty as the rest of us, regular as Wonder Bread or peanut butter.

Nevertheless I felt bitter toward the author. Hemingway had killed Robert Jordan, and the loss, the tears I shed, were not trivial, not at all. King Lear, Ophelia, Hamlet, Beth in *Little Women* had to die. Some literary losses you absorb as the price of admission. Some you resent. Robert Jordan should have lived (because I loved him), but of course he couldn't.

Robert Jordan, like Nick Adams before him, is Hemingway's own voice, thinks his thoughts, and fulfills his fantasies. His cause is lost and it isn't such a good cause to begin with—which Robert Jordan knows. He goes on anyway. It is this going on, both heroic and silly, romantic and profoundly male, that rivets our attention. From the very beginning Jordan knows that blowing up this bridge just before a surprise offensive by the Loyalists is so dangerous as to be virtually suicidal. He also knows that the guerrillas who must help him, a mountain band led by a morally weakened man named Pablo and his fierce wife, Pilar, have themselves committed crimes—murdered most cruelly priests and bakers, barbers and merchants whose only sins had been to support the temporarily vanquished fascist side. He knows that the soldiers who search the mountains for the Loyalist bands are themselves decent men of the villages and towns, not monsters but human beings whose sisters write them letters and whose death when it comes will not be more or less deserved than his own.

When I first read this book I had barely heard of the Spanish Civil War. I had seen Picasso's *Guernica*, black and white twists and turns, horses' eyes opened wide in agony, and great swirls of fear and burning lanterns racing across the wide canvas. Then I had thought the fascists, allies of Hitler, were the only evil ones. Robert Jordan knew better. Evil is in the human condition, and all political creeds carry its germ, express its form at one point or another. In a scene in which Pilar describes to Robert Jordan the rounding up of the fascists in her town and the humiliation and murder of these ordinary men, we understand exactly the madness of the mob and the nastiness of the political animal with a gun in his hand and the crowd on his side.

My love for Robert Jordan was predicated on the goodness and hopeless valor of his allegiance to the Loyalist side. The simplicity of Hemingway's plot was deceptive. *For Whom the Bell Tolls* is a far wiser and more complicated novel than I could ever have understood on first reading, before my sixteenth birthday. Then I still believed in pure good and absolute evil. Robert Jordan, as I considered him again and again and compared him to the real boys around me, became my ideal of manhood, manliness, maleness. This vision for better or worse served like travel directions, sometimes misplaced, on my own far less well shaped journey.

This is a war novel that never forgets nature's sweetness: the earth smells, the sun strikes the leaves, the seasons move on.

> Robert Jordan pushed aside the saddle blanket that hung over the mouth of the cave and stepping out, took a deep breath of the cold night air. The mist had cleared away and the stars were out. There was no wind and outside now of the warm air of the cave, heavy with smoke of both tobacco and charcoal, with the odor of cooked rice and meat, saffron, pimentos and oil—Robert Jordan breathed deeply of the clear night air of the mountains that smelled of the pines and of the dew on the grass in the meadow by the stream. Dew had fallen heavily since the

wind had dropped but as he stood there he thought there would be frost by morning.

Wind, stars, dew, mist, the smells of man, man eating and drinking repeat themselves in the book over and over and within this fold, embraced within, lies the killing and the death and the waste of human life. And the simplicity of the words, the somber rhythm they create, becomes attached to the soul of Robert Jordan so that the man who is the hero of the novel is also the landscape or the air around the story. And the man that I loved, Robert Jordan, was made of this combination—place and destiny, land and sky. Who could resist such a pounding in the brain?

There is a passage in the early pages of *For Whom the Bell Tolls* that foretells the end. The dynamiter who had been with the guerrillas a few months earlier has died in another action. Robert Jordan is taking his place. Someone in the band asks what has happened to the man sent from Loyalist headquarters in Madrid who had helped them blow up a train sometime previously. Pablo, the husband of Pilar, the leader of the band whose will to fight is slipping, answers the question: "He is dead since April. That's what happens to everybody. That is the way we all finish." Anselmo, a good peasant, adds, "That is the way all men end. That is the way all men have always ended." These words, said quietly in the mountains, outside the cave the band uses for home, under the stars and the large pines and the rock boulders, are both ordinary and grand. They have the effect of a prayer repeated so often that the meaning is carried by the echo rather than the actual words. They console us, the way a hand on an arm consoles or a piece of music or a familiar voice.

Now it's easy to parody Robert Jordan and it's easy enough to listen with an ironic ear to his words on life and death. They are not original. They are not phrased with the gorgeousness or preciseness of an Emily Dickinson or a Gerard Manley Hopkins. They do not uncover secrets like the words of James Joyce or Virginia Woolf. Out of context they sound almost silly, obvious. But with the smell of violence just over the hill's crest, with the wine pouring from a flask, with the bridge waiting to be blown up, with the Fascist guards smoking in their sentry houses, with the Loyalists planning a doomed venture, with the stars overhead, the stoicism, the fatalism, the bravery of men catches at the throat. Yes, these lines are sentimental, lacking in wit and sophistication, far from Noël Coward and Oscar Wilde, far from Dorothy Parker and Alexander Woollcott, and yet they hold and echo and demand respect. They are true, in the way that elemental things—breathing, eating, loving, hating—are true, beyond comment, just are. In context they move us like the massive rocks at Stonehenge. They are not laughable. The author himself is not pulling our legs or twitting us with irony. They are intended exactly as said. They apply to us too even though we are not on a mountaintop about to blow up a bridge in a war that was meant to preserve the socialist vision which wasn't worth preserving and had already been subverted by the communists whose ruthlessness was a corruption in itself, corruption incarnate.

Cynicism in Robert Jordan is reserved for politics. Man is noble or sometimes noble, and in that vision the character is dead straight on. And that's why after Robert Jordan died I felt a special desolation that hung on long after the last page of the novel had been read. Later I understood it. Ideology of the left and the right had failed us. The difference between good and bad had been blurred. The side of the angels had been defeated in Spain. There were no angels on either side and now there was no more Robert Jordan.

A character in a Hemingway short story says, "There is no sense in mouthing things up." What he means is that every little thing doesn't have to be analyzed, examined, and placed into a sentence. Some things should just be experienced, lived, understood. This is an odd statement for a writer, whose task, after all, is to put the undercurrents, the complexities, the things we see and feel and know and fear into words. But it is very much a part of Robert Jordan's maleness— this hoarding of words, this not saying too much. This is often a masculine manner. It's akin to not crying. It's a stiff upper lip and a put-into-action-not-into-words response to the needs and the longings and the disappointments of living. So the hunter walks in the woods and doesn't report on all the pangs of indigestion he is feeling from the rapid gulping of his too-dark cup of coffee. He strides, he looks, he focuses on the task before him. He isn't maudlin or embarrassing or overly precise in his use of words. He is male. His silences are intended to speak volumes.

There are many descriptions of trout fishing in Hemingway's novels and stories. Robert Jordan also fishes. Nick Adams fishes. Jake Barnes of *The Sun Also Rises* goes on a trout fishing trip before the bulls begin to run in Pamplona. Trout fishing is about watching the water for the sign of the feeding fish. It is about silences and shadows and the shifting patterns of the sun, the rising and falling of insects in the dark underhangings by the river's edge. Robert Jordan watches everything as he moves upstream or downstream.

My spouse is a fisherman. Not cut exactly from the Hemingway cloth, he began as a boy in Sheepshead Bay in Brooklyn, fishing with a bent pin and an earthworm dug up in the park. Now on his August vacation he fishes for blues off the shore of Long Island, and for many years he surf-cast from the ocean's edge in the dawn and the dusk, standing in the foam of the waves, trying again and again, winding and tossing, hoping and losing hope. Once he caught two fish and the moment stands in our mutual history as one of miraculous fortune, as if an angel had struck us with a floating wing. We have fished in Moosehead Lake in Maine. We searched for bass in the Everglades. Once when we stayed at a ranch in Santa Fe, he fished for trout in a stocked pond and we had them for dinner. He has taken small boats out into the wet-smelling fog and he knows how to hit the fish on the head as it lies flapping with desperation on the floorboards of the boat, how to bleed it so it will taste fine in the frying pan. He knows just as if he had been born in Idaho how to skin the fish and cut away the bones. Sometimes his hands smell of fish for days. We have fished for salmon and he has stood on a small island in Togiak National Park in Alaska following the running fish, upstream and back down, stumbling on the stones beneath his feet, red with excitement, tense with concentration, fierce in his desire to have the fish, this fish, his worthy adversary.

We are city people. Guides must come with us when we wander in lonely wildernesses. Robert Jordan would need no guide. Nick Adams would be a guide. But my spouse as he stands patiently waiting for me to take his picture with his fish is ripe with a joy that splashes over on me. The emotion that wells up is a leftover, a remnant, from feelings that first were connected with Robert Jordan, with Nick Adams, from a romance with men who want to pull from the water the scaly, ugly, gill-widening and -closing creatures. When I ask my mate what is it, what is the great excitement, the victory in the thing, he says nothing. His eyes look bright. He touches my back, my arm. He wastes no words. This experience is beyond words.

Hemingway is an author so he must use words, but as sparingly as possible, no gooey adjectives, just the essentials as if the fishing were relayed to us the readers by a heavy stone sunk under the ripples or a weed drifting in the current. He describes the bed of ferns where he places the trout he catches and he describes the chill in the air or the sun on his back. He does not use more words than necessary. He does not tell you what the fisherman is feeling at any given moment. The experience enfolds and overcomes words and exists as action, feet walking, eyes watching, nature being itself, shadows falling, fish swimming, jumping, large or small, escaped or caught, cooked, time passing.

For Hemingway this not mouthing it up too much is a writing technique, his hallmark style. We also know that men for the most part do not discuss their emotions as easily with the same kind of dissecting interest and passion as most women do. Almost every girlfriend or wife has turned to her male partner at some time and asked, "What are you thinking? What are you feeling?" Men, even the most verbal among them, tend to a kind of Hemingway gruffness when it comes to the flow of everyday irritants, interests, attractions, sadnesses, tooth pains, etc.

Once we were at our Thanksgiving table, and my husband was reading aloud the poem of an absent child, one who was very sick, and suddenly he couldn't read anymore and in the silence everyone at the table felt the lump, the swallowed tear, the unacknowledged tear. It was like the silence following a door slamming. The power was in the trace of the unexpressed.

Robert Jordan, through whose head most of the novel *For Whom the Bell Tolls* passes, does not waste words. His maleness is mixed up in this. He allows just so much of what he thinks to pass his lips. He allows himself to think only that which he can tolerate. A woman attached to this kind of male needs to learn how to hear the unsaid, to interpret the smallest of sounds, to divine the signs from the slimmest of evidence. But somehow, perhaps because I once loved Robert Jordan and Nick Adams and hung over their shoulders while they went fishing far away from civilization, out on streams and rivers that offered them silence and dignity and elemental matters, like fish scales and rain or wind, I find in the nontalking, the few words as necessary—a dearness, a sweetness, a boyness, an otherness that draws me close.

Of course when I am close I say, "What are you thinking? Tell me." But I don't expect an answer. I accept that the male, the Robert Jordanness of whatever male I am with, is avoiding mouthing it up too much. Perhaps this response to the male silence is only realistic, or is it reactionary in a postfeminist world?

Of course, it is reactionary. Hemingway's vision of the man without too many words is only a stereotype, a prison in which we incarcerate our genders. But that said, Robert Jordan, lying on his blanket under the night sky, his coming death accepted without whining, complaint, explanation—a paucity of words—is a male to be loved ever after. I can't help that. I am a woman of my time and place, and I read *For Whom the Bell Tolls* for the first time while I was still a virgin and the death of all civilization seemed to be imminent. Ducking my head under my desk, hiding my eyes from the bright light of the hydrogen bomb that might fall, I feared that the end would come before I had a chance to love a man or understand how it was done, part to part, generation to generation.

For Hemingway the elephant or the bull, the walking, the brush, the gun: these are the footprints, the signs along the trail of emotions. They are sufficient. They do not need expansion or elaboration or close analytic examination. If Hemingway is the anti–Woody Allen, the anti–Proust, the primal American frontiersman, despite the transplanting to Europe or Africa or Cuba, then maleness, this kind of maleness, is in fact subversive, anti-urban, anti–talk show, and still glorious and still with us.

What is particularly appealing if paradoxical: the close-mouthed male hero appears in a book, whose only reason for existence is to talk to us, the readers. The Hemingway male wants to communicate what he knows (most of them are writers like their creator). They want you to know what they feel but they are under a restraining order to do it with as few words as possible, with as little fuss as they can. There is a poignancy in this contradiction that informs the way we respond to the work, that makes us love the man who is trying to tell us that he loves or needs or hurts even as he can't bring the words directly clearly out. The tension between the urge to say and the need to say as little as possible creates a sound like a lamenting saxophone. This leads to a semi-mute man, a hero with a muzzle on, whose purpose is to tell us something important but reluctantly. The muffled quality amplifies the emotions. Robert Jordan wants to be a writer if he returns to civilian life. What woman would not want to be at his side?

Robert Jordan did have a love, his first real love he said. It was Maria. Maria is with the band of guerrillas in the mountains. She is the schoolgirl daughter of the Loyalist mayor of a town that has been taken over by the Fascists. They have killed her mother and father. They shaved her head. Brutally they raped her. She was a prisoner on the train whose tracks had been bombed by the guerrilla band, and in the confusion of smoking steel and bent doors and railroad cars upturned, she escaped her captors. She was unable to talk, stunned and terrorized by her experience, when Pilar, the woman leader of the band, found her and took her along into the mountains. Her hair has barely begun to grow back. She is still afraid when Robert Jordan comes to the cave. Jordan feels her wounded soul in her eyes, in her limbs, not in her conversation.

Maria and Robert Jordan become lovers, and this love is both ridiculous and romantic. I reject its reality and I adore it at the same time. I suspect that when I first read *For Whom the Bell Tolls*, I didn't know enough to see the romantic exaggeration. Maiden-like I hoped it would happen just so to me.

After the first night of intercourse under the stars on a blanket in the mountains as the group waits for the moment to blow up the bridge, Maria is told by Robert Jordan that the earth has moved for him. It has moved for her too. Could this be the origin of this much-mocked expression? Did Hemingway invent it for Maria and Robert, or was it something people said all the time in those days? I don't know. What I do know is that Maria, childlike, trusting, offering to wash Robert's clothes, to fold his equipment, to hold his horse when he goes into battle, is a man's fantasy of a woman, a sweet offering, a loving hand, willing to have intercourse even when her genitals hurt if it will give him pleasure.

No wonder Hemingway found his real wives less than satisfactory and kept replacing them. Maria is a cross between the ideal geisha, the innocent daughter, and the sexual lover who is always available, a woman ready to serve. It is the fact that she has been harmed by the Fascists, that she is the wounded orphan of the war, that makes her so captivating as well as the fact that she is so trusting, so eager to serve him. One does not imagine that Eve in the garden was equally gracious to Adam. This earth moving, this offering of the innocent, this coupling in the night just before the battle at dawn, is romantic in all the worst sense of the word, and yet was I also not ready to love with the fullness of my heart? Would I too not give myself to the man who wanted me and would promise me protection and lead me through mine fields? For all this would I not be grateful?

During the blowing up of the bridge, Jordan insists that Maria stay on the far side of the danger and wait for him. After the bridge has been blown up, a futile act because the enemy has already learned of the Loyalists' plans and has prepared its own terrible counteroffensive, Robert Jordan arranges for Maria to escape safely while he, wounded, accepts death, staying behind to shoot at her pursuers.

Yes, I know reading *For Whom the Bell Tolls* some fifteen years after it was published, in the safety of my apartment, with doormen and elevator men to watch over me, in a big city in America, I could hardly need protection like Maria with her animal-like luster and her dark eyes in the mountains of a Spain at war with itself. I was not in battle. What was the danger that I wanted protection from? Why did I want it from a man? In truth I could learn judo or get a gun permit or make myself safe in my single bed. But these are thoughts from this time, looking back on that time. Like it or not romantic dreams have stubbornly persisted, drawn by the cart of biology or habits formed in millennia past when someone had to hunt the horned beast and someone had to stay by the hearth waiting for familiar steps on the path below. There is no absolute answer to this question. All I know is that Maria is a one-dimensional character whose beauty and soul, whose innocent wounds, charmed Robert Jordan instantly.

Willingly I would have been Maria. I would have abandoned any other dimensions I might have been harboring. I would have charmed Robert Jordan if I could—not just because he would protect me or make the earth move under my blanket, although those are good reasons, but because there was redemption in this love that burned holy at the center of the novel. Male and female made he them, me too, me too, I called out in the privacy of my mind. Could love redeem the mess, the murder, the war, the limbs lost, the devastation wrought, the wiping out of village and priest, could love even if it only had three days to be, could love do that? I hoped so. I still hope so.

Nowadays we make fun of the macho man, silent, tough, chasing across the terrain doing what he feels he must, acting within a clear moral universe, a John Wayne, a Lone Ranger, a Robert Jordan. But do we really think this is ridiculous, or do we still hope to find this man, bending toward us, lifting us up to the back of his horse, out of the flames, out of the range of danger: tender, gentle, tough, and hard, the too-heavy drinker, the constant smoker, the eyes that have seen the unsayable, still capable of survival, capable of ensuring our survival under the most hostile of circumstances? How bad is that? How silly is that? Pretty silly, I reluctantly admit.

Of course Maria is a child-woman. Of course Maria is damaged and still in shock when she meets Robert Jordan. Hemingway's creation of a good woman for his macho man leaves most of us cold. We are not childlike, at least not past our childhood. We are not so traumatized or frail as Maria. Our beauty is not in our compliance or our willingness to love. We are more than that. But if we are honest, we know that we are also that. So sex and love remain a many-times-painted-over picture, layered with old versions, lying just beneath the surface, filling our mind with things just out of sight, things not so politically correct or reasonable or contemporary but impossible to erase just because they have slipped out of fashion and never were so real or useful anyway.

Hemingway writes often about fear. On the surface of his stories he seems to be idolizing the brave and condemning cowardice. But that's the impression you get from a fast read, not a careful one. Actually what impresses Hemingway is the way a man can live with fear and still do what he feels he must. In his own life he hunted fierce animals with sharp horns. He ran with the bulls at Pamplona. He admired bullfighters the way some of us admire neurosurgeons or physicists. He wrote about war and courage and cowardice over and over again. But this obsession with behavior under pressure is more interesting than it seems at first glance.

At the end of *For Whom the Bell Tolls*, the point of view shifts to Andrés, one of the band in the mountain. Andrés is making his way toward Loyalist headquarters to warn them that the Fascists are prepared for the offensive. Andrés who runs with the bulls in his town every year and is known for his bravery in hurtling himself directly over the horns acknowledges to himself that each year he hopes for rain, listens for rain on his roof, in hopes that he will not in fact have to run through the streets. He admits his great fear of the bull and the task before him. As Hemingway writes this, we see that the man's bravery, his courage both on the streets and in the war, is all the more valorous, worthy, because he has felt fear.

Pilar the older woman, tells Robert Jordan of her love affair with Finito, a famous matador. "Never have I seen a man with more fear before the bullfight and never have I seen a man with less fear in the ring." The struggle then is to control the fear, not to deny it. In a short story that seemed incomprehensible to me when I first read it and now seems particularly nasty, "The Short Happy Life of Francis Macomber," a man shows cowardice out on a hunt in Africa. He bolted "like a rabbit," from a lion. He is ashamed and his wife expresses her contempt for him. But on the next day he finds his courage and shoots a buffalo and feels excitement rather than fear. He has found a way around his cowardice. Hemingway has the white hunter Wilson say admiringly, "Fear gone like an operation. Something else grew in its place. Main thing a man had. Made him into a man. Women knew it too. No bloody fear." But Hemingway didn't mean absence of fear; he meant fear faced and conquered, and courage was the action that was taken despite the fear. The story ends with Mrs. Macomber, angry at her husband's new-found manhood, shooting and killing him perhaps accidentally, but more likely not. Hemingway sometimes sees women as the enemy, as the castrators, the destroyers of all that is beautiful in a man. Mrs. Macomber is the anti-Maria. Both versions of women are not entirely alien to any honest female.

Today we make fun of the great white hunter, and we in America hardly see the need to test ourselves against the horns of a bull, but we still understand that a man must be brave and willing to risk even his life for the things that matter to him. In our urban computerized world of malls and meat under cellophane, the need is still there to make a man's life worthy, framed by his courage. A man must still be brave, not foolhardy, not careless, not drive drunk down a highway at ninety miles per hour but find a dignity within himself, a bravery that is different in kind and stripe from female courage or female bravery.

The man whom I love doesn't have to be a boxer or a solo pilot or a firefighter. In fact it would be hard for me to love such a man because so much would be lost between us, so much of who I am and what runs through my very citified mind, but still any man I love must be brave. What can that mean now that we don't test it, now that we tend to mock Macomber flushed with pride facing a charging buffalo, Jordan sitting still waiting for the last moment to release his dynamite? Today the bullfighters and the trout fishermen and the heavy drinkers are as out of step with the times as the *Tyrannosaurus rex* trampling through the forest primeval.

The easy answer: I like to believe that if the need arose, the man I am with would behave with Robert Jordan courage and shield my body and take my hand and lead me out of danger and give me a blanket if I were cold and even take the jacket off his back for me. The easy answer is that a man I love in today's world has only to give me the illusion that he would hunt for me and kill for me and that fear of death would afflict him but not stop him from doing what might be necessary.

But that's only part of the answer. The other part is that a man has to be there when a woman loses a breast, loses a baby, loses a job. He has to brave the knives and daggers of the world of his work and survive and he has to be of comfort when she is undone and he has to be prepared to face his own death or hers with courage and conviction that the good thing between them will endure through the darkest of experiences. Brave is not ignorant, not unfeeling or unflinching, it is just constant, revealed in suburbs, in PTA meetings, in hospital corridors—a quality of a man that lies under the surface, not tested for the most part, but there.

Is this bravery different from that required of the female? In many ways not, and yet it has a different tone. It rests on a premise of physical courage, of action and aggression. The courage required of a male is qualitatively different from what we expect of women, from what I expect from myself. If a man turns to putty, lets failure overcome him, allows reversal to still his ambition, his desire, then he is not brave enough, not brave enough for me or mine. This remains so. And women when they select their mate know this, perhaps without words, but they know that they want a man who will stay strong when the floods come because come they will.

Cowardice and fear: bravery under pressure. This is the heart of the bullfighting matter. Death is in the air: stare at it, conquer it, kill or be killed. This is what fascinated Hemingway. Hemingway observed the religious ritual of the blood rite of the bullfight and he loved it because it encapsulated the drama, the murderous drama that is nature, species against species, self against the indifferent sun. The ritual contains the fear and the joy, and the excitement of killing the bull is the overcoming, the undoing of the beast, the one within, the one without. The form, the style of the bullfight is the human contribution to the primitive morality play we are all engaged in, like it or not: to live or die, to harm or be harmed. Every time we eat, every time we chop down a tree to build a house, or drain a lake to bring water to our cities, we announce ourselves, killers and victors.

Despite the phallic symbols and the biological references to sex, the bullfight is not for women or about women, and when in *The Sun Also Rises* the bullfighter is seduced by Lady Brett, she sullies his beauty, despoils the purity that was there. The bullfighting that so obsessed Hemingway is a male rite, a thrust of the sword against fate, against the will of God, against the massive, dark beasts that haunt us in both reality and imagination.

I have not asked of my Brooklyn-born husband that he fight a bull but I know he was a soldier in a war that needed to be fought. He volunteered after his first year at the university. He will tell me nothing about it. He tended a radio decoder and was brought up right behind the front lines all the way from Normandy to Munich. He wasn't a hero and he didn't kill anyone with his Army-issue gun, I don't think. And yet he was a hero. He was there. All of our long married life I have known that he went to war as a very young man, barely shaving. That fact is in the curve of his spine as we lie together in the bed we share. I know he would not let me die without a fight. I know that he will help me to be brave when I must die and I know that whatever afflictions come our way, he will enfold me within his ferocious and sometimes territorial stance.

It is not fair to Hemingway, not fair at all, to think that he was singing the praises of the testosterone-pouring, aggressively growling male beast. *For Whom the Bell Tolls* contains a strange and wonderful conversation between Robert Jordan and an older peasant member of the band whom he likes and trusts.

Robert Jordan asks, "You have killed?" Anselmo replies, "Yes, several times. But not with pleasure. To me it is a sin to kill a man. Even Fascists whom we must kill. To me there is a great difference between the bear and the man and I do not believe in the wizardry of the gypsies about the brotherhood with animals. No, I am against all killing of men." "Yet you have killed." "Yes. And will again. But if I live later, I will try to live in such a way, doing harm to no one, that

it will be forgiven. . . . with or without God, I think it is a sin to kill."
. . . Jordan repeats, "But still thou has killed." The answer is, "Yes.
Many times and will again. But not with pleasure and regarding it as
a sin."

There is then this moral dimension to the Hemingway male. He is
aware of the value of human life, and while he may kill or be killed because of what he deems a necessity, he is not a random murderer. His
killing is not simply an expression of rage or blood lust. This moral
struggle, whether it is about the behavior of men in war or about the
way a man pays his bills, is central to the thing about a man that ren-
ders him worthy, valuable, sexually interesting. In the everyday lives
that most of us lead we make moral decisions all the time. We don't
cheat on our taxes or we do. We don't betray friends or we do. We
honor our obligations even when we are not pleased to do so. When
we can't honor our vows or our duties we ache with guilt and regret.
We visit old dull relatives or we travel an arduous distance or stay up
late at night because someone needs our company. In the most banal
of lives, roads have been crossed, deeds have been done or left undone, self has been pitted against other. This clean moral core, the
hardness of it, the dependability of it, embedded in a male who will
act, who will drive forward when it is necessary, has its own power of
attraction, its own worth.

Robert Jordan in all he says and does is a man of moral rectitude.
This is different from a woman of moral rectitude. It requires less social smarts, less language, less excitement. It is simply a matter of contained goodness and decency and the intention of making acts in the
world conform to a vision of right (what God would want if there was
a God), that never fades, slips perhaps, but is never erased.

I would not ever have married a doctor who wanted only to make
money from his patients. I would not have married a man who did not
honor his children. I would not marry a man who did not see himself
in the world as a person whose life should bring something, no matter
how small, to someone else. This is Hemingway in urban garb. His
values translated into the world in which I live. Once after we had
been married a long time my husband and I went to Israel on a tour.
We were in the Galilee and were visiting a small farming settlement.

My husband said to me, If I had my life to live over I might have become a general doctor traveling from kibbutz to moshav, vaccinating, watching over sore throats, bringing antibiotics in the trunk of my car. Now he didn't exactly mean that. But he did. And as he said it my hand went to his and I held on as tightly as possible. There was something in the vision he had as we stood among the tomatoes covered with long plastic sheets in that dusty earth-smelling field that was romantic, yes, but not out of character, not discordant with his person, something that bound him to me and me to Robert Jordan.

Hemingway who did not lead his own life with specially fine loyalties or moral choices did understand what it was that a woman could love in a male, love year after year. In fact I think he understood what makes a woman attach herself to a male just as well as he understood how to find a trout in the dark shadows at the side of the river bank.

The hunting and the fishing that Hemingway so enjoyed and wrote about again and again reveal much more than the use of his sporting interests in his work. Yes, he did not as a young man believe in the Gypsy bond with the nonhuman forms of life. He had no sympathy for the bull killed by the matador or the steers gored by the terrified and angry bull. He was not squeamish and animal blood did not make him close his eyes. But as he aged, his point of view seems to have shifted. In *The Garden of Eden*, published posthumously in 1986, he writes a story within a story about a boy horrified by his father's tracking and killing a grand old elephant who has moved through the forest, past the young boy, a presence of dignity and grace. The boy despises his father, and the hunt as viewed through the child's innocent eyes becomes a dirty alienating form of murder. In *The Old Man and the Sea* (Pulitzer Prize, 1953) we see the fish as a worthy opponent, as a creature deserving of great respect, a mystical fish perhaps who has its own reasons and its own strengths and its rightful place in the universe.

This expanded empathy, this late-in-life identification of the writer with the animal, may simply be the mark of Hemingway's middle age, of death approaching, but it may also reflect moral emanations from the center of the Robert Jordan world. Back to Anselmo: cruelty should not be random, unnecessary; death is always awesome, even if it is of a small trout, gills flapping uselessly in the dirt.

Most people I know think of Hemingway as the Great Satan of gender stereotypes, the perpetrator of the dominating male as hero. But here too the story is more complicated than it seems. We can turn to psychoanalysis and knowing that Hemingway's depressed mother dressed him in girls' clothes until he was five, a barely acceptable custom of the time and place, we can see that his male huffing and puffing could be in defiance, in denial, in repudiation of his early male anxiety. But on the other hand the fantasy of being whole, by being double gendered, is right at the heart of Robert Jordan and Maria's lovemaking. This dialogue takes place inside the sleeping bag the night before the blowing up of the bridge, the end of the story:

"Was it well?" she asked.

"Yes," he said. "Take off the wedding shirt."

"You think I should?"

"Yes, if thou wilt not be cold."

"*Qué va*, cold. I am on fire."

"I too, but afterwards thou wilt not be cold?"

"No, afterwards we will be as one animal of the forest and be so close that neither one can tell that one of us is one and the other the other. Can you not feel my heart be your heart?"

"Yes, there is no difference."

"Now feel. I am thee and thou art me and all of one is the other. And I love thee, oh, I love thee so. Are we not truly one? Canst thou not feel it?"

"Yes," he said. "It is true."

"And feel now. Thou hast no heart but mine."

"Nor any other legs, nor feet, nor of the body."

The lovers admit that it is a good thing there is some difference between them but they express the wish we have to merge in love, in sex—even the most sophisticated among us. I learned this I think from Robert Jordan. I too have been one creature, the humpbacked one. I know this image is romantic, even sentimental, but it is comforting nevertheless. We are too much alone, too single in our beds, in our bodies. Sex, of the kind that Robert Jordan has with the tawny-haired frightened girl he has nicknamed Rabbit, allows escape. Expressed here is the platonic version of the human condition— the split halves searching for each other. Only in deep love is the double-sexed creature restored to its wholeness, to its true self.

Some Hemingway women are passive, childlike Rabbits. Some are vicious hard-edged destroyers like Mrs. Macomber or Frances, Robert Cohn's destroying girlfriend in *The Sun Also Rises*. Robert Jordan befriends Pilar who by becoming the leader of the band has emasculated her husband, Pablo, and crossed into the other gender role. Jordan admires Pilar. For this I respect him.

In good novels you don't get your cake and eat it too. This love affair with Maria is doomed, not because of the moth-holed character of the partners, as is the usual case, but because death will have the last word. Perhaps their love succeeds so well because it will be so absurdly brief. It's not easy inside a Hemingway novel. It's not easy outside either.

Hemingway is not unaware of how women feel. He grants an entire scene to Pilar who is no longer young and beautiful and allows her to express her hurt feelings on being rejected as a sexual object by a young man. He creates a brave little sister in the Nick Adams stories who is the true companion of our hero's heart, a precursor perhaps of Holden's Phoebe, or a female doppelganger of the hero. Hemingway is not a woman-hater. His masculine stereotypes, while they smell of boys' things and range over streams and mountains, pass the hours climbing and fishing and hunting and drinking hard, are backed or surrounded by the gentle touch of a girl's hand, the female love, sexual or pure, that he included inside his writer's persona. How else could he write it, Robert and Maria, write it so well?

Today, now that we women have broken free of so many of the restrictions society placed on us, we can reread Hemingway and let ourselves be touched by the male wish, the male fantasy of the all-loving woman, of the Rabbit, and we can let that fantasy rise up in our minds without fear of being returned ourselves to the kitchen or reduced to frightened girlhood. We can hear the primitive elemental chord this fantasy strikes in us. Love me, yes love me like that so I can love you like that. There was a time when the feminist movement surged into our consciousness, probably mid-sixties and early seventies, when it would have been hard to appreciate Maria, so pathetically childlike and dependent. We would have rejected Maria, Jordan, and the whole story. The maleness of the fantasy would have made us uncomfortable, left us outside, complaining. Why was the only strong woman in the novel (Pilar) beyond sexual attraction? But now we can play. We don't need to go to work in suits with ties and we don't need to stifle that part of our sexuality which remains, for whatever reasons, embedded in flirtations, dependence, girl-daddy images. Now that we know that we are not Marias, at least not if we don't want to be, we can allow her to live in our imaginations at least some of the time. It seems that our sexuality is not so easily subordinated to our political wishes. The entire range of dominance-submission, helplessness, girl-woman, man-father, boy-playmate, can be tossed around, in fashion, in fantasy, in movies and books, enjoyed at no risk to our earning power or intellectual achievement. A girl doesn't have to be a cheerleader all her life to enjoy lifting her skirts and screaming at the big game. With this shift Maria and Robert Jordan under the blanket once again can become food for fantasy, pleasure, lump-in-throat anticipation.

Writing, being a writer, was part of the Hemingway romance, part of the hero he presented to us again and again. Nick Adams, the first of his alter egos, wants to write. Robert Jordan promises us that he will get rid of the terrible pictures in his head, the war visions, when he is able to write about them later. Jake Barnes is a journalist and the narrator, therefore writer, of *The Sun Also Rises*. David in *The Garden of Eden* is also a writer; so is the dying hunter in *The Snows of Kilimanjaro*. Ah, to fall in love, to be loved by a writer, a Hemingway man, a man floating across Europe, a hard-drinking, heavy-smoking man who had a notebook, who had a story to tell.

There was a time in my life, after I had read *For Whom the Bell Tolls*, when I confused the writer with his product and I confused writing well with making love. My hard nonromantic perspective exercised itself only in regard to quality of prose. Just as a Hemingway character was good at hunting, understood the bulls, knew the lay of the trout at the shallow side of the river, so his writer characters were good at what they did too. Their stories, which in some way were the stories we were reading, were always fine performances, daring, like the matador standing in the center of the ring staring into the eyes of the bull.

I went to Europe the summer I was twenty. I was studying French with a flock of girls at a school in Paris, or that at least is what I was supposed to be doing. In fact at the Deux Magots café the first week of July, I met an American boy who had been on a Fulbright to Finland and was now traveling about the summer before his return to the States. He had curly dark hair and sad eyes, brown as the dirt, hard like olive pits. He was broad chested in his T-shirt. There were muscles in his arms and his hands were ink stained and a notebook poked out shyly from his back pocket. He started drinking with breakfast and he was not entirely clean (I considered both these attributes a sign of writerly virtue). He was a writer or intended to be and had spent his Fulbright year working on stories. He invited me to travel to Spain with him. His name was Larry and I thought I might love him and in a small hotel room above the rooftops of Montparnasse I offered him all I could and then I met him at the railroad station and we went off together to Barcelona. I left behind a selection of postcards for my friends to mail to my mother from time to time. It's easy to lie on a postcard.

We were walking down a very narrow street in Barcelona, so narrow the sky was reduced to a small stripe of milky gray floating high above, washed sheets hung from terraces, and a smell of urine spilled from a pot hung heavy in the air and the dark lace of ironwork on the balconies seemed like a scribbling all around when Larry stopped with his back pressed against the gray stones of the wall. He suddenly froze. He couldn't move at all. He trembled as sweat streamed down his face. He had seen a bat hanging from a balcony up above. He was afraid of bats. I had to lead him step by step, encouraging him to lift his feet, along the cobblestones until we reached the corner and there was a wide plaza with children playing and a fountain in front of us. His muscles slowly relaxed. I lit a cigarette for him. His hands were shaking and the match kept falling. He told me at the café where we stopped for beer that he had been bitten by a squirrel in the park as a child and had then received a twenty-one-day series of rabies injections that were delivered by a long needle right into his stomach.

This psychic wound, this fear of small winged things, this connection to the child he had been, made my affections glow, a lubricant to my love. Robert Jordan's father had killed himself. This was his wound. Larry had wounds too. He drank beer all day long and wine at night. He was always slightly drunk. I thought that this is what writers did. I thought it was because he was brewing a story that he needed to drink. I understood. We stayed in a rooming house with prostitutes plying their trade next door. I was intrigued. Their bright clothes, their lipstick, their loud voices calling out to one another made me feel as if I was alive at last, beginning.

Every morning a man selling rope from a basket called up to the housewives in a deep-throated hoarse terrible animal wail of words you couldn't catch. His tongue had been cut out, the concierge told me, by the Loyalists a long time ago. The groping choking call of the man selling laundry line seemed a reproach to my American softness, my come-too-late-for-real-tragedy birth, showing me that in this Spain of the late fifties the remains of Robert Jordan's Spain existed and they weren't pretty or picturesque or romantic. Something horrible had happened here. I knew about it because I knew Robert Jordan.

Larry had carried with him to Finland and now down to Spain a small portable typewriter and in the morning with the ever constant beer by his side, he would sit on the bed, smoke from his cigarette whirling over his head, and write. There I was a fugitive from my life, wearing the pink lace silk slip from Bergdorf Goodman my mother had packed for me to take to Paris, standing on the balcony and staring at fish bones thrown in the garbage in the side alley when Larry gave me his story to read. I was Lady Brett. I was his muse. I was Maria, I was his love. I was content with the narrow ribbon of turquoise Barcelona sky I could see straight above. Starlings flew between the buildings, rising and settling on cornices and griffins carved from stone. There was sweat flowing down between my breasts. I could smell my own body, the beer on the table, the stale water that dripped from a pipe at the side of the stone building, the half-eaten orange on the terrace below. I read.

The story was moribund, flat, dull, and overwrought. The writer was not a writer. He was counterfeit, an imposter. I knew it as I knew the skin on my body, the moles and the dry patches and the shape of my navel. As soon as I could I went back to Paris. I took my love back from Larry because his story was clumsy, hopeless. Robert Jordan on the other hand, Jake Barnes certainly, would have written something that made me glad of breathing, eager for the next morning. The prose itself was part of the love I felt for Robert Jordan. This I admit. There is nothing to be proud of in this anecdote.

It could have been worse. What if Larry hadn't given me his story to read and I had stayed with him so long I could no longer tell if he wrote well or not?

There was a difficulty for me in reading Hemingway. I jumped over the problem. I skirted around it. I pretended I didn't see it at first. It ached sometimes like scar tissue, or I poked at it sometimes the way one does with a sore in the mouth. In *The Sun Also Rises* the antihero, the man who spoils the perfect dance of the others and smashes the face of the young bullfighter, is a Jew named Robert Cohn. Jake reports that Cohn had his nose improved in a boxing match at Princeton, and Hemingway has his character Michael say: "No, listen Jake, Brett's gone off with men they just weren't ever Jews and they didn't come hang around afterward." None of the men in the group object to Brett's promiscuity, only to her choice of a Jew: "He's got this Jewish superiority so strong that he thinks the only emotion he'll get out of the fight will be being bored." At the fight Jake asks, "Does Cohn look bored?" The answer comes, "That kike." When describing Cohn's former girlfriend, Frances, he says, "She had a Jew named Cohn." As the group meets in Pamplona, someone says, "Go away, take that sad Jewish face away. Why don't you see when you're not wanted." In a discussion about Brett's finances, Jake says, "She gets five hundred quid a year and pays 350% in interest to the Jews."

Cohn was based on a real man. He was from a wealthy Jewish family, had been educated at Princeton where he was continually excluded and ridiculed as a Jew. He financed a literary journal for a number of years, publishing many of the same writers who despised him because he was a Jew. He went to Paris and was a writer in the expatriate group. In Hemingway's novel his character is presented as unattractive. His love for Brett is pathetic. His desire to join or be an accepted part of the group is repulsive. His Jewishness is his sin. This open and enjoyed anti-Semitism cut me to the quick when I first read the book and still stings, a slap in the face, a wound inflicted by a loved one, a harshness that is hard to understand.

This anti-Semitism must have seemed so normal, so well deserved, so commonplace that it was no more remarkable than a C sharp in a Noël Coward song or a Coke ad hanging above the counter in a local drugstore. It was the common attitude. It shocked no one. Certainly neither Christians nor Jews reading the book when it was first published in 1926 saw anything odd in mocking Cohn as a Jew or in creating him as the outsider whose presence spoils the grandeur and the rightness of the traditional ritual of the bullfight. But for me, a Jewish reader, reading this years later, I cannot say with some critics, "Oh well those were the times, that was the commonplace view," or "You can't take it out of context. That's just the way it was."

I was reading the book after the Holocaust, when the social anti-Semitism of the Americans and English in Paris had been echoed and underlined by the furnaces. The book appeared a decade before the Nuremberg Laws but was nevertheless connected to them, yoked by a leash of snobbism, social exclusion, and the well-practiced habit of dehumanizing, demonizing. The exclusion of Jewish athletes in the Olympics, the stripping of Jews of their citizenship, the refusal of the United States to grant entry visas, this all was connected, hard-wired to the words of Jake Barnes: "That kike."

For me with my own hide and the hides of my grandchildren to save, the matter is still grave and threatens my attachment to the books, the author, and his characters. Was Robert Jordan's idealism and humanity, his death for the life of the Spanish republic, phony? This attitude toward Jews compromises and diminishes the morality of Robert Jordan and the beauty of the trout fisherman and the hard-to-bear fate of Jake-the-Wounded-in-the-Worst-Place-of-All.

Hemingway stood outside the communist pieties and saw that in Spain the party was party to a disaster. He stood outside the American dream and saw that it had cheapened decency. He knew that religion was not salvation. He questioned the existence of God. He swallowed no political ideologies hook, line, and sinker. He saw through so much. He went to Paris and danced with the most avant-garde of artists. He partied with Gertrude Stein and Alice B. Toklas, he drank with Fitzgerald and Gerald and Sara Murphy who had left proper society behind to its own devices. He had a most sophisticated palate in wine and food. But he took with him society's most fundamental cruelties and profoundest human error.

When a Jew reads these insulting remarks, a Jew has a choice: put down the book or rush over, half reading, half not, the libels against the self and the people of the self. It is possible to shield one's Jewish heart against this hurling of stones by reassuring oneself that they are not in fact stones, but rather sponges, mere prattle of the times. Of course a reading Jew tries this approach, to brush the insults off, so common they can't hurt anymore, but they remain to haunt, they affect the reading of the rest of the work. Damn your bullfighter I think, damn your damaged penis, as I come to the end pages of *The Sun Also Rises*. So what makes you think your death matters, I mumble against my beloved Robert Jordan, so many more deaths to follow.

I want Hemingway to explain himself. Why couldn't you see that the Jews, just like the innocent and decent villagers you describe, were also just eating and loving, having children and growing old and giving birth like everyone else? Why couldn't you see our complex flawed humanity too? Hemingway was not a car salesman on America's brainwashed Main Street. He wasn't a Lion or an Elk or a Rotarian. But nevertheless he took the very nastiest canards of anti-Semitism in his writer's mouth. This hurts. It really hurts.

There are two parts to this wound. The first is personal. Hemingway's words make it clear that I and those I love would be despised as inferior: whatever we did or said would be painted with the same dark brush. Our sorrows would be mocked, our loves become the object of jokes, our finances assumed venal, and our attempts to sit at the table with others would make us like Robert Cohn the object of ridicule. The second part is less personal but more alarming. The casual and thorough dislike of the Jew that soaked the world made possible the killing of small children, the smoke of Auschwitz. This frightens me for the future. It frightens me as a Jew, and it frightens me for whatever other group, nationality, or religion will become the butt, the ostracized, the unwanted.

The personal insult is palpable. The group threat is like a drum beating in the hills. The savages will rise again and storm the small shelter we have created. When I think of Robert Jordan I also hear the drums.

Still, if I were Maria, I would have welcomed Robert Jordan in the night.

Hemingway was a travel writer and made some good money at it. But more than that Hemingway was able to create a romance with Europe that lasts to this day. It's the names and the words he uses. Place names and names for food and drink, non-English words with wonderful rhythms and evocative sounds. Words for places like Cádiz, Le Grau du Roi, Camargue, Hendaye, Nîmes, Calle Vitoria, Escorial, Burgette sing along with words for drink like Armagnac, absinthe, Manzanilla, marismeno, a drink with garlic-flavored olives, Perrier-Jouet, Lanson. Food like jamón serrano, ham from pigs fed on acorns, or sal chichon, dark sausage from a town called Vich. Street names like Plaza Santa Ana and St. Etienne du Mont are among the thousands and thousands that roll through the Hemingway books. His characters are always eating or drinking in a kind of sensual orgy of displaced passion. They are skiing in the remotest of mountains or riding on trains through peasant towns drinking wine from leather flasks. The objects and the places named in Spanish and in French take on a magical aura that words like Peoria, New Jersey, St. Louis, Albany just don't have. The food words overwhelm with their promise of something exotic, something ancient, something rich in texture and taste. They are unlike the words of our supermarkets: Wonder bread, peanut butter, Jell-O. It is their foreignness of course that makes them seem so fragrant, so filled with possibility. In a sense this is a cheap trick. Of course the everyday foods of another place carry resonances that our own have lost through familiarity, through overexposure. Of course the names of cities and towns ring with beauty that has faded from those along our own commuter routes. Hemingway counts on this. He also counts on the fact that he is writing about a Europe that seems to be groaning under the weight of culture, swinging on the arms of history, old and venerable, rare and pock-marked, oozing with memory, especially compared to our own America, so shiny and new, so commercial and flat and upbeat, so without patina, paths that haven't been trod by Goths or Visigoths, monks bearing illustrated manuscripts, merchants with spices from the East.

We Americans have felt ourselves to be coarse, broad, boorish, no counts or lords or castles among us. Our grandest stories have been reduced to cartoons: Paul Revere one if by land, two if by sea; George Washington chopping down a cherry tree; Paul Bunyan, Johnny Appleseed. They don't compete with Joan of Arc, Martin Luther, Vasco da Gama, Caesar, Henry the Eighth, Napoleon, the great queens Victoria and Elizabeth.

Our Hudson River school, our Ashcan painters, were fine indeed but compared to Leonardo, Botticelli, Turner, Ingres—well, what are we Americans but philistines? Commerce is our gift and our fate. Our cathedrals small, our roads infected with billboards, our vulgarities legion.

When we read Hemingway we lean over his pages, bars in Madrid, falling into bars in Barcelona, bars with bad girls, bars with shiny gold banisters, bars where the *patrón* brings a special wine to the table. We are captivated by the non-America, the anti–Norman Rockwell. We understand why Henry James removed himself. We know why Edith Wharton's characters took long boat rides to spend the season in Paris.

After World War I Americans flocked to Paris because it was the other place, the better place. After World War II Americans flocked to Paris because it was the place where expatriate artists had learned their craft, because it seemed as if its otherness would inoculate, vaccinate a person against the flat, crude, harsh nonbeauty of the American Main Street, because culture was there and not here. Their history was deeper, more veined with human efforts and glory than ours, chiseled with ancient pain and pounded by the hooves of Roman soldiers, religious wars, emperors and dictators marshalling armies that charged and retreated across the fields. Their history was etched in time, while ours was rash and shallow, imitative and tinny, displeasing to people of taste and soul. That I believed too. We all believed it. True or not.

Hemingway with his wanderlust, his daring of the African continent, the island of Cuba, the constant taste of drink and food that you wouldn't find in the drugstore on Main Street USA, he set a tone, set a pace. It didn't occur to me until late in life when I found myself on a raft down the Snake River that the rocks, the canyons, the red stones and the mesas, the white sand, the long highways, the oil rigs on the New Jersey Turnpike, the gas stations with their Mobil, Shell, or Texaco signs, the dogs and the horses, the wildflowers and the jagged skyscapers were themselves worthy of my love. I had been distracted and deceived into thinking my land was like a door-to-door vacuum cleaner salesman: loud and soulless.

In Paris in 1957 I wore a blue beret. I smoked Gauloises cigarettes. Was Henry Miller still walking by the Seine? Was Jean-Paul Sartre at a nearby table? Was I free of the dull and the boring and the terrible fate of those who lived in suburbs and paid for life insurance? I would never carry a camera because I didn't want anyone to think I was a tourist. (I know, Holden. Phony.) I drank pernod, a taste so foul my stomach cramps at the memory. I missed the point that Jackson Pollock was about to make, that Andy Warhol would bring forward: all objects, all shadows, all colors, all places, all the fadings and rippings, drippings, and curlicues of design and commerce, soup can and neon sign, are all expressions of the human face, are in themselves overbrimming with vitality, all bearers of our truth.

This excessive Europhilia of course cannot be blamed on Robert Jordan who went to Spain for justice's sake and was killed, another twentieth-century statistic. But my desire to find my own Robert Jordan, to merge like Maria into his arms, to taste the sausages and drink from the wine flask and climb in the mountains, was not as harmless as it might seem. The boy next door didn't have a chance considering the visions that floated through my head.

It was a narrow view. In God's eye it was no better to be drunk in Montmartre than to be drunk in Minneapolis. In God's view the pungency of life was the same from Louisiana or Virginia as it was from the Basque country or the shores of Normandy. It took me years to grasp this. I pressed my nose to the window of Hemingway's Europe where everything had a flavor that would rise to the tongue if one only knew, if one only had the right words in a foreign language to name it. This pleasant conviction, bound up as it was in the unpleasant sense of inferiority as an American, was part of my original love for Robert Jordan, fighting for the Loyalists in the last gasp of the Republic of Spain.

To imagine oneself inside a Hemingway novel is to invite parody. The style seems easy to imitate, the images so strong and simple one would think anyone could do it. But when you actually try, you quickly see that the Hemingway rhythm is created by overlapping broad strokes but nevertheless more dependent than it might seem on a real but often buried still-taut narrative line. This is the strange personal Hemingway heartbeat that turns to ash when others steal it. He worked hard to achieve it. It rips with tension, the author's private tension, the particular duel with his own demons that was not healed by drink or writing well or women. So knowing that it can't be done, I am going to do it anyway because like the best of Hemingway's characters I will not be stopped by fear of failure, and because despite his wise words, I can't help mouthing it up too much.

• • • •

In 1936 I was actually in utero but now in my mind's eye I am twenty-two and I have gone to Madrid as a journalist for the *Herald Tribune*. I got the job because I filed a good piece on the bread lines in Newark and because I slept with my boss, a married man who was anxious to terminate our friendship before something of unwanted consequence occurred. He sent me to Spain. I have a room at the Gaylord Hotel where the other journalists are staying along with some Americans whom I'm told are on mysterious missions for the Loyalist side. I mingle with the communist columnists, the anarchists, the Loyalists, and a former monk turned spy or so the whisper is. I am not a communist. I just hope I am. I want to be good, unselfish, and valiant. I loathe the Fascists. The war has been going on long enough so that there is an odor of regret and vomit, wiped away but not thoroughly, in the corridors. The jokes at the bar are stale and the journalists themselves sometimes file their reports without leaving the hotel. They begin to make things up but the things they make up are as true as the things that they have seen and so it hardly matters. One evening just as night is coming on and the generator of the hotel wobbles with its usual faint-of-heart start-up I am joined in the bar by an old friend and his companion who is leaving for the front tomorrow. My friend introduces me to Robert Jordan.

He is a large man with a sweet, self-deprecating smile. His eyes are not easy. They shift away from me, over my shoulder, to the door and back. He has a certain shyness. It shows in the way his hands grasp his drink as if someone were about to take it from him. It shows in the way he leans forward toward me but I cannot quite catch his eye. I tell him for no particular reason, except that conversation is required, that I am from New York City. There are shadows under his eyes. They darken as he considers New York. He tells me he is from Montana, a former teacher of Spanish. I nod. He looks at me. I shift my legs under the table. "I only have tonight," he says. I nod. He orders another drink. "Do you have a gun with you?" I ask. "I always have a gun," he says. "Will it ever be over?" I ask. "Never," he says. The waiter brings us Armagnac. It burns the throat. The waiter wipes his hands on his apron, waiting for a tip. The mirror behind the bar has a crack where some journalist in the midst of an argument hurled his ashtray the week before I arrived. The room is hot. The fan overhead swings around too slowly to cool the air. Jordan and his friend discuss a trout fishing trip they had made together in the mountains the summer before the war began in earnest. They don't say much. They talk about the trout, five I think, that they carried back to the small hotel they were staying in. They smoked and I smoked and there was a nicotine heaviness to the air. Robert Jordan asks me to go for a walk with him out on to the plaza. I go. His legs are long. His body is hard, used to climbing and walking. Not a city man's body, soft in the middle, all face. "Have you been with a man before?" he asks me. "Yes," I say. "Good," he answers.

Later on the hotel bed we lie beside each other. "Do you have to go tomorrow?" I ask. He doesn't answer. We both know he has to go. Outside in the corridor we hear the brawling of two men. There is pushing and name calling. "It is not peaceful here," I say. "It is not peaceful anywhere," he says. And that is true. As the dawn comes up, I wake and hear him dressing. There are shadows on the cobblestones as the sun drifts through the leaves of the great oak that stands in the center of the Plaza Maja. Robert comes to the bed and sits at its edge. Bending over, he touches my hair with his hands, gently the way you might the mane of a familiar horse, one that has journeyed far with you. "Tell me one thing about you I can remember forever," he says. "I am Jewish," I say. He stands up startled. He goes without saying another word.

. . . .

3

...... Dick Diver ......

Dick Diver

F. Scott Fitzgerald's
Tender Is the Night

A hot and steamy tale of incest and wealth, of gigolos and psychiatrists, in which the wages of sin are paid by some but not by others. It should have been a miniseries.

Dear Dick, sweet sad ineffectual well-meaning, ambitious, coming out of nowhere America to the height of expat sophistication, into the maw of the wealthy, entertaining, anxious to please, smart enough to go to Yale but not smart enough to survive the deceits, the power grabs, the sharp splinters along the rungs of the social ladder. Dear Dick, you didn't deserve such harsh failure. I wish you'd never had a drop to drink. Oh Dick, it should have been otherwise for the likes of you. Perhaps if you'd just stayed in America, perhaps if you'd just been less of a crowd pleaser and more of a hard worker, an intellect rather than a taster of fine wines. Oh Dick, you really are not such an admirable soul. You were not all that I would have hoped. You were considerably less than you would have hoped. But still I have a soft spot for you. I wish we had had, you and I, once before you married so unfortunately, a moonlight-on-snow crunching startling-white-beneath-the-feet walk together with fir trees standing guard and stars above, stars without a trace of mockery in their glitter. I would have tried to tell you about discipline and how it keeps chaos at bay.

True, I have you mixed up in my pantheon of men-to-muse-upon with William Powell as the martini-guzzling Thin Man, with boys I used to know whose promise shone from their newly shaved faces like a nouveau riche lady's diamond ring, maybe a ring as big as the Ritz.

It was not as easy for me to fall in love with Dick Diver although he was elegant, charming, raffish, as it was for Rosemary, a seventeen-year-old movie actress who joined Dick and his beautiful but not so mentally stable wife, Nicole, in their intimate group at Juan-les-Pins when she came with her mother for a summer holiday. Rosemary thought Dick was the last word in male sexual power because he arranged good parties and watched over everyone, and could converse with the assembled cast with the ease of a magician pulling a rabbit out of a hat. Rosemary joined the scene with the balmy breeze of a convent-school girl and the bouncy morality of a tiger cub. She desired Dick, thought he was perfect, after merely a morning on a beach in the South of France.

Love, unconditional love for Dick Diver, did not arrive, thump thump, like that for me, an independent modern woman doused in today's feminism. Certainly my love did not come as quickly as it did for Nicole, mental patient at a Swiss sanitarium, fragile beauty, motherless wealthy American girl from Chicago with a daddy who unfortunately thought he was Lot.

I'm as much of a sucker for Irish-American charm, grandiose designs, reddish hair, slightly pointed noses, and blue hard flashing eyes as the next person. But there was something off-putting about Dick Diver. His creator was not bamboozled by his flaws. The attentive reader can sense them long before they actually appear. If I'm going to fall in love at first sight, the fellow needs more of a hint of toughness about him than Dr. Dick Diver, Rhodes scholar, would-be healer and classifier of the mentally ill, could ever, even in his most excellent prime, have mustered.

Yes, I'm interested even to the point of marrying one, in those who struggle with the daily debris of the florid, the depressed, or the destructive but I have known enough psychiatrists in my time to regard them without awe. Many of them are commonplace, intelligent enough but frequently slightly damaged: why else their fascination with tumors of the mind? So I wouldn't have loved Dick Diver just because he was a very intelligent doctor who wanted to contribute to the science of the mind and make his reputation among his peers. This ambition to make a difference, to achieve the pinnacle of professional success, is attractive in a man but only in one who can take care of himself. Dick Diver as it turned out could not. That particular psychiatrist most assuredly could not heal himself, and modern psychiatry, or Fitzgerald's somewhat cockeyed and naive examples of it, lumbered around with the finesse and effectiveness of the doctors who bled with leeches a few generations earlier.

As *Tender Is the Night* slowly unwraps its dark core, we see a train wreck in slow motion. We readers see it coming way before we hear the whistle or notice the smoke puffs rising into the sky. Nevertheless, despite my open and early resistance, somewhere along the plotline, Dick Diver became a man I took into my heart, have over the years been involved with, ached for, wanted to yell at, to divert from his destiny, save, puzzle over. Not entirely admirable as a man, not a comrade to go to war with like Robert Jordan, not a fellow traveler on the adolescent skids like Holden, but a man nevertheless who leaves a mark, a sharp memory, carved out for himself a place where affection for him has lingered, someone with a story that lasts, reverberates with one's own, a story that is tragic without conforming to our ideas of classical tragedy. This story is not bloody. It is completely without catharsis. It contains little howling on the heath. It simply leaves behind, after the last page has been read, puddles of pity to dampen the mind.

I read this book first in the 1950s in English class at an all-girls school. I read it again just now when in this autumn season of my life I know everything I'm likely ever to know (maybe not). Then I had to struggle simply to follow the bare facts of the story. (I also didn't get the joke of most of the *New Yorker* cartoons. A person who doesn't get those cartoons should not be reading Fitzgerald, not yet.) What had happened to Nicole in bed with her father exactly and why did that drive her crazy, or did it? Was Baby Warren, Nicole's older sister, a good character or a bad one? I wrote a paper on that question but I can't remember what I decided. I had a 50 percent chance of being right. I liked the way Baby Warren rescued drunken Dick Diver from the Paris police, so confident, so persistent, so strong, but I knew her inability to marry, her self-infatuation and very worldly competence, were not admired by the author. Was she the evil protagonist in the story? In those days I believed in good and evil as split apart, night and day. I just wasn't sure which was which.

It seems to me in English class that we discussed symbolism. We were always discussing symbols, of ice and snow and flowers wilting. But nobody explained to me why Rosemary spoiled Nicole's marriage (it said that on the back flap) or what exactly made Abe North, the alcoholic writer, carry on like that. I read the book from the vantage point of my own virginity, a virginity that was not only literal but included an untouched soul, eager for love but not yet bent or damaged in its hurricane gales. The tale was rich in exotic places and activities—skiing in the Alps, swimming on the Riviera, hotels in Paris, cafés and restaurants, rail stations and countesses, psychiatrists with Germanic names, sanitariums with scenic views, dinner parties in Mediterranean ports—but poor in meaning. What was this story to me and me to it?

Our very mannish English teacher, heavy oxford shoes, tweed suits with padded shoulders that never seemed to fit, pale stringy blonde hair that seemed not quite washed, whose faded blue eyes like unthreaded needles rolled about the room, who eventually in March of my junior year began to hear voices calling her a communist, accusing her of something dirty with the headmistress, and was forced to leave the school and enter a hospital for the mentally ill, didn't explain. She couldn't because of all the things in this book that no teacher could then discuss with a class of girls wearing blue gym uniforms with matching heavy cotton bloomers beneath. Now, however, I know why Dick Diver has remained for half a century in my head.

Certain books should not be examined in English class at all. They should be saved for Elderhostel and the terminally ill, who will see them resplendent in their glory. It may take a lifetime to love Dick Diver fully and see oneself mirrored in his fate. It certainly takes a few bad choices, wrong turns, and hard moments before a reader can easily grasp that beneath the glamour of Dcole's (Dick and Nicole signed their notes that way) life, a very unglamourous not-so-pretty erosion was taking place.

Back then I did not understand that money and romance were connected in any way at all. This is odd because I was myself the child of
a frozen-in-mid-strangle marriage in which a man, my handsome father, had seized economic opportunity by marrying a young woman,
my anxious mother, of no small means. So imbued was I with the
American myth of romantic love and living happily ever after that I
couldn't see the evidence that lay right before my eyes. Money was
not discussed as a motive for romance except in musty novels of other
centuries. I assumed the idea had never crossed the Atlantic—that
America was the country of individual happiness and self-determined
lives—in the exact same way that sex was not, in the back end of the
1950s before Erica Jong's *Fear of Flying*, associated with female pleasure, not openly at least. Class, upper, lower, middle, was not a polite
subject for anyone but a Harvard academician. These subjects were
outside—did not apply to the self. We were all equal in America or
should be, and romantic love was connected to that equality and no
one would have been able to convince me otherwise.

Eventually I figured it out. Marriage can be a form of economic
opportunity resulting frequently in a lemon of a life—if the man is the
supplicant and the woman holds the portfolio everyone is in for it. In
true Shakespearean manner, the world is out of tilt and disaster follows (true at least in that prefeminist world in which, no choice of
mine, I will always have one foot). So imbued was I with the romantic
ideal of marriage that I found myself shocked just a few years ago
when a friend of mine, talking to my grown daughter, said, "Marriage
is not about love but a way to arrange your life." My first impulse was
to rush over and put my hands over my daughter's ears. On second
thought I admitted that I had, after all, read my Jane Austen, my
George Eliot, my Thackeray, my Trollope. I knew that marriage was
often about economic matters, two families merging funds as well as
genes. Romantic love like a blind fish deep in the ocean exists of
course; it swims along down in the murk but is hardly the only fish in
the sea.

I should not have been surprised that the wealthy were not happy.
My classmates included many blue-book names that Edith Wharton
would have recognized. These well-bred daughters were not exuber-

ant or carefree. They had the pinched anxious faces of girls who were going to make their debuts in white dresses, and then free-fall in surprising ways. They were very well mannered. They had as few opinions as possible. They knew how to jump horses and play volleyball. They played tennis at Piping Rock Country Club. They came out at cotillions and went to house parties on Long Island. The smart ones went to Bryn Mawr and studied Homer. The dumb ones went to junior colleges and then did volunteer work in hospital gift shops. For our yearbook we had our photographs taken in ballgowns at Bachrach with radiant light bouncing off the satin drapes that hung behind our heads. The corsets pinched. The smiles were forced. There was fear in the eyes of the dull ones as well as the bright ones. Selected Aztec maidens at least knew their destiny for a certainty. We were confused. We could read Virgil in Latin and knew what the pluperfect subjunctive was in French but didn't know that Dick Diver's dazzling way with a group, his ever-present lightness, was a truly alarming sign of inner blight. Our English teacher never told us.

One girl in my class, niece of a prominent cabinet member, had gone off to boarding school and returned with boils all over her body. It was rumored that she suffered a nervous breakdown like Nicole. She wore white clown's makeup to class, dark sunglasses, and a strange polka-dot bandanna on her hair. Her legs were trellised with running sores that climbed above her bobby sox. I avoided her because her masked face frightened me. Before we became twenty-five she was murdered while a patient at the Menninger Clinic in Topeka, Kansas. I certainly knew that coming from a good family, free of money worries, only created a space for all the other woes of life to dwell within and be fruitful. But what surprised me was that charming, brilliant Dick Diver was reduced to rubble for reasons that were not so reasonable or clear.

In those days before the recovered memory movement, before five out of every ten novels had an incest experience inflaming the joints of the plot construction, I didn't know that sleeping with your father could turn a girl mad. I still am not convinced that this explanation of Nicole's schizophrenia, if it was truly that, was quite sensible. What I did understand was that Nicole's wealthy father had abused his trust and was banished ever after from seeing his child. Was this justice? Did the psychiatrist who pronounced this sentence really know what he was doing? Nicole sought a new protector, a doctor who could scare away the demons of mental illness and preserve her in the world.

I felt sorry for Mr. Warren. He was lonely. He had done a bad thing but would no one forgive him? I was ready to forgive my own father for his indifference, his temper fits, his dark headaches and cold manner. A simple smile would have made me, like Rosemary Hoyt, who at age seventeen had starred in the movie of that name, "Daddy's girl," in a moment.

When I first read *Tender Is the Night* I kept waiting for Mr. Warren to reappear and for a touching reunion to take place and for his true soul, redeemed by the love of his daughter, to shine through. Was I in the wrong book and on the wrong page! Then I ached for the banished Mr. Warren. Today it is very clear that Mr. Warren is a male beast, a destroyer of little girls, and he probably deserved whatever terminal liver damage he got.

However, on first reading I wanted a tender reunion. I wanted a rapprochement that Fitzgerald did not provide. I had come to *Tender Is the Night* not so many years after reading *Daddy-Long-Legs* and *Little Lord Fauntleroy*. Like fatherless Rosemary I wanted wisdom, protection, attention from a powerful source devoted to my well-being. My hope for Mr. Warren's redemption stemmed from my own story, but then it could simply have been my tenacious blockheadedness that extended hope where hope, if it is as the poet said, "a thing with feathers," was as dead as the chicken in the fricassee.

When *Tender Is the Night*, begun in 1926, was finally published in 1933, some critics attacked it for concerning itself with the rich at a time when the country was suffering through a depression of mammoth proportions. The social conscience of some in the literary world recoiled at the idea of offering sympathy to the flotsam of the American capitalist system. Of course the movies too were filled with tales of mansions and poor little rich girls all during the thirties. It comforts to know that the rich are miserable too and that a healthy bank account doesn't keep away TB or guarantee wedded bliss. But if one thinks of Dick Diver, son of a southern Protestant clergyman raised in provincial Buffalo who goes to Yale, wins a Rhodes from the state of Connecticut in 1914, gets his medical degree at Johns Hopkins, trains at a clinic in Switzerland, and writes a psychiatric diagnostic book that while he is very young makes his reputation, whose future knows no limits, the story becomes not about the rich setting in which it is placed but about the dark hole that awaits the young and the brilliant, about the corruptions of a world America was unprepared for, of the weakness of character that brings down the brightest among us.

The book is very much a depression-era story. It is about failure after great success (exactly boom and bust like the American stock market). But it is no accident that the story takes place in the glitter of a Europe that seems to be attending a ball, one being held on a frozen lake deep down in which the bodies of the World War I dead are buried. Dick takes his group on an excursion to visit the actual burial grounds. They are tourists who return to an evening of gaiety in Paris, but the horror is so close it can be touched. The war dead in their graves haunt the living through the rest of the book. Fitzgerald, party boy himself, was too much of a real writer not to make it quite clear to the reader that the personal tales of his characters were shadowed by the inability of nations to save themselves from extraordinary savagery. It is this visit to the graveyards of the war that begins to mark Dick as a man with a soul, a memory, a capacity for understanding far greater than his playboy image would apparently admit. Here my love for him begins in earnest.

When I first read *Tender Is the Night* I didn't know anything about transference and its consequences but I was warm to the idea that what every sick woman needs is a doctor in her bed, on call at all times, ready to be the sun and the moon and the earth of his patient. When some years later I married a psychoanalyst, I knew that his profession lent him a general's rank in the war against my own nibbling devils, although I had no money to offer and he in fact supported me, allowed me to curl against him night after night. I don't think Fitzgerald was clear on transference either. The couch had not yet hit the American heartland, and Freud's ideas were so new here that they shimmered distantly like constellations in a foggy night sky: yes, yes, but where exactly is Orion's belt?

So Nicole, still speaking nonsense, not quite in touch with the real, broken apart, angry and fearful, caught (butterfly in a net) in her illness, sees Dr. Dick Diver and speaks with him. She attaches to him all her hopes for recovery and imagines that he will save her from herself and this emotional conviction she names love. This is understandable. What is harder to understand but crucial to the matter is Dick Diver's response. First he intelligently tries to remove himself. He understands he has an unfair advantage over a sick and beautiful young woman already exploited by a sexual predator. He knows that any involvement with Nicole is dangerous even if he doesn't have all the protective armament against the relationship that a present-day well-trained psychiatrist would surely have.

He is told he is part of the reason she is getting better. She writes him garbled letters, jumbled thoughts, signs of real disease: not lovable but pitiful. She focuses on him as her rescuer and she does regain some balance. When he sees her again she appears normal if somewhat unreal, pasted together, pretending at a life that seems scripted rather than genuine.

He tries to avoid Nicole but when she finds him again at a ski resort and her beauty holds him transfixed (and the needs of the plot line require it), he agrees, despite knowing full well that he has been bought, purchased, to marriage.

"Dick don't do it," I would warn him. "It will destroy you." The weak have a strange power over the strong. They can ruin everything using the moral currency inherent in their very helplessness. You don't know her. You don't understand her. You might not like her if you knew her. Dear Dick save yourself for a woman who is strong, will love your children, will do her part in the world, who would never try to kill you by deliberately steering a car off the road. Dear Dick, you could have a wife who will be a partner on your journey, who will say intelligent things to you and spur your work on, instead of a wife who is more anxiety than pleasure, more image than substance, a woman whose illness has stolen her energy and left her flat as a soiled sheet waiting for life to come to her bed.

By the time Fitzgerald writes the scenes in which Dick moves into marriage with Nicole with the nasty breath of Baby Warren on his back, the author himself knew more about mental illness than the rest of his crowd. His wife, Zelda, taught him that the broken mind, with its strange associations, terrible compulsions, voices, sleeplessness, neediness, rages, and withdrawals, is not a pretty thing. He knew a good deal about covering up and pretending all was well. He knew down to the minutest detail what it was to turn from lover to care-taker, from friend to enemy, from partner to competitor. He knew he was condemning Dick Diver by giving him Nicole for a partner.

I too once chose a husband who could not love me. I looked for trouble and found it. I could not have imagined the details. But I could have seen that my fascination with a glamourous talented trou-bled soul was not, as I had thought, a credit to my adventurous cre-ative spirit but a nod in the direction of self-inflicted grief. I have seen how friends have selected from all the men who would desire them the one who was most likely to leave them, harm them, grow de-pressed or drunk or penniless. I have come to think that the American version of romantic love, free choice, is an oxymoron. Our choices are never free of our past, and love in all its sweet hilarity is too risky a business to found a future on. The American vision of romantic love is as chock-full of truth as our self-congratulatory slogans about equal-ity and brotherhood.

The ways in which real life determined this novel's direction can't be pushed out of the readers' head. We know too much. Here is a book that tap-dances between invention and reality, a real high-wire act. Ordinarily this kind of inquiry is motivated more by gossip than seri-ous concerns. It should, in an ideal world, make no difference where the author's well of inspiration was found. The actual facts are impor-tant only insofar as they illuminate the inventions. That's true as far as it goes. But none of us is so pure that when reading of Nicole and Dick we don't see two other couples shadowing their every step. The first couple, Gerald and Sara Murphy, were all unknowingly sitting for their portraits while living in the South of France and partying with the Hemingways—Hadley, Paula, and Ernest—the Pablo Picassos, and Zelda and Scottie. The Murphys, he an artist, she a calm aristocratic beauty with a long string of pearls always draped around her neck (like Nicole), had taken avant-garde Paris by storm. Gerald, heir to the Mark Cross store on Fifth Avenue, was a serious painter who not only did the sets for Diaghilev and Stravinsky but hung his work in the most prominent exhibits and received approving applause from the art world. Sara was Sara Wibourg, the daughter of a midwestern industrialist. She had been presented to the queen, come out at the most social of balls, and frolicked at theatricals at the Maidstone Club in East Hampton. The Murphys had the first apartment in Paris with true spare bare-bones white furniture in it. They did everything with style, with endless warmth and generosity toward their friends, and like Dick Diver, Gerald Murphy would rake the beach each morning so it would be free of stones when their friends and guests came down to the water to swim.

One can understand the Fitzgeralds' interest in the Murphys. Their life seemed so perfect, so unsullied by money worries, so devoted to pleasure and family and style that something black just had to be waiting in the wings. The novelist saw an opportunity to scrape at the surface of these lives. Perhaps he was egged on by envy. Perhaps he was intuitively sensing the tragedy that would follow these golden times at Juan-les-Pins when the Murphys would lose two children to illness and Gerald would stop painting entirely and his homosexuality would burst forth and need to be contained again and the most charmed of lives, lived by the most charming of people, would turn out to be a matter of compromises, ordinary in that.

Fitzgerald when he played with the Murphys in the South of France was already drinking way too much and creating scenes at their parties. He was already aware of the illness of his wife and his inability to heal her and he was already fearful that success had passed him by. He needed money. He needed infusions of fame and both were in scarce supply. When in 1926 he began to write *Tender Is the Night* he had in mind some use of his friends Gerald and Sara, some critique, some bitter biting, one suspects. But it never came about because instead of the story following the Murphys' star-crossed journey, the book instead soaked up like a blotter the spilled ink of Fitzgerald's own disaster. Into the story of Gerald and Sara came the drama of the author and his wife, Zelda. So the book is something of a quadrille. Dick Diver is Fitzgerald's own alter ego as well as Gerald Murphy, and Nicole looks like Sara Murphy but is mad like Zelda. This combination makes it hard for a reader to get a fix on the story. It complicates. This is not a writing flaw; it is writing with many coats of paint. What you see covers something else and the something else is still visible, affecting the patina of the whole.

This is part of why Dick Diver haunts the imagination. He is Fitzgerald disguised as a psychiatrist whose life falls apart due to drink and despair and lovelessness, as will the author's own. He is also Gerald Murphy, disguised-as-heterosexual homosexual, the artist who stops being an artist, who loses the fame that was in his hand. All he had to do was close his fingers around it. He didn't. The poignancy of this double character loss and failure is the life-giving oxygen of the story. It makes the book so profoundly American, so sadly about us, so richly about the way we run away from our fate and run right into it. It is also about artists—how delicate a thing creativity is: how it can come and go, be welcomed or refused.

Fitzgerald was a fine portraitist. When he was writing about Gerald Murphy, a.k.a. Dick Diver, he captured his style, his grace, his sweetness to friends, his charismatic social skills, impresario, counselor, leader of the pack, but he also captured, without I suppose conscious intent, the slight effeminacy that marked the character, gave him his love of style, his unusual way with clothes, his dandiness. It is this effeminacy, a whiff of it, that made me love Dick Diver primarily in ways that are not so directly sexual. It explains why it took a long time for Dick Diver to win his place in my soul and why on first reading I couldn't quite see what it was that, fatherless herself, Rosemary so desired.

Fitzgerald surely wanted to be the best novelist who ever wrote. He wanted to wipe the floor with his predecessors and his contemporaries. Diver's ambitions too are in the beginning of the book huge and very American: everyone can make it, come from the wrong side of the tracks, imagine yourself what you want to be and go get it, social position, education, wealth. He tells the head of the psychiatric clinic where he wants to work, "I want to be a good psychologist— maybe to be the greatest one that ever lived." Early success such as came to both Fitzgerald and Diver makes it hard to calm down, to accept the reverses almost everyone experiences. Here is Fitzgerald in "The Crack-Up": "One should . . . be able to see that things are hopeless and yet be determined to make them otherwise. This philosophy fitted on to my early adult life, when I saw the improbable, the implausible, often the impossible come true. Life was something you dominated if you were any good." This is a little like buying a lottery ticket and spending the winnings before the drawing. What if failure follows? Perhaps even accomplishment is considered failure if measured against such outsized ambition, such extraordinary plans.

The night my first husband's play opened in a small theater above a Ukrainian club on the Lower East Side and the reviews came raving in and the applause wouldn't stop, we celebrated 'til dawn. He was twenty-five and I was twenty-four and we walked along Broadway with the set designer, the prop girl, and the director, floating, joyous, giddy with having cracked open the door. We walked past the stage door Johnnies with their flowers still waiting, past bums on the corners, dancers with their bags slung over their shoulders, a hum, a buzz filled the streets, above us the Camel sign puffed out smoke rings, lights flashed and floated by. We were in the history books or so it seemed. There was a magic about the theater then, a glamour that spoke of adulation, hits, pictures on the wall of Sardi's, a table at Toots Shor's, the Great White Way lay at our young feet. And in the months that followed we went to parties at famous directors' homes and spent country weekends with names that were on the marquees in lights. Agents and newspaper people called. Photographs of our baby appeared in the *Daily News*.

And then it all cooled off, and the play he wrote next was damned and the one after that caused the critics to talk of lost promise and suddenly the magic carpet was pulled out from under, midflight. My husband, like Dick Diver, like F. Scott himself, consoled himself with long binges, nightly drunks, obliterating thought, trying to overcome the smell of defeat, the defeat he had always expected anyway, with the more powerful odors of scotch and nicotine and bourbon and beer.

Then I knew what Dick Diver must have suffered when he considered that once he had written an important book and had been hailed as a young genius and now was no more than a dissipated doctor who had married Nicole Warren. Bitter, bitter, it tastes: poisonous and barbed become the former laurels.

For writers and artists the extremes of success are quite sudden and the reversals loud, public, and profound. But everyone hits the ceiling at some point, has gone as far as he or she can go. The wealthy man looks up and finds someone wealthier. The brilliant mathematician finds his creative period has ended. The real estate developer is outmaneuvered by the new guy on the block. For some, like John Updike's Rabbit, early high school fame is followed by a life of tawdry second-rateness. For others like Dick Diver, once cast out, once returned to the minor leagues, nothing is retrieved. Shame shines down with each morning's sun and lasts through the circling of the evening moon. On the other hand I suspect we all start out with exaggerated hopes. All writers want to join the pantheon of greats, and all scientists daydream about Nobel prizes; all philosophers want to be Plato and all soldiers want to be Alexander the Great. It is hard to accept one's mediocrity, ordinariness. But if you can't shrug off your vainglory then you go under. If you flinch, if a lesser place in the hierarchy of your choice spoils your appetite for life itself, then you'll go under, achieve nothing at all, drop out, be wiped out.

Alas Dick Diver I feel sorrow for you just as I felt for my first husband, dashed on the shoals, drunk at midnight, bleary-eyed at dinner. It's your own fault I know. But who's to say why the will was weak, the staying power without wattage? As when watching a lame bird lurching across a field trying to escape the oncoming fox, one resists the inevitable, feels a gentle astonished grief for the bird.

Dick's failure when it comes is gigantic. He returns to a small town in upstate New York, becomes a simple country doctor, and drinks and drinks. With his collapse he loses his children. He closes off his opportunity to make a significant mark in medicine. Alone he moves from one small town to another, probably chased from place to place because of some flagrant drunken error of his own, some disgrace he has created for himself. Social mobility goes two ways, and the American dream is a very fragile fantasy indeed.

I believe in self-invention, upward striving, and class jumping. That's why my grandparents on all sides came to America. If the streets turned out not to be paved with gold here, a person could always take the alternate route. My father, by marrying a woman considered to be an heiress, although it was only a shirt company and not a kingdom, used his good looks to move away from his immigrant Hungarian parents, his father a traveling drug salesman who sometimes made a sale and sometimes didn't, to a life of golf and tennis, squash and stock market tips. My father married his silver spoon. Unlike Nicole who used Dick and then tossed him away, my mother never threw my father back into the pool of American dreamers, where he would most likely have met Dick's drowning fate.

My first husband's mother was determined that he make it into New York society. She was from a once-good southern family (one or the other of the Carolinas) that had fallen on hard times due to a gambler grandfather and a scoundrel daddy. She herself had run off to New York at an impressionable age with a piano player, an impulsive act she most likely regretted for the rest of her life. Soon divorcing him, she lived with her mother and her son in cramped quarters with a window on the fire escape of a brown brick building near the elevated subway in Jackson Heights, Queens. Her only remaining hope was that her handsome and brilliant son would marry some girl with a blueblood pedigree and a daddy rolling in railroads or steel. She obtained a scholarship for him at a Manhattan school known for educating the children of the properly connected, the top of the social order. He traveled there by subway an hour and a half each way. His food and his clothes were paid for by his grandmother's work at the Lane Bryant department store for fat ladies. His new friends went on vacations to warm places and had doormen in uniforms guarding their hallways, where oriental rugs ran up and down floors with burnished wood leading to endless rooms with views of the park and armchairs covered in chintz and bookcases containing silver trophies earned by sculling down the Charles River or playing football, tennis, or track on a New England campus where the libraries and the pools and the gyms and the laboratories were donated by alumni with the same names as the current students. My first husband never invited anyone to his home across the bridge. He attained invitations to coming-out parties where he might have had his pick of the year's debutantes. He was following the most American of paths. He was inventing himself and inserting himself into a picture in which he did not by birth belong.

There is a heroism in that. For him as for Dick Diver, as for F. Scott, only the top would do, where the people with the financial power and the glamour of good times and good wines resided. My first husband invented for himself an English accent, very Oxford. He smoked with a long black cigarette holder. He was part Oscar Wilde, part Orson Welles, a poet-philosopher Horatio Alger who wanted to be either famous or so drunk he wouldn't notice that he wasn't famous.

Behind this ambition lies a very American chronic condition of humiliation. If anyone can succeed, if anyone can own a big car, a big house, a stock portfolio, what of those who don't? The trouble comes with the downside of ambition: failure. If you fooled the admissions committee, faked your pedigree or your Purple Heart, they may one day find out and expel you from the promised land. The stench of failure hangs around, noxious fumes polluting our neighborhoods. Shame is the most brutal of all the sticks that do in fact break our bones. Dick Diver who got himself to Yale on his own brains sees he has to scramble to stay up with the others. He is not proud of his minister father who did not have the get-up-and-go to become a master tycoon in a turbulent America.

But his own life as the spouse of the very wealthy Nicole also humiliates him. He is not his own man. He is more powerful than Nicole because he is her doctor, the guardian of her sanity, yet he is weaker than she because he is a kind of family retainer, a servant after all. In this is a humiliation that he can't endure, not well, not without a wearing down of his character, not without a turn toward self-destruction.

The search for success, Gatsby's and Fitzgerald's, is fueled by some terror of being humiliated, shamed. Out there in the social world, some primitive circle of wolves is forever selecting top dogs and letting others slink away into the forest, cast out from the pack. Charming Dick Diver was not really a top dog. His anxiety, the holes in his swiss cheese soul, let the cold air of loneliness and fear in, and he drank and drank and brawled and lost everything. Weak American man, bad little boy. Dear Dick, I would if I were one of the Fates who spin the threads, pick you up, dust you off, dry you out, send you on your way with a kiss and a rub and a whisper of my eternal regard. But I'm only a reader. *Tender Is the Night* is only a book. Fitzgerald lost everything and died.

Nicole shops with Rosemary in Paris and we see that Nicole shops the way a child splashes water in the bathtub. Rosemary has earned her money, and her relationship to objects is very different from Nicole's. Fitzgerald points this out so we don't miss the point that Nicole is buffeted, protected by her wealth from the ordinary constraints and limits that press on most of us. Fitzgerald, who had money worries all his life except briefly after his first flash of success, is bitter and perhaps envious of those whose birth allowed them to avoid the struggles of commerce. The rich are not so much admirable in his eyes as lucky, and their luck is undermined by their hesitations, their moral failures, their common humanity or lack of it.

Fitzgerald is fascinated by money and he feels superior to the rich even as he presses his nose up to the glass behind which they are dining. This is very American. This is the beginning of the celebrity culture we have today. Art, a writer, may have meant everything to him, but money mattered too and he couldn't help but write about money, make it grind the wheels of his plots just as surely as if he had been a socially aware left-leaning John Steinbeck or a William Saroyan reporting from the gutter the griefs of the hoboes and the laid-off and the fringe people who lived in motels and ate in diners along the road.

My second mate is of far better character than the first but he too saw that America is a ladder and climbing, not baseball, is the true national pastime. He was born in Flatbush of Yiddish-speaking parents who never lost their foreign inflections. He used the public schools to make himself into a boy of the Enlightenment, a reader of Tolstoy, a follower of Darwin. He was very good at the things that teachers admire and determined to rise in America, to do and to be more than his father. He became a doctor through his own hard work and considerable mind. He went to the movies on Saturday afternoons, and watching the double features he listened to the sound of American English and taught himself how to speak as if he came from the heartland, not the ghetto.

He read and he studied and he joined the Army and made it out of his neighborhood into his own doctor's practice in Manhattan, into a home by the beach, into an America where his father would likely not have been comfortable. I admire him for that, just as I admire Dick Diver for wanting to contribute something important to the field of psychiatry, for wanting to be someone of prestige and worth. All over the country people are still scrambling up out of back streets, crossing the tracks, and taking up residence high on the hill. Ambition is a good thing. It keeps us growing. It makes us prove our mettle. Whatever manner a person has been born into, that person can make it to a better manner, richer, more powerful. That's all right.

Failure—Dick Diver's collapse, failure to hold on to your newly won position, failure to hold the spotlight—is bitter, breaking, and turns the night from tender to brutal, and Fitzgerald knew it. In 1929 failure was just a little spin of the stock market away, while for a writer like Fitzgerald it was a spate of bad reviews and rejections from magazines, the open pit of disaster was always waiting. It was only one or two books away, one review away, one roll of the dice you're out, you're the butt of the joke, not the star of the show.

Fitzgerald equated his own success with America's boom years. Ah what a glorious firecracker of a success he had after the publication of *This Side of Paradise*, a handsome charming young man he was with the whole world in his hands, smiling at him, throwing bouquets, raining gold down so that he could marry his beloved Zelda and sail forth to Europe ready to duel with the best. Mirrored in his own crack-up, downslide, he saw wagons tipping over, sending their occupants down into ditches, the depression, the crash, ambition's hang-over. Like the country, Fitzgerald, a.k.a. Dick Diver, lost his helium. Like a balloon drifting too high in the thinning atmosphere he burst. But this analogy is far too simple. Dick Diver himself knew that it was character, choices, moral lapses that brought him down. The process of personal collapse began long before the economy wobbled, tottered, and fell on its head. What were his flaws? A person like me who is extremely fond of Dick Diver, wishes him only the best, can still see how his collapse was not an act of the gods for which he holds no responsibility. Love for a man can be sustained without blanket ad-miration forming like a mist from the sea, covering all in a romantic dampness.

Dick Diver had tried all along to maintain his financial indepen-dence. He knew he shouldn't be simply a bought man, a decoration on the Warren family crest. But he lived too well. He allowed the family to buy him too much, even a half-share in a clinic that he couldn't himself have afforded.

Nicole traveled with enough luggage for a princess. There were servants everywhere. The fine quality of clothes and hotels, of flowers and restaurants, wines and toys and dogs, was natural to her. This grand style was adopted by Dick and became the leash by which he himself was led. How could it have been otherwise?

He wasn't a heavy drinker until his marriage drained him, ex-hausted him, emptied him of his energy and natural delight in things around him. He had to pretend too often, and in the effort to keep up a pretense, of love, of calm, of control, he weakened himself, used himself up. He was putting on a show, a show of his good life and Nicole's and hiding his anxiety that she would behave oddly, lose her hold on reality, scream, collapse, speak nonsense, turn vicious or weepy. He was always aware of her fragility. It was as if he walked through his day with an additional shadow, his own and hers. It wore him down. It turned him toward drink. It left him empty of pride, of authenticity, of genuine feeling. It left him feeling trapped.

Early in the book, Rosemary sees a large chestnut tree in full flower uprooted and strapped down, being carried on the back of a truck down the Champs Elysées. This refers to her condition, of course, as a starlet, as a female, as a beautiful person more done to than doing, but more significant and far more apt it refers to Dick Diver himself, uprooted, being moved about while no longer moving, a wonderful tree with great leaves, but headed now toward death, no longer planted in the soil. Dick arranged for a party in the car of the shah of Persia. He arranged for good wines in fine restaurants. He was the master of ceremonies, the clown of the jazz age itself, but as with all other clowns he was hiding a pale face beneath the colorful makeup.

In every marriage the seesaw exchange of dominance and submission goes up and down. But the outside eye has no way of knowing what are the true stakes, which way is up and which is down. So Nicole has money and position but she also has her trump card: her illness. Dick must be careful to protect her from undue excitement, pain, turmoil. He must create a world for her in which she can be comfortable, that will hold back unreason, hysteria, the so-called push of her illness. Nicole's weakness is also her card to play in the marriage. She can drag on Dick. She can be cold to the children. She can withdraw when she feels the need. She can threaten to make a scene. Nicole has in her illness many ways to make her side of the marital seesaw rise and rise again.

Finally Dick understands that he will not be admired by his colleagues. He will not be able to devote himself to his work as he would like. Nicole loves him, but her love is tinged with ownership and limited by her own soul's smallness. Her illness, even when it is not florid, has tightened her responses, made much of her behavior artificial, brittle. Fitzgerald says about Nicole, "She had not much memory for people and forgot them easily." What he is describing is the self-absorbed nature of illness. There are those attracted to the most neurotic and darkest of souls for reasons of their own. But eventually they find themselves locked out of the other person's inner drama and no matter how loudly they knock at the door, it is not opened. That is in the nature of mental illness. Dick is bored and lonely because his wife is frozen in some self-regarding ice. His entire way of life—his homes, his work, his vacations—is constructed around her needs. His own, now-shelved, rile and ache lead him toward his daily drink.

There is the matter of Dick's supposed love for Rosemary. The thought of her with a boy behind a closed curtain turns his stomach. His betrayal of Nicole with Rosemary is the first step on his downward spiral. But how much did he really love Rosemary? Was his kiss, with its consequences, just a faithless act or was it more a search for health, for his own young possibilities? The story is told here from Dick's point of view, and we see him pursued and offered a new flower. We see him afraid of Nicole's delicate balance. Rosemary is tempting him where he may not go, not ever again. Originally he cannot have Rosemary because he is bound to Nicole. Later she will not have him because he has lost his aura of power; the grace of his style has turned shabby. Later Rosemary, grown up, has her own pleasures and pursuits and can see that Dick is no longer a charmed being. Then she treats him no better than she had treated her dismissible Yale boyfriend in the early days of her friendship with the Divers.

Rosemary is the catalyst for Dick's recognition that he has made for himself a bad bargain. As he was lured by Nicole for the glitter from her surface, he is lured by Rosemary for the same lame reasons. He cannot be in love with Rosemary's spirit, intelligence, wit, insight, or character. She is rather too ordinary, too banal, too selfish to be the object of a man's deepest love. He is attracted to her gorgeous surface and the shimmer of immortality it holds for him. This is his weakness. This is his lack of understanding. It leads to his roaring in pain in a Paris jail.

Dick Diver was finally angry at what had become of his life. Nicole was sick, too sick to tend his sores, and there were many of those, there always are. The effort to pretend to love after love itself had been burned up in the hours of nursing the irrational mind, when dependence replaced the flirtation, the love gestures, the intimacy of the marriage night, that effort exhausted both Dick and Fitzgerald. Debauchery seemed like the only escape. The party turned malevolent. The guest was not polite. Drink became a necessity. Fitzgerald says of Abe North, the drunken writer who is being chastised by a very uncomfortable Nicole, "Often a man can play the helpless child in front of a woman, but he can almost never bring it off when he feels most like a helpless child." It is drunken Dick who becomes a helpless child in Paris in front of his vengeful sister-in-law. It is drunken F. Scott who becomes a helpless child and while needing extra infusions of love behaves so badly that many of his friends shun him.

It is this helpless child that moves me. Dick Diver, boy wonder, man on the skids, the mother in me wants to save you, succor you, feed you, warm you in my arms. This, I know from experience, is never a good idea. Men do not appreciate their mothers, although they never stop needing them. Mothering a man is as good an idea as hitting a policeman. It will gain you nothing and cost you dearly.

A very big part of the tragedy involves Dick and Nicole's children, Lanier and Topsy. Their fate is echoed in Fitzgerald's story "Babylon Revisited," written in 1933. In this story an ex-drunk, jazz age party man Charles Wales, who has lost everything in the crash, tries to reclaim his daughter, who after his wife's death and his own drunken years, is now in the custody of his sister-in-law in Paris. The girl is named Honoria, the name of Gerald and Sara Murphy's surviving child.

In this story, despite the father's love for his child, his desperate need to reclaim his role as a father, to be near his own flesh and blood, she is not returned to him because some drunken companions from an earlier time ruin his chances. In *Tender Is the Night*, Nicole tries to kill her family in a mad fit, as she purposefully turns the steering wheel of the car, causing it to run off the road. Nicole seems to treat her children like accessories to her costumes. Fitzgerald observes that his heroine led a lonely life, owning Dick who did not want to be owned, bringing up children she could only pretend gently to love. The author says that the Diver children were in fact guided orphans. They are part of Nicole's normal appearance toward the world but not part of her soul.

Dick tries harder. He thinks about his son. He tries to be interested in his thoughts but he fails and we see this in the child's insistent questioning of the father about the size, quantity, and manner of objects and natural phenomena. These questions are really attempts on the boy's part to find his father. Are you there? he asks in a million different ways. Dick isn't quite there. When Dick jokes with eleven-year-old Lanier, "If you're not careful I will divorce you," Lanier laughs out loud so absurd is the idea, but when a little while later Dick is sent packing and the children are sent to England to live with Baby Warren and never arrive to visit in America, Dick has been forced, in fact, to divorce his children, and it's not a joke. He does not have the material or moral resources to fight the Warren family. He does not have the emotional strength to reach out to his children, take pride in them, enjoy his time with them. When he is with them his warmth is wan indeed. When they are absorbed into the Warren world, Dick is too weak, too dissipated, to claim his own. This is not lovable. This is shameful. This was written to underline, to outline in red, Dick Diver's shame, his humiliation, his failure on all fronts.

Dick's capacity to love if it had ever been robust was certainly attenuated by his life with Nicole. Fitzgerald described Diver as the marriage headed for its end: "He had been swallowed up like a gigolo and permitted his arsenal to be locked up in the Warren safety deposit vaults." He was unmanned as both a father and a husband. He became paper thin of spirit, detached, keeping himself alive by pretending to love all the pretty girls he sees. He had lost his own reality—if he had ever had it. Was he always a decorative figure, a kind of one-dimensional character out of a movie or a magazine? Possibly. Nicole while normal appearing was also without a rooted, firm reality, more like a model in a picture, a society lady photographed on the slopes. What did she really feel? Anything?

Fitzgerald himself was struggling with his inability to create a home for his own daughter, Scottie, who had not lived with him for several years when he wrote "Babylon Revisited." He too drank too much to provide a household for a child. Zelda was institutionalized. The child was taken care of by his agent and his agent's wife. Fitzgerald was hardly proud of his fathering limitations. Dick Diver was punished like Job. He lost his wealth, his work, his wife, and his children. All that Fitzgerald spared his hero was boils and would-be comforters.

But here in his pathetic end a reader can't help but feel the punishment outstrips Diver's crime. He was a lush. He made scenes in public. He did dissipate his gifts. He did drown out his feelings of dissatisfaction. He got into one ugly fight with some police in Paris, and he howled in the night from a jail cell in a way most unbecoming an American gentleman, but was he so evil, so ill intentioned as to deserve to lose all? He handed Baby Warren the means to remove him. After she rescues him from the French courts, she thinks, "Whatever Dick's previous record was, they now possessed a moral superiority over him for as long as he proved of any use." Here is the American capitalist's daughter exercising her stiff-necked, heavy-booted-warrior view of the world. A man like Dick who was weak but not calculating would never have owned a major company and made millions in steel.

But it must be said on Dick's behalf he didn't give up easily. Fitzgerald says, "It was not without desperation that he had long felt the ethics of his profession dissolving into a lifeless mass." But dissolve they did. He lost his clinic. His professional hopes for distinction, for creative contribution, were over. Once his children are gone, once the financial means that allowed him to live so elegantly, travel so well, stay in the best hotels, are stripped away, all that he has left is his drunkenness, so perhaps he should be forgiven for holding on to it.

Nicole appears to be on the upswing at the end of the book. She takes up with an old admirer, Tommy Barban, a mercenary soldier, a fighter who doesn't mouth it up too much, a man without capacity for introspection but with a certain simple effective virile combative approach to both women and war. Fitzgerald seems to allow Nicole to outgrow Dick. She no longer needs a therapist in the bedroom. She needs a man who will make decisions, take her boldly, love her without complications. She seems no longer on the verge of collapse. She is better, or so it seems. The irony is that the one who had been her nurse is now sick.

There is a problem with this ending. The severe mental disruption Nicole suffered from time to time throughout her marriage to Dick was closer to the troubles that afflicted Zelda than to a mild case of consumption cured by some seasons spent in the mountain air. Nicole, insofar as she was patterned on Zelda, was in for more hospitalization, destruction, dark and sleepless nights, commitment to an asylum, not a happy future with a mercenary soldier. Tommy Barban was a not quite believable deus ex machina rolled out by the author to humiliate Dick Diver further and hammer the last nail into his waiting coffin. There is a reproach buried here against Zelda. Nicole is not lovable at the end, only tougher and apparently capable of survival. Dick is wronged. Our sympathies are with him.

He is not wronged because of Nicole's infidelity. After all, he was the first to betray the marriage vows; Rosemary was a yummy hors d'oeuvre. He is wronged because despite his odd passion for Rosemary, he tried so hard to be a good doctor, a good husband, a good father, and in the end the effort was more than he could sustain. In the end he found himself used up, dried up, done in—in much the same way that Fitzgerald himself would find himself while looking into a mirror in Hollywood several years later.

I had married my writer in Paris when I was twenty-one. I tried so hard to ease his way, to help him avoid the things that produced panic, that wore him out, that made him strange and withdrawn. I worked as a receptionist and I sold my wedding gifts so he could binge whenever he felt it necessary. I was caught in this ever-tightening web of my own design. My original love turned to a silent anger, a rage such as Dick felt screaming in the streets of Paris. I was suffocating under the weight of his existence, his needs for fame or attention or booze. My love, which had been quick (cupid's-arrow-piercing-the-chest-bone kind), as well as fatal for my well-being, dried up in the process of coping with the daily demands of money and food and minimal order. I can understand what happened to Dick Diver. He has my full sympathy. It is very hard to be the healthier, more viable partner. The less healthy partner resents you and that resentment smolders and glows, ending in arson. Any love that may have lasted evaporates. At the end Nicole hates the beach. "She resented the places where she had played planet to Dick's sun." This sentence may refer more to Zelda than to Nicole, who has shown no previous signs of wanting to be the center of attention. Zelda's disease fed her ambition to become a ballet dancer although she was already too old for such a career. Her wish to become a ballerina reveals how much she covets center stage. Nicole's distant, frozen contempt at Dick's horrible failure at waterskiing is produced by his weakness, not Nicole's desire to hold attention.

But the imbalance of power between doctor and patient, between sane and less sane, creates a misery for both partners. Problems of the mind are curiously infectious. The healthy partner does not so much mimic the sick one as find ways to cover his or her own despair behind the calamities of the other. Dick Diver and I were brother and sister in our missions. We both failed.

Men or women who dream of finding lost dogs and nursing them back to health are a dime a dozen. Many of them get into bad trouble as the object of their affections resents their ministrations or resents the dependence that follows. Often the rescuer is really on a mission to rescue himself or herself disguised as the other. This never works because real people refuse to remain stand-ins for parts of someone else and something unexpected always goes wrong.

Here's a rescue fantasy: mine.

· · · ·

What if we had met? What if the boat that Dick took back to the United States was the very same one that I had sailed on, a young woman psychiatrist, returning from a year in Europe, having completed a short analysis with the Doctor in Vienna? What if we found ourselves side by side leaning over the railing, watching the foaming wake and the sunlight splitting like glass in a path toward the horizon's edge? What if I have in my hand a well-thumbed *The Future of an Illusion*, by Sigmund Freud? Dick sees the book. He asks me in German how I come by it. I tell him, in English. We discover our colleagueship. His eyes are sunken. He seems not to have slept in weeks. His hair is matted. There is a sour smell about him. Still I can see that he was once a man of parts. He sighs as he looks at me. "Can I help?" I ask him. I am a compulsive helper. Dr. Freud has explained this dangerous habit as a disguise for other less nice thoughts that rise in the presence of the opposite sex. Accurate though the interpretation is, it did not stop the offer from being made on that transatlantic trip. Dick introduced himself. I had heard of his book. "Why no others?" I ask. This is rude, but out on the ocean the rules change, time is limited. The social dance cut short. We sit down on the lounge chairs and pull the blankets up over our legs. He tells me. I listen to his story about Nicole and Baby Warren and the wasting that has come over him and his children whom he left behind and I let the melody of defeat float over both of us, surround us.

He suggests we go have a drink in his cabin. I put my hand on his arm and look into his frantic eyes. "Let's not," I say. He settles down, the way a horse frightened by a passing owl will rear up and then regain his rhythm. The sun slides over his arms and I notice his elegant hands. "Shall I tell you my story?" I ask. He nods. As I talk he sits up straighter. I see I have his attention. In part it's my curly hair and dark eyes. I know the effect they have. In part it's my knowledge of his profession, our shared interests, or at least interests he used to share with me. I know that he is thinking about my body. I don't mind that. I lean forward and shift my legs. I see him look at my ankles. I go on talking.

At last he begins to ask me questions, to attempt to charm me with his frankness, with his own acquaintance with our subject. He asks about Freud. "You should have your own analysis," I say. "Really?" he says. "Really," I say. "With you?" he asks. "No," I say. Some protective instinct, some newly learned wisdom from Herr Doktor allows me to see that I might have better uses for this man than to make him my patient.

What if we return to New York and instead of going upstate as he had planned, we continue our shipboard romance? He stays in rooms at the Yale Club. I take him to a jazz club on Morton Street. We shout to each other over the music. "Why did you love Rosemary?" I ask. "She was perfect, new, shining. She adored me." "Really?" I ask. "Or were you a prop, a carpet on which she could walk up the royal stairs?" Dick slumps forward. His skin seems to sag. "What did she think about?" I ask. "How interesting was she?" Dick doesn't answer. He changes the subject. "You should have known me," he said, "before, before Nicole." There are tears in his eyes. It's not smoke. "Dick," I say, "you're the weakest man I've ever met." He looks away from me. Of course he's offended. At the end of the set the waiter comes by. The booze is illegal. It is not unattainable. Dick orders tomato juice. "Tomato juice?" I say. "Yes," he says. "I'm not without spine." I put my hand on his, covering it. I look into his eyes. They are such a blue, a cloudless blue. "I think you could do anything you want," I say, "but you have to try, to believe you can, not just showing off for me, but truly." He shrugs. I offer a little free analysis. Why not—I am heady with the pleasure of insight, tipsy on my royal roads to the unconscious. "Dick," I say, "something made you pull the house of cards down on your head. You outdid, you transcended your father and then felt guilt." Dick stares at me. "It's Oedipus," I say. "Fear of castration, that sort of thing." His eyelids twitch. He takes great gulps of his tomato juice. "You were afraid," I say, "of your own power. You had to ruin it." "It was done to me, not by me," he mumbles. "Rot," I say. "You have to take responsibility, you just beat yourself up, mea culpa, mea culpa. That may get you into heaven but it does nothing for you on earth, and now you should take responsibility with resolve to move on. You don't have to be a poor whimpering Warren-whipped creature, not in the least bit." Dick looks at me. "I'd like to be analyzed myself," he says. "Do you think it's possible?" "It's possible," I answer.

What if, at my suggestion, Dick does enter analysis with A. M. Brill, five days a week, and I open my own office in the town house that belonged to my great-aunt and became mine on my mother's death? Dick himself joins the clinic at Bellevue Hospital. He stops drinking except for those occasions when I am too busy to see him. On those nights I sometimes return home to find him sitting on my steps, a bottle of whiskey in a paper bag sticking out of his coat pocket. I am not charmed. We talk about it. I will not marry him until he has been sober for a long time. In this story Dick Diver is the bedraggled cat and I am the ASPCA. But unlike Nicole, Dick does not despise his rescuer and unlike Dick I do not grow restive. We have sufficient money but no excess. We are not glamourous and we live simply. We have that musty psychoanalytic frumpiness that values the sites where antiquities are found more than nightclubs where sharp clothes and a little fame will get you a table. We go to conferences in Chicago and Boston and introduce Freudian ideas along with our colleagues in the universities. Dick publishes papers on the subject of object loss and melancholia. I am the first to read his papers and I comment; my notes fill the margins. He says he needs my help but that is affection speaking more than intellectual need.

Dick is not the strongest man in the world but he has a sweetness that increases when he feels comfortable. Now he often sings show tunes to himself to calm down instead of drinking. His hands no longer shake. Of course he still feels bitter about his children. As he repaired certain flaws in his character in his own analysis, he became more capable of love for his children, whom he no longer has to love. He is cracked inside but does not fall apart. The crack lends him dignity, wryness, irony, grace to imagine the pain in others. Now he listens more than he talks. He is not the life of every party although on occasion he can take charge and make everyone in a room feel exceptional, desired, connected. We grow accustomed to each other's company.

I'm a bad cook. I tend to overintellectualize. I have nightmares that I insist on analyzing in the middle of the night. I have been cured of most anxieties, but some are still with me. He knows my flaws. I know his. This too is love, love that seems to expand with time. What if Dick after several years decides to marry me—not of course until I had begun to date another young analyst, who was becoming insistent, but that's a novel in itself.

Even after the war we never return to Europe. We take our vacations with our children on Cape Cod.

* * * *

In reality Dick had no capacity to turn himself into a real man, even if all the psychoanalysts in the old and new world got together and tried. The odds of success for all the king's horsemen putting Humpty Dumpty together were greater than for Dick Diver to find his footing on his life's path. There was a rattle about him, a social need, a weakness of purpose, and an excessive draining striving that would have kept him from change. Sad but true. Neither will Nicole have the happy ending that Fitzgerald seems to imply in the last pages of *Tender Is the Night*. But common sense tells us that Tommy Barban too will tire of caretaking, and he will wander off as he has always wandered from battle to battle and Nicole will not stay symptom free and the end of the story will find her as compromised as ever. That's the way it is and Fitzgerald probably knew it but couldn't write it. It is a hard thing to ask an author to pass as bleak a judgment on his own future as this would require.

4

...... Rabbit ......

Rabbit

John Updike's *Rabbit, Run; Rabbit Redux;*
Rabbit Is Rich; and *Rabbit at Rest*

Neither bunny nor hare, and especially not the Easter or the Energizer,
not Thumper, not Wabbit (Bugs) or Welsh or Br'er, not Peter Cottontail,
not Harvey, not Monty Python's Deadly, not Watership Down's, not Alice's
White, not Disney or Beatrix, not Milne or Aesop—and not a Playboy.

Ah, Harry Angstrom, high school basketball star, Hassy to his mother, Rabbit to his fans, hero of John Updike's novel in four parts, failed Harry, confused Harry, bad Harry, adulterer, ever looking to satisfy a sexual itch, mediocre of brain, worse of morals, muncher of cashews even to death's door. Sweetheart of mine despite it all. When a monster pain breaks across the chest of this American Don Juan, this clumsy Toyota salesman, this man who once saw God in the soar of his golf ball, while he plays a game of twenty-one with a black kid in Deleon, Florida (searching for the mythical fountain of youth will kill you), I do not judge him. I do not admire him but I grieve deep in the bones, back behind the eyes where sorrow waits to turn into water, I flow forward into tears. I gulp. My nose turns red. My own heartbeat races.

Rabbit, Rabbit, I think. Wait, not yet, please don't die. The sadness and the beauty of living, his tiny petty compromises and his large terrible ones fly through my mind. I try to distance myself from his form, lying flat on the ground, awaiting the ambulance. He was shallow. He betrayed those who trusted him. He was immature and lustful. He was selfish and incapable of discipline. He couldn't stop eating fatty foods even when he was told what they did to his arteries. He was not my kind of man. He couldn't make his way through a history book his wife had given him: two paragraphs and he fell asleep. He betrayed more than one woman. He made a mess of his son, he slept with his own daughter-in-law. He took to the road whenever he felt trapped. He faced no consequences. He ran away from everyone who cared about him.

Nevertheless nothing will ever shake my love. I would defend Rabbit against all comers. I would, if I could, snatch him from the cruel hands of his creator and give him a better ending—something tender, gentle, radiant, something with grace in it. No, more than that, I would give him a better life, one without the ungenerous, not beautiful Janice who wouldn't feed him a decent meal or vacuum the dirt-stained rug and drowned his infant daughter while drunk. (Yes, I know he gave her cause.) I would give him a son who didn't become a cocaine addict and bankrupt his dealership. I would give him a mistress who was more than his fourth choice. I would give him a sister who didn't become a friend to gangsters in Las Vegas. I would give him a way out of Brewer, a town decaying with moral rot and the dark unclean side of American tawdry plastic unloveliness ("Acres of dead railroad tracks and carshops, stockpiled wheels in the heart of the city—sole new buildings are funeral parlors and government offices").

I would have let him land his golf shot on the green, kept him out of sand traps and water holes. I would have had the police find the neighbors who set his house on fire and I would have had the black man who abused his trust at least apologize. I would have spared him the guilt for his wife's drunken state the night that his child died. If his consuming desire was to put his big Angstrom hands, his ex-linotyper once-ink-stained hands on Cindy Murkett, young wife of his golf partner, I would have arranged it. I would never have put Rabbit through so much to learn so little.

There is nothing maudlin or sentimental about my love for Rabbit. I know he was never intended to be a hero. He's no Robert Jordan dying for a cause he once believed in, protecting his friends and his lover. He doesn't have Dick Diver's intellectual gift. Honor is not his strong point. He is no Holden aching for a just world, seeing too much for his own good, filled with goofy energy. He has no outstanding marks of mind or talent that might lift him out of his place and let him soar limitless in the wide American sky. I understand perfectly well that Rabbit is a stand-in for America's failure of moral courage, paltry attempts at spiritual life, coarse bestial behaviors in roadhouses, motels, gropings in the back of cars. I know that he and his friends are vulgar, uneducated, bigoted provincials. I know that the book is ironic and satiric sometimes. I'm clear that Rabbit is an updated woebegone Babbitt slipping on the banana peels littered across America's Main Street. He has a den and some yellowed newspaper clippings of his high school triumphs and not a lot more to his name. Still. Who could resist loving Rabbit? Not me.

The Rabbit novels—one novel really—appearing in the bookstores over a thirty-year span, 1960 to 1990, cover an adult lifetime: the significant part—mine and Harry's. From childhoods spent safely in America during World War II to coming of age in the retro-dinosaur-smothered don't ask, don't tell, don't think fifties, to the hell-broke-loose, the antiwar protests, the hippies-on-the-march, racism-discovered sixties, to the Ronald Reagan eighties, we aged, gained weight, lost some of our sparkle, placed our bets on grand-children. Our plotlines stalled before the finish line. But that's just the outer shell, the first peel of it all.

We were in fact different. I pushed a stroller in front of the White House with a sign in my hand that said, NO, NO NAPALM. Harry in his basic and sweet belief in the goodness of his government and the citizenship he had learned in fifth grade was instinctively for the army whatever it did. He made a lousy cynic. I, New Yorker that I am, took to it like a fish to water. We both watched the evening news each night. His was local; mine was national. I don't play golf; he kept trying to improve his game. Our differences are too many to count. And yet our similarities are there. They shimmer beneath the facts, hover over the plot. Why else read?

Throughout all four of the Rabbit books, we are largely inside Rabbit's head. The observations made, the feelings reported, the view are Harry's. When he first takes the car at age twenty-six and runs away toward the South, toward some vague blurry vision of freedom and sultry satisfaction and abandons his pregnant wife and two-year-old son as well as his job demonstrating salad shredders in a local department store, the reader sees the road unfolding down through Amish country through his astonished hopeful eyes.

There is a problem here. Harry himself, big cloddish Harry, thinks thoughts of extraordinary delicacy. He watches the lengthening shadows. He catches the birds dipping on the telephone wires. He remembers the look of his mother's hands and his sister on a bike. He's a killer with a metaphor. He is thinking with the observational skills and the literary brilliance not of Harry Angstrom but of the author himself, John Updike. This is disconcerting.

Yes, Harry is the usual alter ego character, the author's mouthpiece, the author's shadow, so to speak, but Harry cannot without pushing the edges of our credulity think with the sharpness and breathtaking ease of Updike whose language loops across a page like the frozen strings of ice strung from branch to branch in the most northern forest after a storm has passed. Harry is thinking Updike's thoughts while living his own life in his own nonliterary Flying Eagle Country Club, Toyota lot opposite the Pizza Hut, place. Everything is somewhat coarse, TV influenced, broad, dull in Harry's life except the extraordinary language that runs and runs through his head.

There is an incongruity in this, almost a novelist's mistake. Here is Rabbit thinking about his father-in-law, Fred Springer, "that slippery quick salesman's smile of his, Rabbit can see it still. Like a switchblade without a click." Would Rabbit really have thought up this precise, brilliantly searing image? Not likely. But by sleight of hand, by sheer weight of language and force of story, Harry and Updike become one. The author's own literary mind and Harry's duller, dirtier mind merge and we the reader believe, follow, allow, gasp at the flight of words that are Updike's alone. We follow the fortunes and misfortunes of Harry burying Krugerrands, taking home to his deserted house a hippie girl and a black revolutionary, examining with lustful prying interest the physical parts—breasts, nipples, legs, skin, noses, ears, hair, teeth—of almost every female who passes before his eyes.

This mind meld works because we readers are hooked on the lumpish, clownish human being that is in fact Updike's invention. It works because we wouldn't have been brought so close to Harry, allowed inside his brain and body, without Updike's verbal pyrotechnics. Hemingway may have warned that mouthing things up spoils, but Updike paid him no attention. He mouths everything. He uses Harry as his Charlie McCarthy—his puppet.

All right. There is more than one way to create suspense, empathy, awe in a reader. Hemingway knows a path, but so does Updike. So when I say I love Harry Angstrom, I mean I love Updike in Harry or Harry in Updike. One without the other would not mark my heart so indelibly, so profoundly. Also to complicate matters I love Updike for having given me Harry. Not exactly the way I love my spouse for having given me my children but not so very differently either.

Yes, there's sex, a lot of it, in both Rabbit's mind and his real life. I am mesmerized, like a real bunny in front of a headlight, by Harry's endless sexual rising and fallings, his penis feeling good or bad, pushing or planning or remembering some sexual moment. I wasn't brought up that way. True: I always knew that boys were after that; my mother told me to beware. But if I believe Harry, this sex obsession is worse and far more serious than I had ever in my girlish innocence imagined. Harry in seventh-grade social studies class is looking at Lotty Bingaman as she raises her hand to answer a question in class, and he sees a peek of her bra under her arm, "that sweet strain of cloth and zipper against thick blood," and a slight glimpse of her armpit, and he has an erection in the seat behind her. Now if I had known that just a glimpse of bra above my blouse arm line would do that to a boy, I might have gloried in my power—or I might have been terrified of it. I would certainly have made a habit of raising my hand. I, however, thought they were worrying about baseball scores. I thought they wouldn't like me because I wasn't sure which team was which. I had it wrong.

If I had known that they were thinking about me in dismembered parts—lips, thighs, pubic hair, nipples, round curve of breast, an inch of showing bra—what would I have done? Nothing to do, of course, but I would have been aware that I was holding a crucial card in the game we were playing. I would have understood that it wasn't about conversation or affection or values or the presence or absence of God at our dance but only about the lace edge of my slip, the slope of the dress where it folded beneath the waist. I would have allowed Rabbit to look at me all he wanted if that's what made him happy. Lotty Bingaman didn't know the score and neither did I. Pity.

It's not clear that Updike (or Harry) really likes women, loves the humanity in them, but it is clear that this irrepressible duo is driven nearly mad by the smell, glance, tilt of women's bodies. The descriptions in the books are in the thousands of female moistness, rashes, pimples, full cheeks, limp hair, odors of sweat, garlic breath. It certainly isn't indifference. Rabbit speaks of the grainy feel of the inside of a woman's vagina. Aha! I think. So that's how it would feel if I were not me but him. Grainy? What's grainy? Are we like health bread inside? Is the route to the uterus sandy like the shore? Makes a kind of primeval sense.

Rabbit speaks with enormous gratitude of a woman who takes his penis in her mouth. I'm not sure why this seemed so special. It must have been a huge taboo in Brewer from the way he fusses. But something about the acceptance in the mouth, something about the fact that the pleasure for the woman is not equal to the pleasure for the man, made this act a gift—or so Rabbit thought. Ah, poor Rabbit, so in need of caress, of acceptance, of the squirting of his fluids into a female, that he is overcome with victory and tender surprise when a woman holds his organ in her mouth.

This is sex up close and real, precisely real because it so frequently fakes the emotional connection while being exactly true to the physical act. Rabbit can bury himself in his first mistress Ruth's heavy thighs and still leave her at a moment's notice when his wife goes into labor. He can leave his wife when he sees signs of her ageing thickness under her chin. He can have sex with an underage hippie wanderer and share her with a black fellow who is a very boring revolutionary. When the hippie girl dies in a blaze he hardly mourns. A little guilt nags at him.

This is not the behavior of a man who might arouse affection in the female reader's heart. But he does. He does because in each sexual encounter, in each bestial coupling, in all of his rambling imaginings of sex even with old ladies and waitresses and wives of friends, he reveals what he barely understands himself: the intensity of his need to be loved, to be contained, verified, justified in another's body. This animal groveling, the sensation-seeking of his body, the constant rising and falling of his well-observed penis: this is the means through which his benighted awkward restless soul seeks ease.

Of course he really wants sex too and receives a lot of it. But the tragedy here, the part that makes a reader croon into Rabbit's unhearing ear, "Peace, peace," is the underneath neediness, the little-boy loneliness, the damned condition we live in since thrown out of the garden of Eden, the sad soul isolation that all that fucking cannot, will not, cure. The boy must leave his mother's breast. The cold air of separation, autonomy, flows in between safety and adventure. This Rabbit male is Oedipus, Lear, Attila the Hun, Paris, and always Achilles with a very exposed heel: also he needs his precious blanket, which was, whenever it was, untimely ripped away. Updike knows this. All of it. He writes about loneliness with the same pornographic clarity that he writes about sex.

Damned we are, not because we can't find physical pleasure in the world, but because love itself is so difficult, so fleeting, so mingled with our ever-demanding flesh. Pitiful is Rabbit in his physical thrashings and yet glorious is his questing. What reader is not on his side, no matter how badly he behaves?

There was a brief period in my life in the mid-sixties when I was single in New York City and moving in a crowd of painters and writers. The sexual revolution meant less to this group than perhaps to America at large because most of them had, long before it became a subject on talk shows, accepted its premises: life is short, rules are for the dull and slow of step, the artist needs experience and is entitled to take advantage of opportunities. Artists do not tend to believe the pieties of the masses. They had girlfriends and wives and children, of course, but they were led like a flock of geese by the pied piper Henry Miller, and they believed that a certain lawlessness marked the perimeters of their turf. As dogs may circle the yard urinating in the corners to ward off danger, so these artists spilled their seed in as many women as possible to keep depression at bay, to remind them of their power, to release energies into the night and like Rabbit to ease the ache, the thing inside that would not be soothed and contributed unmercifully to the hangover the next morning. Also they were gluttons, wolves of the night, sloshed and frightened, boasting and red-eyed. They mistook sexual sensation for the saw baked inside the prisoner's cake, the instrument that would free them.

Conventional life—commuter life, mowing the grass, and going to PTA meetings—was not for these cats who along with the Owl and the Pussycat were headed out to sea. The wives went home before midnight. The divorced and the single women stayed on to play. I was one of those. There was much drinking. There were some drugs. There was some fighting now and then as one man or another would pull his fist back over an imagined or actual insult. No attachment seemed permanent. We were all caught in a whirling flush. It was fine to be miserable or crazed. It was considered in this crowd a sign of intelligence, a prerequisite for good work. They did not talk about their golf handicap as Rabbit's crowd might have. They did not discuss insurance or car sales or baseball scores, but they had their own words for success and failure, and the high-stakes game of reputation and admiration and competition continued into dawn as the ashtrays overflowed and the music got louder and the dancing turned lewd and clothes were left in piles behind doors.

One night after the revels ended at whatever house we were, I brought home to my bed a man of charm and gift who had consumed many substances but still wanted me. That was all right. I had grown used to my own disorder the way a voyager on an ocean liner grows used to the tilting of the waves and the expanse of the horizon, knowing that one day land will be sighted. I woke the next morning with the man's hand on my stomach. He startled as he felt me stir. He looked at me. "Who are you?" his eyes said. "Where am I?" His mouth kept the words inside but I heard them anyway. Later as he stood at my apartment door, he said, "Do you know what I am worried about?" "What?" I asked. I thought I knew. I hadn't. "One day," he said, "I will see you and I won't remember your name. I can't re-member the names of the women I've had. I won't remember being with you. Forgive me for that now," he said. He said it sadly. Of course I agreed. It wouldn't be his fault. (It was the sixties—a time to snatch the wings of freedom and drive on out, forth, never mind inspection checks on the vehicle.) I didn't care if he remembered me. Or did I? Was his a boast or a confession? Was my response sheer bravado? But as the elevator rose to my floor, as my child called for her breakfast, I caught his grief as if he had flung it to me across the hall. The hall stank from our unloved bodies. No shower would wash away the stench. Rabbit too needs perpetually (for all eternity because he's stuck in the pages of these books) far more than he'll ever receive.

The Rabbit series serves as America's mirror in which we catch the re-flection of its sea-to-shining-sea angst. This angst is unsuccessfully self-medicated, but in the try-and-try-again mode of American can-do, much overtreated with booze and drugs. Alcohol, hard and soft, drips through Rabbit's life story like the waters in an underground cave darkly staining the walls, leaving puddles on the stone floors. I'm a person with a low tolerance for drink. It makes me sleepy. It makes me feel weirdly distant, as if I were an eye on the ceiling of the room rather than a participant at the table. But I have known hard drinkers, real drinkers in my day, and so it doesn't surprise me that Janice would turn to her Campari to get through the afternoon or that her daughter-in-law Pru sips creme de menthe the way a baby sucks its thumb. Rabbit's pals don't just watch beer commercials; they carry six-packs around with them. When the golfers decide to swap wives, a pitcherful of Caribbean rum props them up, so they can overcome their shyness, embarrassment, sense of transgression. It wouldn't sur-prise me if the bar bill for Rabbit and his golf partners at the Flying Eagle Country Club could pay for the orthodonture of half the town of Brewer.

Rabbit himself is not a drunk. That is not to say that many a night he doesn't have something, swallow something liquid—but not so much that he can't feel the pain. He has other methods to help him muddle through. Janice, on the other hand, is a real tippler. Janice has been drinking too much since the early days of her marriage and occasionally gets blind. That's the state she was in when Rabbit went back to Ruth for a very brief encounter and Becky, the Angstrom baby daughter, was drowned in the bathtub. If this happened today instead of back in the fifties, the Angstroms would have sued the appropriate booze manufacturer for damages done. Great lifelong damage was done.

When Janice speaks to her son trying to figure out what ails him, she needs a drink in order to hear his confession that he needs cocaine. When Rabbit takes in Jill and Skeeter from the hippie world, they drink, they drug, they smoke more than tobacco and surround twelve-year-old Nelson with a road map of mind-altering routes. Street drugs have a starring role in this story. Jill and Skeeter take drugs the way the more conventional golf players take booze—casually, constantly, and with a sense of entitlement. This is all very American, and Updike observes our banal habits with his usual brand-name eye, exact down to the label on each package of poison. But what Updike-Harry doesn't tell us (a novelist's job is not to explain but to describe) is what is causing this rush to tipple, snort, guzzle, suck. It certainly isn't a search for fun. There is no character in these novels who would believe that excuse if you tried it out on them.

Nelson becomes a crackhead and ransoms the Toyota business he is running. He goes hundreds and thousands into debt. He steals from Toyota. He steals from his parents. He becomes an indifferent, nasty, and incapacitated father and husband. It's a very American story, this betrayal by the children of the parents, of men of their wives and children, of women of their husbands and children, this slipping into drugs, rehab centers, NA meetings, the middle-class child sledding along on a downward mobility ride. Rabbit who married up has a higher status in life and a far higher income than his workingman father. Nelson who is sent to college should have outdistanced his own father, but in a perverse, punishing, angry way, he falls down the social escalator to join the punks, to dally with the thugs, to become juicy jailbait.

Updike uses this plot twist to turn the knife in our American dream. See what has happened, he says. See what we have created.

The author is bitter. Harry is confused and angry. I understand Harry's fury. The child he loves, whose two-year-old sleeping head roused him to such tenderness he could hardly bear it, has turned into his enemy, the destroyer of his property, the taunter, the miserable haunter, finger pointer of his life. That's Rabbit's side of the story.

Nelson has his own. Rabbit fled the house when the boy was barely walking, and Janice fled when he was twelve, and though both parents returned, they simmered and stewed in the aftermath of their actions, the resentments, the boredom, the lack of real joy between them. The dead baby who hung in the air is the daughter Rabbit would have loved if his feckless travels had not led to Janice's carelessness. Alcohol bathed that night in a formaldehyde preserving forever the costly consequences of trying to drown your sorrows.

Nelson is the child whom Rabbit wants to love but can't. Yes, Nelson is Rabbit's rival for the physical affections of sweet Jill who like a dandelion fluff has blown their way. Yes, the son is also the rival for Janice's affection but in addition to this elemental man-to-boy struggle, this Cronus and Zeus, Abraham and Isaac, Hamlet and his uncle, timeless battle over the herd of females, there is the ugly fact that Nelson holds Rabbit responsible for Jill's death by a bigoted neighbor who set fire to the house while Rabbit was out fucking Nelson's best friend's mother.

Oh layer upon layer of guilt, revenge taken, ripples of dislike and bonds of affection that run beneath this storyline, this is family life. Poor Rabbit, he wants a son to love, a son who would be glad to see him, who would make him proud, who would be like his basketball once was, a thing tossed into the air to the cheers of the crowd. Instead he has a son who holds him responsible for the death of two girls, a son who does not forgive his father for being taller, who cannot wait to dethrone the man from his Toyota dealership, a thorn in the side, a reminder that the world is not necessarily getting better.

I too have had a child who turned to drugs. I know what that is like for a parent, a hand squeezing at the throat, to attend a family counseling session at the rehab center. I know about the coldness in the child's eyes and the anger that overwhelms reason in a parent's mind but is subsumed under fear and pity and guilt. I know about that pity:

how it rends the capacity to see clearly, to protect oneself from ma-
nipulation, from exploitation. I know what it means to feel as if you
are losing the biggest game of your life, the next generation. I know I
am not alone on this train.

If I had met Rabbit at the rehab center, big Rabbit, with his pale
face sealed now because of a shyness, an odor of failure floating off
him despite the decent suit, I would have sat with him on a coffee
break while his wife was in the ladies' room wiping her eyes and cleaning her face from the running mascara and I would have said to him,
"It's all right, Mr. Angstrom, we're responsible all right but other
things are responsible too. We've been failed too. Our children could
have made other choices. There's nobody to hate. Maybe God."

Of course because I had read the Rabbit books, I would know that
while I was saying those words he would be looking at my sweater
lying loosely over my breasts and he would be thinking about the
color of my pubic hair and he might be wondering if he came to New
York would I meet him somewhere, a Holiday Inn or a Marriott that
wasn't too expensive, not way out of line. It would be this bouquet of
sexual heat that he would toss me that would make me laugh, forget
how sorry I was that I was myself, that I had a child with needle marks
in her arm, at least for a moment.

It would be this flirtation that would remind me that we stumble
forward in eros and in shit. It would be hard for me at that moment in
the corridor of the rehab center's family room with its card tables
strewn with pamphlets: *how to recognize when you have a problem, sniffing, pupils dilated, running noses,* etc., information I had received too
late, not too late to love Rabbit who had once held his sleeping child
on his shoulder and trembled for him, longed to keep him within a
safe perimeter. Rabbit who grieved because his child would be short,
too short to play varsity sports, Rabbit could be my brother, my twin,
except that he would be thinking about my hips, my old hockey-
playing well-developed calves. Would he know that when I was a girl
I played outside my apartment building bouncing a ball against the
wall for hours on end? I would like to tell Rabbit about that, about the
sun on the bronze mailbox that was attached to the building's side,
about how if I missed, the ball would roll under a wheel of a parked car

and I would lie on my belly and reach my arms around the tire and scratch the ground with my fingers for my ball.

Rabbit kills himself with salted nuts and fatty foods and the weight he keeps putting on. The mouth is the hole of destruction here. This too is abuse, not chemical exactly but substance abuse all the same. Peanuts after all are a substance. "No," I want to say to Rabbit, "don't munch on that. No, have a celery stick instead." But Rabbit can't hear me or his doctors or his daughter-in-law who say the same thing. Janice doesn't stop drinking. No one avoids the poison of their choice. Why?

When in Hemingway's *The Sun Also Rises* the group of expatriates drink themselves barely conscious in an orgy of wine flasks, brandies, and Armagnacs just before the final bullfight, we see the flow of liquor as almost Dionysian, ritualistic, awful but correct in some odd geometry of the lost generations, in some homage to the place and the out-of-placeness of the Americans. When Hemingway characters drink, they seem to be playing a role on the world's stage. Even when tragedy is on the horizon, even when the liquor makes the characters stupid and cruel and badly behaved, there is something romantic about the drinking. This must come from Hemingway's own view. Bars and cafés, drinking on open-air buses, always drinking, the Hemingway characters seem valiant if suffering from diminished capacity, living while impaired, whereas the Updike crowd makes us wince, the way we do when a forest animal has wandered onto the highway and lies there flattened, red guts spilled, flies buzzing around.

When Holden Caulfield prowls the Manhattan night spots, he tries everywhere without much success to get a drink. For Holden the prospect of drink is the green light, the go of adulthood, of mastery, of belonging. Holden also needs a shot of booze because young as he is, the snarl of things, the disappointment, the unreachable, the discontent, the guilt of all varieties, survivor guilt, disappointing parent guilt, leaving fencing equipment on the subway guilt, has hit him and hit him hard. He may be underage to get his scotch but he is the right age to need it.

When Updike's characters in cheap bars, in faux-paneled dens, on the patio of the country club by the pool drink, we see despair, a pure

American form of despair, of boredom, of ends reached, of sexual failure, of disappointment, of a brave smoke blowing in the distorted haunting face of the inner demons. When Updike characters drink, it is like listening to the scratch of chalk against the blackboard. Stop it, we want to say; stop please! knowing it can't be stopped.

Updike is not the spokesperson for your local AA chapter. Rabbit could not make do with a twelve-step program. He would need a million-step program and giving up his particular vices would be the least of it. One day at a time is more or less the way he always lived. That's part of his problem not his solution. The way America drinks or drugs or relaxes by the mind-numbing TV exposes the infection at the tongue's root. Something is eating at us, chronically, perpetually. The bacteria of the mind are of the resistant sort. Poor Rabbit it's not your fault. That's just the way it is.

So when Nelson, Rabbit's son, witness to his mother's dereliction, his sister's death, his father's desertion and return, and his mother's equally sudden desertion to a room across town with her lover, turns on too often, we feel that the author is not just describing a wacky kid but a wacky world in which the weak are eaten up from within. Janice never can get mad enough at Nelson, partly because she loves him as mothers love sons, without sensible conditions, but also because the sins he commits against property and person are hardly writ larger than her own.

No one ever gets really angry at the right person at the right time in these novels. Everyone, even Rabbit, is stingy with their affections, unable to reach over and rub a leg, hold a hand, rumple a hair. It's as if expression of warmth must be sexual or it doesn't exist. It's as if praise, pleasure, attention to the other would take away something precious from the self. The air around Rabbit lacks oxygen. Stingy grandmother, stingy grandfather, stingy Janice, stingy mother, stingy father, shabby town. Poor Rabbit trying to find God on the golf course.

Admission: the Protestant stiffness of Rabbit's world which seems to take for granted a swallowed expression, as if people had no tongues or throats to force the scream through, is not mine. Our Jewish prayers are weighed down with layer upon layer of feeling, imploring, remembering, grieving, beseeching, howling sometimes, and often crooning. Our history is too extreme, too irregular. Our response could hardly be composed, refined, repressed. We have been crowded together in shtetls, in steerage, in tenements, in refugee camps and other camps, in exile, and are accustomed to the human noises, the smells, the color of emotions.

In *Bech: A Book*, Updike writes of Jews. He calls them overexpressive. This is meant as an observation, not precisely as a criticism, and from the author's vantage point must be true. But from my perspective the people of Brewer and Mt. Judge are underexpressive, muted, fogged in. Their God gave in so easily to the self-help mumbling of those who might sit through the whirlwind that came upon Job and hear only the refrigerator making ice cubes. The TV so quickly provided their songs, their jokes, their dramatic relief. Their myths seem few, their heroes shallow; their history has lost its heroism, its lyricism. But this is Updike's complaint. This is his view contained within his subject, his themes. It is his objection not mine.

The narrator in *Bech: A Book* is a Jewish author who describes a Jewish woman with a faint mustache, a nose too long, intelligent, alive eyes. She is part mother, part clinician, and Bech, noticing this, says to himself he should have more to do with Jewish women. He refers to "the forgotten downiness of Jewish women, their hairy thighs." This is somewhat surprising. All Jewish women do not have long noses. Some do of course; so do some Italian and Greek women, Lebanese and Brazilian women. The hairiness he remarks on (furry upper lips) is true of some of us. Dark and frizzy, we are some of us, the anti–Grace Kelly, but this is not true of others. With these descriptions Updike is not insulting me exactly and I would never demand of him political correctness or conventional restraint, but his observations of us (Jewish women) squeeze us into a racial type, slightly closer to forest animal than goddess and that makes me uncomfortable.

When Rabbit buys a condo on the Gulf side of Florida he meets many Jews. He notices that the women make noises when they speak, a habit Janice picks up. He notices the funny-looking men and the plump women with bad legs which he somehow thinks are Jewish legs. Here I really object (my legs are just fine, thank you), but at the same time he admires his Jewish golf partners. They have a life energy he drinks in, they seem to have a knowledge of things that he doesn't. He even asks them to help him understand his son, his family. Kindly they try. They fail him but he doesn't blame them. This is not anti-Semitism in the usual sense. It is simply the way the non-Jewish world, and after all most of America is not Jewish, views Jews.

They do speak as Rabbit does on several occasions of Jewing some-one down. They do regard Jews with a mixture of admiration and sus-picion. Why are they so rich? And they do think that Aryans are more beautiful—tall is better than short, blue-eyed better than dark—while still wanting a Jewish doctor in an emergency.

As a Jewish reader I shrug it off. But "overexpressive"? Come on. The exquisitely written Rabbit books are a testimonial to the failure of underexpression. The author loves language, but his characters are inhibited, isolated, and say much too little, or little of real importance, to each other. Updike documents the sad lonely run of Rabbit who can't tell anyone what he needs and is kept in the dark about what oth-ers require. The Rabbit books, with extraordinary verbal exactness, portray America at its most inarticulate core: another irony. The Rab-bit books are Protestant in every last fiber of their invented world. I now understand why a fellow like Harry Angstrom would look to a golf game for relief from what ails him.

But it would be absurd to take Updike's rudeness to Jews very seri-ously. He is rude to everyone. He notices ear hair, chin sags, preten-sions and absurdities in ministers, cars, houses, old women, young women. Children don't escape his critical eye and the horrible Roy, Rabbit's grandson, is described with the same excruciating close-up as the Jews and blacks he encounters. The fact is that Updike is not a people person. No flaw of surface or character escapes his scathing tongue, his searching eye. Often he is as nasty as the mirror in a gas station bathroom with a high-wattage bare light bulb hanging down from a cord.

Rabbit has to carry this cold vision in his head and sometimes it seems too much, too cruel, too terrible. But Rabbit himself, even with the icy Updike eye, is still the boy searching for escape, looking for grace, wondering when God will come to him with a sign. There is a particular poignancy about this Rabbit who must protect his soul against all the corruptions of the flesh, all the cruelties of the other characters, all the tawdry pictures on the TV while walking around with Updike nonstop talking in his head. No wonder he has such a hard time.

Here is why I love Rabbit. He is trapped in his life, once a fine athlete who played easily, gracefully, not just tall but smooth, like a dancer, now bumbling in the net, himself the ball, no longer the star. Around him everyone is dulling their brains with whatever they have. Rabbit still, despite betrayals of his own, betrayals of friends, looks for the rise of the moon, the lengthening of the shadow, the growth of a bush, the memory of the pretty girl who lived next door and undressed each night, a silhouette across an alley. He is treading water, trying to keep his head above, and all around him the flow of alcohol rises higher and ever higher. Rabbit takes the measure of anxiety, loneliness that has been our especially American lot. The rivers of alcohol rise along the malls, carrying the french fries, the car dealerships, the talk shows, the game shows, the baseball games that fill up our time in their wake. In the light of this, Rabbit stirs me.

My mother took a scotch with a squirt of water every day at five o'clock. My father came home and headed for the bar in the art deco blond chest with a blue mirror that hung above it in a corner of our living room. They drank in art deco red glasses with a white design. They drank more at parties, when they went out to dinner, after a game of cards, after a game of golf. They liked manhattans and martinis and whiskey sours. They had a silver ice bucket with silver tongs and sometimes my mother put her cigarettes out in the melted water at the bottom of the bucket. They drank like Myrna Loy and William Powell when they were angry or sad or bored—in other words often enough. Sometimes it contributed to their troubles, sometimes not. They weren't alcoholics, hardly. They just weren't comfortable, easy, surefooted.

I'm no puritan teetotaler. Everyone needs some kind of cotton wool between their head and the real world. This is America where prosperity came to so many of us and left us needing a drink at the end of a busy day. This is America where the drug war is exactly like the war against North Vietnam. It is long, engaged in by an ambivalent population, in a swamp, corruption on all sides and within. The drug war is itself all American, a moral pose covering immoral opportunities: a good try but not good enough.

My first husband couldn't leave the house without a good jolt of scotch. He drank at parties to remain charming. He drank until the early hours of the dawn, reeling down the pink neon blinking streets of Manhattan searching for bars with vinyl booths and ads for beer hanging from ceiling fans, relief for his irregular heartbeat, relief that could not be found inside the apartment he shared with me and his newborn child. Yes, it was a disease, so I've been told. Naming it a disease should help clear up the confusion but actually it doesn't. Calling it a disease is probably good for those who claim recovering as a permanent state and need to fill out insurance forms, but no matter what we call it, we are left with the seething, the searching, the itching in place. Drinking too much leaves us flattened, dulled, medicalized because the disease has a cause and the cause is the thing we need to remove. Substance, bottled or in plastic Baggies, is only the Band-Aid that covers the cause, the thing we can't name.

We were in our early twenties my first husband and I. I had a baby on my hip, he was cracking inside. He needed to run away. Go, go, I finally said. Home is a trap. Without home the fear rises. Inside it the fear burns and burns until it burns down the home. Is there a country in the world without a bar on every corner? Is there a place without opium, beetle juice, mescaline, dream food for those who have settled for too little? Janice and Nelson overdo it. The sixties overdid it. The fifties hid it but they also did too much. The rest of the century went on building rehab centers that filled up as fast as the new highways with new cars. All the commerce in cars, TVs, computers, refrigerators is dwarfed by the sales of designer novocaine intended to numb the heart.

Oh Rabbit I wish I could have found a way out for you.

• •

Here are the things that Janice did to Rabbit that I would never ever have done:

1. She didn't understand his humiliation when he was working selling salad shredders. He had been a basketball star. Now in the real world he was a lowly employee, no respect, no challenge, just boredom faced him each day. He was a cog in the American sales machine by which the economy purrs, yes, but the heart is taken out of a cog. Janice took his paycheck but she didn't even try to compensate him for his bruised pride, his diminished soul. She is angry when he is late. She has retreated behind her own defensive walls, sipping something with a goodly percentage of proof.

2. She was a slob. She never had food for him in the house. I would have kept my part of the marriage bargain. Dear Rabbit, I would have made him cookies and roasted meats. I would have set the table with a candle each night. I would have swept the floor and sprayed Lysol on the toilet seat. I would have turned off the TV when he came home so he could tell me what was on his mind. I would not have left him alone in the American economy, working for me but not with me. I would have let him make love to me any way he wished. I would have found out what I liked and told him. I would have let him know that he might be a lowly salad shredder salesman during the day but at night he was superman. I really would have.

3. Janice never openly expressed her guilt at her baby's drowning. Instead she allowed Rabbit to take it all on his shoulders. Her family blamed him. Everyone blamed him. She should have taken her share of the guilt, the lion's share in fact, because it was her drunkenness that killed the child both of them needed and would have loved, would have increased their portion of the world.

4. She ran off with Charlie Stavros, perhaps to get revenge on Rabbit for leaving her for the last three months of her pregnancy and living with a former prostitute, Ruth, but tit for tat is not justice. It's more like a temper tantrum. She left her child, not yet a teenager. She watched the boy from behind a curtain when he would bike over to where she was living and wait for a glimpse of her. She felt bad, ashamed perhaps, but she didn't move out the door to sweep her child in her arms.

5. When Rabbit's house burned down, killing Jill and ending Nelson's childhood with a nasty stink, she reabsorbed Rabbit, a Rabbit with his tail between his legs, into her family's home. Rabbit went to work at the Toyota lot and moved into her old room in her parents' house. Rabbit was in the house on sufferance. He wanted a home of his own. I would have helped him get it, gone to work to save for a down payment, understood how cramped, how unpleasantly cramped he was between her mother and her father. He wanted light. The house was dark. Janice didn't care what he wanted. Not at all.

6. Janice owned the lot. Ma Springer left everything to her. Janice felt that the lot belonged to Nelson. Rabbit had worked there for years, and yet he owned nothing. Janice let that stand. I would have made Rabbit my full partner. I would never have allowed him to feel as if he, after all those years of work, was a drifter, a decoration, nothing but a pile of old newspaper clippings that told the story of his high school triumphs.

7. When Rabbit sees a young girl who he believes might be his daughter by Ruth, Janice is so offended when he mentions this to her that he nurses his hopes in isolation and renewed guilt. I understand why a woman would be angry at the idea that her husband's child from an adulterous affair may have surfaced and threatens to enter their days, especially a daughter, a fact that reminds her of the one she drowned, but she pays no attention to Rabbit's need, his yearning, his hope for a girl who would carry his genes on, walk with his walk, bring solace to his mind. I would have swallowed my fear of the situation. I would have told Rabbit to pursue it. I would have let him tell me what he expected. I would have looked up birth records in the county files. This would not be easy for me but I would have done it because it would have made Rabbit less alone, brought him closer, protected his heart muscle against the assaults that eventually wore it out.

8. Then there's feminism. I am a feminist. I don't believe that Janice needed to bow under, to play housewife, a role she was eminently unsuited for, as the times changed. Rabbit himself liked her growing decisiveness, was attracted to her new boldness. But then she made it all too clear that the Toyota lot, the Toyota dealership that Nelson later lost in his drug lunacy, was all hers and Nelson's and on top of

that she moved forward toward a career as a real estate salesperson. Well good for her but it left Rabbit to lonely TV dinners, while ensuring that he would no longer have a significant economic function. She rendered him useless as a newborn babe and gave it no thought. She wouldn't let him go home to the house he loved on release from the hospital but made him spend the night in their old bedroom at her parents' house because she wanted to go out to a class and didn't want to stay by his shocked and frightened side. That was the night Pru, his daughter-in-law, got in his bed.

I would have stayed with him, knowing that the first night out of the hospital would be hard for him, that he needed his own bed, his familiar place, and his wife. I would have understood what the loss of the dealership meant to him. I would have understood that he couldn't just play golf forever after. I would have found a way to give him a dignified and powerful role and certainly real choices in his own life. Janice just ran over Rabbit like he was a bunny who chose a bad moment to cross the road. No wonder he slept with his daughter-in-law. He thought he had lost everything. He knew he had lost everything when Janice planned to sell their own house and move permanently back to her parents' home with his son and his son's family. Rabbit knows he has become an appendage. All is lost, dignity and self-respect gone for good.

When Janice says she won't forgive him for sleeping with Pru he runs away to Deleon and manages to strain his heart 'til it breaks. I could make a good case that Janice killed him. I would never have treated him so shabbily, sending him headlong into bowls of salted peanuts and candy bars: her fault.

Yes, there is another side to this story. I see it. Poor Janice, one might say. Her young husband is already right there in the first pages of the first Rabbit book looking at her body and marking its loss of tautness. He runs whenever there's a problem. He runs with his feet and he runs with his car. He runs before he considers. He causes embarrassment and havoc as he presses down on the gas pedal. He left her seven months pregnant. He returned and left her again the night after she comes home from the hospital, a long difficult birth, with their newborn daughter. He leaves her with a two-year-old. He leaves her without saying good-bye, or a word of when or if he'll ever be back. Janice's leaving Rabbit after his angioplasty is a revenge for Rabbit's return to Ruth after Janice's delivery of Becky. What goes around comes around, so they say, so novelists agree and build their plots to prove it.

Further sins of Rabbit: he lusts after every woman who enters the lot. He especially lusts after the girlish wife of a member of his golf foursome. He takes another mistress, a sorry lady with lupus, who will die before him, but die wanting to make him happy. No one forced him to have sex with his daughter-in-law when she offers herself to him after his angioplasty operation. This is hardly upright behavior and morally unjustified whatever excuses may surround the deed. Rabbit, like the lead wolf in the pack, may be weak in the legs and ready to be deposed by a younger more virile beast but he still shouldn't sleep with his daughter-in-law. Some rivalries are better played out in the unconscious than in the bedroom.

Whatever his reasons Rabbit's morality is slipshod, his ability to consider consequences almost nonexistent. Finally he runs to Florida just as he has always run. He is a coward and he turns his head away from things one had better look at. It is as if he sent a boy into his life to do a man's job.

Ah but the sweetness of him holding his newborn granddaughter on his lap, an infant all swaddled in pink—the love in him, the hope in him. "You can feel in the curve of the cranium she's feminine, that shows from the first day. Through all this she has pushed to be here, in his lap, his hands, a real presence hardly weighing anything but alive. Fortune's hostage, heart's desire, a granddaughter. His. Another nail in his coffin. His."

Ah Rabbit.

Another nail in his coffin? What's that? Updike-Harry is ambivalent. Every time he loves he feels trapped. Every time he's trapped he tries to escape. Here we have the little boy who must leave his mother's side but still needs her. He wants to be engulfed and enfolded in her arms but he wants to get out, as far away as possible. This double contradictory desire makes men mock and fear domesticity, hate women for their clingy needs while at the same time they call out, Mommy, Mommy are you there? I need a drink of water, they call into the dark. They hold on to us, request their favorite foods, complain about the sniffles while pulling away into the TV, resent their own children, carry on adventures in their heads, watch James Bond films in the early hours of the morning. This connect-disconnect, this resent-and-feel-guilty-for-resenting dance is as sad as it is common. Rabbit and Janice lived with it. They deserve credit for that at least.

I realize that I haven't made a convincing case for Rabbit as a man worthy of our affection. I want to stick up for him but I keep noticing the way he lets everyone down. As a woman I get embarrassed by his all-consuming obsession with sex and his pervasive lack of fidelity, but Rabbit has his reasons: a defense can be made on his behalf. Rabbit started life with pride and pleasure—sweetness toward his sister whom he rode on his bicycle bars, mute, raw love for his mother, pride in his effortless leap toward the basket, affection for the first girl whose body he virginally explored under her skirt in the back of his car, a girl who married someone else while he was in the army in Texas. Now I'm not blaming the girl. No reason why first love should be honored ever after and no reason that all the bad things that followed his forced marriage to Janice would not have happened if he had married Mary Jane instead. But Rabbit suffered too. Everyone's life contains knocks on the chin and comeuppances that pinch the aorta, and Rabbit had more than his share.

Rabbit never made it in American terms, not on his own anyway. He lost his job as a linotyper as the industry automated. He never owned a real share of the capitalist enterprise. He was the working stiff who stood in Janice's place and made car deal after car deal. His partial climb up the economic ladder was more illusion than reality. This was not because he was immoral. It was because he was an average guy, muddling along, wanting to have a few goodies, but not mean, not pushing, not without a soft spot in his heart for angry black kids or drug-taking hippie girls or even plump women who needed a hand on their backs and reeked with their neediness.

So my case for Rabbit rests on my appreciation of Freud's *Civilization and Its Discontents*. A very simple thesis really. We all have animal instincts, rages. I want, I take, I need, I can do what I want. Take the prettiest woman, the biggest piece of meat, the prize spot in the sun, and if anyone gets in my way, I'll mash them, smash them, remove them from sight. But humankind can't live like that so we make rules and the rules constrain. You can't move your bowels at will and you can't crush your neighbor's skull when he annoys you. But the rules don't always rule and the instincts sometimes go away so far that they take our life juices with them. So this project of civilization has a problem, built in, alas. Rabbit sees a green glass egg in his in-laws' house and thinks he might bash Janice in the head with it. He doesn't. The impulse passes. We understand the impulse. Through the four volumes, the glass egg reappears from time to time, always to tempt Rabbit with its lethal power. The point is that Rabbit is trapped in civilization. He can't live comfortably within the rules and he can't live without them.

He can't help his lustful yearnings. He can't help wishing he could flee his house. He can't help himself at all: athletes other than a few stars are no longer needed in our society. If we were still tilling fields or chasing buffalo Rabbit might rise to the top of the pack. But with an average mind and a lack of education, he flounders. But the good thing, the lovable thing about Rabbit, is that he never becomes resigned, dulled of expectation. He looks at everything around him. He says that God has turned into a raisin buried somewhere inside his stomach, but he remembers God once was out there. He longs for something else, a whiff of life, of understanding. He is ready to love again—Cindy, a rich man's plaything, his own phantom daughter, his granddaughter Judy whom he wants so hard to please that he brings on his first heart attack while sailing with her on the ocean despite the fact that water frightens him. Oh what an ironic stroke that he should almost die by drowning, that he should almost lose another girl child in liquid. Is Updike sadistic, cruel to his characters? Yes. But doesn't a handcuff always bang against the bedpost, a hollow steely sound, when irony directs the plot?

Who could not love Rabbit as he struggles to sail the boat, turns it over, and thinks his granddaughter is drowning under the sails? He makes a heroic effort to save her. He tries to keep his heart attack from her so as not to frighten her. His tenderness toward the child redeems him, or may redeem him if the judge (Who is the judge? Is the reader the judge?) has compassion, any compassion at all.

Rabbit is an example of the twentieth-century contribution to the crawl of humankind toward whatever awaits us. Not to love him is not to love ourselves.

There is baseball talk in Rabbit. The men use it to pat each other on the back, to make small talk, to build and endure friendships. But the sports watching is real and takes up male passions as the sail scoops up the wind bearing down the line of the horizon. It is vicarious combat of course—combat subject to civilization's rules, so that it becomes metaphor not death. My spouse cares so deeply about his teams that he will turn his back and flick off the television when they are doing badly. He can't bear it. For hours he can go back and forth pacing the threshold of the room, pretending indifference. When it's over he forgets it, whatever the outcome, but while it's happening, the tension rises, something seems to be at stake, something real. It's a leftover from boyhood perhaps. It's a wisp of the child in the man, this game that will go his way or it won't.

It is this remnant of the primitive plains in the man I have married that touches me. When we drive on the highway and someone tries to cut him off he will turn red and scream. He prefers to be first in the line of cars which means passing others as if there were going to be a prize awarded to the first to reach the end of the highway. I would be content to go sedately behind the car that precedes me. He is driving forward. This is a man who has a suit and tie and an honorable profession as well as a fondness for Italian drawings of the seventeenth century. But inside I see the man untamed, the man as warrior, hunter, savage snarl and all. I see him dare anyone to cross the threshold of our cave and I am glad.

Rabbit sees decay everywhere in his home town. His own life which peaked in high school is on the skids even when he appears to be making money. The churches of the town are now staffed by frauds and hypocrites, and God? God seems to be found only in the rehab centers, renamed "Your Higher Power." The deity seems to have become an echo of some former self. If Skeeter who shouts angry black sixties' slogans in Rabbit's willing ear is the prophet and Rabbit is the citizen of Nineveh, then God himself is playing *Jeopardy!* in the great TV station in the sky and is far too occupied to concern himself with the lost Rabbits on the strip malls of America.

Rabbit says to Janice shortly after Nelson's shotgun wedding to Pru, "You sometimes wonder—how badly you yourself fucked up a kid like that." "We did what we could," Janice says,—"We're not God." "Nobody is," Rabbit says, scaring himself. What scares Rabbit is that existential shiver, nobody in charge. What scares Rabbit is that he himself cannot make moral choices, at least not all of the time, not without lapses. This fright in Rabbit is not weakness but insight, and it is lovable. I would turn on a night-light for Rabbit. I would absolve his guilt. If only I knew how. My own as well. I too am alarmed. Wouldn't it be better if someone were God?

Another reason to love Rabbit is that he loves his red-headed granddaughter Judith and wants her to love him. He has trouble. He buys her candy he shouldn't. He can't quite reach her but he keeps trying. The TV interferes, her parents interfere, nothing quite works. The harder he tries, the more he fails. Like a bear trying to put a quarter in a slot machine, he keeps missing his opening move. But he wants, you feel him needing, the affection of this child. What he feels for her stirs him deeply. Yes, she is the replacement for the daughter he lost and the other daughter he thinks he has but who has been denied him by her mother. He has lurked in the woods, stalked the farmhouse he is convinced the mother Ruth, a woman he loved for three months and left pregnant, inhabits. When he finally confronts the woman she denies that the girl he has seen is his daughter but he doesn't accept this. He wants this girl child to be his own with an ache that aches the reader, with a need that is so deep I had to put the book down, so hard it was to tolerate.

So Rabbit as a father is a flop, maybe too selfish, too unsure of what is required of him, maybe too uncertain of his own place in the universe to tolerate the pushing against him of his irritable son, maybe. But he's also a yearner, a dreamer, a man who wants to link himself to the future through his children. He is not a cad or a deserter or at least if he deserts he is willing to return. He is not loved, or so he thinks, by his son. The blow of that he has absorbed, but the bruises left behind are guilt, a bluish-purplish mark across his days, not consciously noticed, not expressed often but there.

I know about that. The newness and the freshness of the baby, the smooth skin, the eyes so searching seem to demand so much goodness from us. Reality intervenes. We are fallen angels after all.

We cannot spare the children what we would spare them. We cannot stop the forward motion of our lives just because the children have joined us. We love erratically, we stray from the point, we become self-absorbed, we make decisions that are not always in the best interest of every member of the family. We grow angry at being tied so tightly. We mutter, we resent. We look at our children and can be pleased sometimes but sometimes not and when not, the displeasure redounds on our own heads. Whose fault is it after all? I see this in Rabbit—the disappointment, the acceptance of the disappointment, the love that continues, the guilt that stains everything. I wish Rabbit as a father were as alien to me as a jellyfish floating in the oncoming waves but he is not, not at all.

Now of course the entire batty sixties, with revolution on the doorstep, emptying the churches, bringing weed into the home, sending the vulnerable into the dark alleys, was as responsible for the headless wonders that emerged as the shortcomings of any individual mother or father. Of course it was in that time of excess that Skeeter came into the house making loud noises about justice and Jill came through talking of vegetables and meditation and Rabbit was confused and lonely and ended up holding the short straw and feeling more guilty. Did Jill die in the fire because he was negligent?

Nelson fudged the car dealership's books. Our daughter took a painting off our walls and sold it on Madison Avenue and pocketed the money while we were away. We made the gallery give us back the painting. We returned their money. But I know what it's like to be taken by your own flesh and blood. It's the drugs of course. It's the bad choices too. It's the times also. But finally it's the pain of the thing, failure.

When first I sent my daughter off to a rehab center in a distant city I felt stunned and ashamed. I went on vacation to a small cottage on a lake in Maine and in the mornings we fished for land-locked salmon and in the afternoons I watched the water ripple with reflections of cloud and bird and once I saw a whole rainbow so perfect that I thanked God and I don't believe in him. But there away from my home, sitting in a canoe, the thought became emblazoned across my synapses and would not fade like the morning's mist that I had betrayed my child, wildly, badly, because I had not prevented, strengthened her, known what to do.

I have more schooling than Rabbit. I know about child development and I have more than a passing acquaintance with the masters of the deep, the scuba divers of psychology. I live in a large city with a veritable circus of cultures around me. I have traveled to Queen Elizabeth's home and watched the changing of the guard and seen the Eiffel Tower. I've been down the Green River on a raft and I've talked to movie makers on the beach at Malibu. But despite all that I understand Rabbit. It's hard—this thing with children—how the knife cuts.

Then there's the matter of the generations repeating, echoing the tragedies of the past. Updike has it right. Rabbit gets Janice pregnant and so has to marry her. He traps himself in a lifelong snare. Nelson gets Pru pregnant and has to marry her. He traps himself. Rabbit tries to run away literally—taking the car south, staying with Ruth, running through the woods away from the funeral of his baby daughter. Nelson runs away metaphorically by snorting coke, by consorting with punks and thieves. Rabbit in leaving Janice alone drives her to drink, which leads to the death of the baby. Nelson pushes the pregnant Pru down a flight of stairs. Pru and Nelson move into the house, crowding Rabbit just the way Rabbit and Janice had moved into the house earlier. Parallels and circles, parabolas and geometric designs, life is messy and disordered and yet if you look closely, you can see patterns emerging. Updike has created them. We see that nobody gets away with anything. Your sins return to haunt you in the deeds of your children.

When we see nervous coked-up Nelson with his son Roy, a child already angry, disappointed, and afraid at the age of four, we see the generations repeating in some terrible downward spiral an almost foreordained disaster. It makes you want to scream it really does.

. . . .

After Rabbit slept with Pru he ran away from Brewer and from Janice and stayed in the condominium in Florida alone. Perhaps in that period of time when he was stuffing himself with salty foods and watching TV and waiting for Janice to forgive him and knowing she wouldn't and the loneliness was on him like a stone, I had been visiting my cousin L who had retired to a gated community in Deleon, Florida. I was giving a talk on Israeli politics to the Jewish Community Center there. I was in Florida for three days. On the second day I go to Mickey's Fruit Stand which is no stand at all but a tourist business where crates of oranges and grapefruits are sent back to sufferers in the cold wilds of Chicago and New York. Large cutouts of cardboard flamingos mark each aisle. A juice squeezer rumbles in the back room. Little green plastic pieces, imitation grass, rest under the trays of fruit. They also sell suntan oil and rubber toys that when inflated become dolphins and manatees with ear-to-ear smiles. Mickey's also sells jellied gingered orange slices and coconut patties covered with chocolate. Rabbit has a fondness for these and we meet on line. I see he has four packages of chocolate coconut patties in his arms. They jiggle, one falls to the ground. I pick it up and return it to him. He looks at me, furry upper lip, frizzy gray hair, my pink sandals with the heels that say to all lookers, Don't count me out, not yet. I smile at Rabbit. Who wouldn't smile at this man with red sun-tinged ears, such a tall man, folds over his stomach, too much weight but a gentle kind of beaten look in his eye? The wait is long. We talk. He walks me to my car carrying the three stuffed orange cats with green glass eyes I have bought as a souvenir of Mickey's for my grandchildren. I tell him I'm a writer. He tells me he's reading a history book on the age of exploration. Leaning against my car door in the hot sun, he tells me that he's alone, hasn't had a meal with anyone for nearly two weeks.

And so it happens that he winds up back at my cousin L's with me. We sit by the pool and I make him a grilled cheese sandwich and when he's still hungry I cut him a slice of coffee cake and we talk about our children and grandchildren. He shows me his pictures. I show him mine. And then before I can explain it I'm patting his thigh, right beneath the long checked shorts he's wearing. He tells me that he's been walking, walking into strange neighborhoods, looking just looking. I offer to go with him. We have nothing in common. I'm married and so is he, sort of. It turns out he hasn't read a book all the way through since high school and even that's in question. He says he wonders what he missed. I have an inexplicable desire to tell him. What book should he start with? I consider what to recommend—Conrad, Melville, Sinclair Lewis, Updike. Would he like Updike? Probably too wordy. My cousin is playing golf and will be gone all afternoon. I take Rabbit into the house and into the guest room. We undress. I have a bad heart, he tells me. No, I say, you have a good heart. I lie with him. We do the usual things that Updike would describe for you in excruciating detail but I will only say that we sweated despite the noisy air-conditioner and we touched and put his hands on my thighs and I put my arms around his big wide hips and I thought of things to do that he might like. He did.

Later we go out to walk. We pass a basketball court where a black boy is throwing a ball into the hoop. Rabbit wants to show me how good he once was. He calls to the boy. I say, "No, I don't think you should, not with your bad heart. Come with me now and we'll have a health food dinner at my cousin's club." As we go down the street, he turns around to watch the boy jumping up for a rebound as the ball circles the rim. He tells me he should have a bypass operation. "You should then," I say. "You think so?" he says. "There's so much ahead of you," I tell him. In telling him this I am thinking that there is much ahead of me too, that it would be a tragedy to die before one absolutely has to. Hold on, hold on with your fingertips, fight for yourself, I think, for me and for him.

After dinner he takes his chocolate coconut patties and throws them in the trash can in the corner. He does this for me. We part. He goes home to his condo in Valhalla and I go back to my cousin's gated community and the next day take the plane home to New York. I liked Rabbit's big body next to mine. Did I give him something in return?

* * * *

5

Nathan
...... Zuckerman ......

Nathan Zuckerman

Philip Roth's *The Ghost Writer,*
The Anatomy Lesson, Zuckerman Unbound,
and *The Counterlife*

Slouching toward Newark.

I *h a v e* your number Nathan Zuckerman. I know that Philip Roth is your alter ego. I know how you roar and rage and suffer from migraines and back pain and neck pain and how the anti-Semites attack you at dinner parties and hit cotton balls at your nose while you're typing and I know that your enemies include Milton Appel, a.k.a. Irving Howe, certain members of the Mossad, an ex-wife with a mannish walk and a psychotic's rage whom you called Maureen, or Lydia, Alvin Pepler of quiz show nonfame, jealous folk and rejected lovers, ex-fans and lunatic letter writers, and I know that at one point the rabbis in America were denouncing you from their high holiday pulpits for writing a book called *Carnovsky,* a.k.a. (in your work even books have alter books) *Portnoy's Complaint,* and now in your maturity, if we can call it that, you get Jewish prize after prize so once again you are the adored, if slightly shopworn, glistening boychick of your childhood.

Newark. I know more about the once-dreamy nostalgia-reeking streets of hard-working families, now replaced by blaring radios, peeling paint, and folks who use food stamps, than seems exactly necessary. I know about Newark even when it pretends to be Camden or Yonkers. I know about your hectoring and hocking father, beloved yes, guiltily beloved, ambivalently beloved, like a Woody Allen dream about the local Cronus and Zeus, Oedipus and Jocasta. I know about your mother, perfection itself, Mrs. Zuckerbird, whistling songs while she patiently goes about her housewifely chores. I know that you asked Sharon Shatsky to put a zucchini up her cunt. I know that you did wild things with more than one WASP from a horsey family, with an Asian hair loss specialist, with actresses and waitresses, Polish refugees, a human rights activist, students from Racine and Rochester, girls at Pembroke and Sarah Lawrence, and city girls and girls in log cabins. In fact I'm worried that just reading you I may have contracted a sexually transmitted disease.

I have known you most of my adult life. I could have been your sister, a fate that would surely have been worse than my own. I could never have been your wife or lover, not even in passing, not on a ship or on a plane, or in a foreign city (forgive the *Green Eggs and Ham* allusion), because I am the very Jewish girl you are running from. Your mother would have liked me: kiss of death, I know. Also I have coarse hair (like Joanie, the sister of your alter ego Peter Tarnopol) and while unlike her my nose and chin might pass your inspection, did not require surgery or massive electrolysis, something less than Aryan in my looks would have made you, once you got out in the world, stare right through me as though I were a pane of glass. I too, like Joanie, am hairy and dark and in this fact you would have read that I had no Druid ancestors, had no Swedish genes, no cornsilk prairie-traveled grandparents, did not fit the one and only ideal of beauty that Hollywood and *Vogue* assumed was IT, the whole of it in those benighted fifties when both of us began our erotic journey.

You would have found me (the winds of the fertile crescent kinked my hair and made my smile slightly buck-toothed, even after orthodonture, open as a leaky faucet, exposing gum disease and crawling with emotions that sprawl and surge, refuse like my hair to stay in place, learn their place) less than inviting. I know that pre- or postnubile or menopausal I could never have possessed the erotic charm that you desired, the royal road to America's heartland. It was, this goy search, a kind of ethnic cross-dressing, free miles, first class on the flight to the real America which, wherever it was located, was not in your neighborhood, that doomed our romance before it could begin. Years ago your scorn would have hurt my feelings but now I think you're entitled, good luck to you, I understand or at least will try to.

I knew a primal horde of Jewish guys like you who looked over my shoulder at the blonde from Wisconsin with the Big Sky eyes and the nose so small you wondered how the air got in. It was a cliché almost, the guys on the lookout for someone with a tribal history that didn't make you weep. When I was seventeen I worked as an apprentice at a summer theater in Connecticut. I fell in love with the twenty-two-year-old production manager whose name was Ed Doctorow, soon to become a colleague of yours. He came from a left-leaning Jewish family in the Bronx. He had a Jewish nose himself and big tragic eyes with bags hanging under them. He ignored me and attached himself to one pale-haired, blank, bleached-out starlet after another. "Look at me," I wanted to cry. "I am your soulmate. I can talk up a storm just like you. I am reading Rilke. I am your proper mate." He ended up marrying the daughter of a minister and living happily ever after. You too, Nathan, you would have enjoyed me if only you could have lusted for me.

All right I did it too, so I can't blame you. I admit it. What I fell for in my first husband was the Scotch and Irish blend, the sniff of England's green and emerald isle, the odor of Shakespeare and Thackeray blended with the master of the plantation wandering ragged and stunned, whiskey and musket in hand, through the hills of Mississippi or some romance like that which proved folly and futile, form instead of substance, leaving in my mouth the bitter taste of rue and shame.

You are off on a dangerous outward-bound American journey, charting new territory, urgently looking for the promised heartland and like a pedlar with his wares in a sack, you drag most of your childhood home around with you. It's a wonder you can move at all carrying all that baggage. You write about escape, about going off to college, about famous actors and writers and politicians. But of course you keep writing about home, about Newark Jews, Newark baseball teams, your mom, your pop, your old girlfriends. You know your past (thank you Dr. Spielvogel, whose real name I happen to know because everyone in New York knew), and you are still condemned to repeat it, at least on the page. This is the strangest Houdini act in all of literature. You manage to get back into your chains time and time again. But you wanted, how sincerely, how urgently to get away, the exact psychological, social, physical place on the planet that would locate you as far from me as the mind can travel and while my amour propre suffers, my brain accepts it. Go friend, ironist, searcher, moralist, soulmate: clown around on some other girl's time.

I get into a cab on Manhattan's Upper West Side and a loud, pushy recorded voice jangles in my ear. It's borscht belt, hatchet-job-on-the-English-sentence, no-nuances-need-apply Jackie Mason reminding me to wear my seat belt. I bend my head back as if there were a way to escape that scraping shoving comedian's rasping riff. I think of Nathan Zuckerman. Even though Nathan went to college at Bass-Bucknell, graduate school at Chicago, studied Joyce, T. S. Eliot, and Milton, irony and the objective correlative, and Jackie is straight from the shvitz baths, tap-dancing his way out of a steamy kitchen—more schmaltz than beurre noir—Mason and Roth are both fiddlers on our not so solid roof, a roof they come crashing through. There's a joke in there but who's it on? Who wants to laugh?

Nathan Zuckerman has spent his entire working life hip deep slogging through the mud of his relationship to the Jewish community, to Jews everywhere, to anti-Semites, to Jewish anti-Semites, to Wasps as they relate to Jews, to Jews as they relate to middle Europeans. Everywhere, on almost every page, boils his Jewish response, his irritation with his brethren, his desire to flee them in the shape of the shiksa, and above all else his compelling need to criticize them, point out all their most shameful flaws, to chastise them, to scold them, to defend them, to woo them. Nathan is a biblical prophet turned jokester, turned vaudevillian, the master of the pratfall, the prodigal son returned sort of, never left in fact. Nathan is our Jonah sent on a journey to Nineveh to remind us that our manners are bad, our class less than upper, our morality suspect, our interest in worldly goods positively shocking, our madness endless.

He is right of course and that's why, if only belatedly, he's become beloved of the Jewish people. Zuckerman did not suffer weeks of starvation and he did not wear sackcloth or sojourn in the barren desert exactly like Jonah, but he did have back pains and breakdowns and a bypass operation. He had divorces and breakups and betrayals. Exactly what you'd expect for an American prophet. Jews prize persistence.

Nathan's role as chastiser, conscience, corrector of the Jewish error began with one of his earliest alter egos, Ozzie. The short story "The Conversion of the Jews" was written in Nathan's first burst of adulthood. It was written before it was clear to him and all the rest of the world what his role would be in America, what kind of a prophet shouting from rooftops he would be, and the wet-behind-the-ears author himself, entertaining us, could have had no idea that this little story foretold the author's own future far more surely than the lines in your palm, or the tea leaves at the bottom of your cup. Ozzie is at Hebrew school and he asks the rabbi why it is that if God could create the world in seven days, a miracle surely, he could not have equally easily arranged the Virgin Birth. The rabbi yells at him, punishes him, refuses to answer him. Another child, one who was not Nathan Zuckerman's alter ego, would have backed off, ducked down, chilled out. Ozzie, like his creator, had no intention of letting the rabbi get away with the sloppy brain work, the ideological formulas that he was trying to feed his students. He climbs up to the roof of the Hebrew school, the irate rabbi running after him, and he threatens to jump if the rabbi doesn't take back his words. Soon a mob gathers, including Ozzie's mother, and the little boy addressing the reluctant and anxious Jewish crowd below, now (and not for the last time) the focus of everyone's attention, insists that all gathered admit that the Virgin Birth was indeed possible, as possible as any other of God's miracles.

Smart Ozzie, smarter obviously than the other kids, smarter than the rabbi, than his well-meaning mother, sees through the hypocritical bias of the not-so-well-educated New Jersey rabbi. Smart Ozzie tells the world what he knows and manages to get everyone's eye focused on him while he harangues them and forces them to acknowledge his rightness and the rabbi's wrongness. Jonah at Nineveh yes—but not so reluctant as Jonah, this little prophet in training is clearly enjoying himself. This Ozzie is clearly the small kid version of Nathan, of Portnoy, the critic of the community, the hero the rabbi wants to smack, who takes his revenge by very publicly humiliating the rabbi. Here amazingly enough lies the scenario for the next forty years of Nathan's life. The rabbi chasing him up the stairs. The writer hero, forcing the world to pay attention, to recant its simplistic views. All that's missing from this early story is the pain little Ozzie would experience being grown-up Nathan: also missing the buckets of tears and semen tossed from that metaphorical roof, enough to cause another flood if God hadn't promised that he wouldn't, not again.

The subject of the disagreement between Ozzie and the rabbi is not so slight as it might seem. The dispute between rabbi and boy is over a crucial matter, crucial to the heart and soul: the survival of the Jewish people. In other words it's a joke that's no joke. The rabbi is trying to preserve the specialness and uniqueness and rightness of Jewish monotheism, a faith that allows for no trinity, crucified sons, or pierced-arrow saints. But what the rabbi is up to has far less to do with theology than one might think. He's actually digging a ditch, an un-jumpable ditch between the outside world, America, and his people. The rabbi's intention is to fence his young charges into a theological system that would permanently separate and define them as different from their Christian neighbors. Ozzie isn't having any.

The information the rabbi gives to the children is that we are right and they are wrong. We define ourselves as Jews by not believing in God in triplicate. Those who do are simply declared wrong and placed on the other side of a rising wall. The wall is the real point of the lesson. The *us* and *them* are written on the young brain as an ab-solute, as a warning, as a dangerous electrified fence that must not be climbed. This is the way Jews stay together, and this is the way group pride tinged with moral superiority supports the persecuted Jew with his terrible history.

Sometimes anti-Semitism alone suffices to keep the Jews together, but just in case the Cossacks sleep in their barns for a generation or two, the message of difference passed on to Jewish children is intended to bind them together, to keep them from straying. The Jew who might wander off is no laughing matter to those who have taken it upon themselves to shepherd the flock, to keep the wolves away, to lead the people toward whatever may await them over the next hill. The religious purpose of Jews is not only in theological conviction but is contained and hallowed in the commandment to stay the course, hang on to history's tail no matter how bumpy or dangerous the ride becomes. Ozzie's raised his voice to ask: What is so logical about the Jewish view as compared with the Christian view? This question is a more fearful heresy than that of the little boy who notices that the emperor has no clothes, and a lot more dangerous to the empire.

America—Ozzie's, Nathan's, mine—was such an inviting temptation, was everywhere around us. Fourscore and seven years ago, these truths we hold self-evident, Ben Franklin, Abe, Grant, Custer, the Wild West, Lewis and Clark, the Donner party chomping on each other, Roosevelts, Teddy and FDR, the Andrews Sisters, Frank Sinatra, Mae West, the Inner Sanctum, the Lone Ranger, the Brooklyn Dodgers, Dr. Christian, the Hardy Boys, Nancy Drew, the Giants, the White Sox, the ballet, the opera, the Metropolitan Museum, the dinosaur bones in the Museum of Natural History, the Planetarium, Carnegie Hall, the Marx brothers (they were Jewish but who cared)— there it was, the whole inviting canvas. America might still have quotas for college admissions but a smart kid could triumph and break down the resistance and out there, where Lana Turner and Ingrid Bergman beckoned, out there in America, staying in the Jewish fold was optional and for those without a desire to commune with God, it was all too easy to let God go his own way without you.

Freedom, this is what America was about or so they kept saying in our American schools. Freedom is what the war was fought over, freedom was ours for the taking. Freedom meant the right to move away, to go anywhere you want, to be anything you could. Freedom did not mean staying in the neighborhood, freedom did not mean being boxed in. *Don't fence me in*, the song went. Fencing in is what the rabbi was trying to do when he wanted to smack Ozzie for suggesting that the Virgin Birth was a logical possibility.

Ozzie, the young American, wants to climb the wall, find the thing in common with the Christian view. They could be right after all; logic does not rule out the possibility of Christian truth. Ozzie wants to get into America and be one with his country and the rabbi wants him to stay put, stay with his kind. This is a battle that Nathan takes to heart, so much to heart that he wages it, all sides of it, in book after book for the next thirty years.

And while we can see the budding exhibitionist in Ozzie and we can see how impossible, what a bother, a purist, a moralist, self-righteous down to his toes, he would be as a friend or a son or a student, we nevertheless laugh at his wit and his nerve and see how he is persecuted for being right, chastised for saying the truth, sympathize with his brave little soul trying to keep its light shining in a world that wants to shut us all up, keep us in place, if we see differently or further than the guy sitting in the seat next to us. We can't help noticing that show-off or not, Ozzie's got a hold of a real problem, and he passed it on to Zuckerman.

We can also notice the budding paranoia in the plot of the story. We see the enemies who would actually smack you, turn your very own mother against you, mark you out, enemies we will encounter again and again as Nathan grows older and gets into ever hotter and hotter water. The enemies list grows by leaps and bounds—the mothers of girlfriends, the frothing-at-the-mouth wife, the state of New York with its arcane divorce laws refusing to free Nathan or Peter from horrid Lydia, Maureen. The meanness of critics, the plague of fans who would pursue and invade privacy, the fear of terrorists, the Mossad that misunderstands the most benign of gestures, the brothers, older or younger, Henry or Sandy or Mo who don't approve. The physical pain in the neck, the physical pain in the head, the migraines, the ache in the heart, the women who want children or marriage or grow boring and follow a man around threatening suicide, taking pills, making it hard to disengage, or the beautiful Irish actress who uses our Nathan as one might a male stripper instead of allowing him to use her as a symbol of the stranger, the powerful lure of the exotic. We can see the paranoid Zuckerman looking over his shoulder, afraid he will be shot like Lennon by a loving or hating fan, the hiding out, the mark of a marked man that seemed carved into Nathan's forehead, our Abel mistaken for Cain, oh cruel and misunderstanding world.

But noticing that does not change the fact that the Jewish communal heartburn has been well outlined by Nathan Zuckerman, perfectly outlined, not solved but exposed, not coddled or turned into comforting rhetoric but examined, poked, prodded until the patient goes numb, the numbness itself a new symptom to report. The fact is that Nathan never escaped, never became free of his Jewishness, not that he was religious, tradition never grabbed him, not a praying kind, too much of the Enlightenment absorbed on childhood's ball fields, but Jewish oh yes, it remained the subject, the angel he was fighting on his ladder, book after book.

In a very real sense the rabbi runs in perpetuity up those stairs long after Ozzie won the argument. Ozzie could stand on the roof and force the Jewish crowd to agree that possibly Mary was a virgin but he could not get down off that roof, end the argument, and go about his business. He's stuck up there and not just because he's a character in a story, but because the terrible truth is that we're all stuck with the problem—rephrased for the time being as "identity politics."

Woody Allen too is mired in the muck of his Jewish shtick and never more than when he courts Annie Hall, Diane Keaton or Mia, and Soon Yi. Note the strange coincidence that Zuckerman himself got involved with Moonie, the sixteen-year-old daughter of Lydia, and after Lydia kills herself he takes girl-child Moonie to Italy, the land of the Renaissance as well as Thomas Mann's sexually crossed borders, broken taboos, imagination. Surely these two comedians did not get together and plan their respective scandals but while one is real only in the imagination and the other only the "truth that is stranger than," perhaps these escapes from generational boundaries, ethnic confines reveal the common salacious dreams of Jewish comedians. They remind us that artists really are hell bent on turning upside down our moral order. A man with his wife's daughter crosses the normative oedipal boundaries and just as Zuckerman claimed he did, the sinner puts the id back in Yid. Anyone who thinks slapstick is just slapstick is going to get a metaphorical thumb slammed in the door.

The balance, a nice, civilized, nonhysterical balance between the particular and the universal, the group loyalty and the general pool of humanity, is no easier to strike today than it was yesterday. We flap our arms in the air, but our feet still stay in the mud. Religion itself with its rules and its manners and its demands and its traditions, beautiful as they may be, rarely makes young inquiring minds burn with excitement, not like Proust or Einstein or Freud or Lacan or Alan Greenspan or Bill Gates. Jews are waltzing with modernity but on very thin ice. That's what Nathan says and I agree with him.

What is it exactly that young Nathan and young Portnoy objected to about the Jewish way of living in America? The materialism yes, the sort of unthinking show-offness of property and goods that Nathan thought was Jewish but was probably just American, a common facet of all immigrant groups new to a little ease and tipsy with spending too much on pink taffeta sofas and tennis lessons. What Nathan wanted was to be upper class, correct in enunciation of consonants and vowels, universal in knowledge, classy as Park Avenue white shoe, American as the steel workers in Pittsburgh and the denizens of Dairy Queens in towns with granaries. Nathan wanted to be as unlike his daddy the hat or shoe salesman as he could be (no matter how many paeans he writes about his father, he himself planned on being the cream rising to the top), unlike daddy, the chiropodist, the dentist, the eighth-grade dropout, the insurance salesman, who all shared the same not-so-high rank in the class system that Nathan, absorbing its particulars with his milk, was intending to ace with one master stroke.

I felt the bite of the unspoken American class system too. I envied friends with oriental rugs on the floor, with mothers who had gone to Vassar and fathers who belonged to restricted clubs. The Jews of the forties and fifties who were exposed and permitted into Christian America felt that upper class was a very desirable state of being. Katie Hepburn in *The Philadelphia Story* was no snob, which is exactly why we wanted to be Katie Hepburn, have both egalitarian ideals and an upper-crust accent and a boat and a life that was very yare (spare but elegant) and still be a Democrat. Leon Uris's *Exodus* may have been sailing heroically toward Israel but many American Jews jumped overboard, the bright and the restless, the skeptical and the funny, the smart alecks and the ambitious, the intellectuals and the social climbers. Me too. How easily most found ways around the gentleman's agreements that blocked their way.

Of course there were Jewish homes in which Friday night candles welcomed in the Sabbath queen and the sons went on to become Torah scholars like their grandfathers before them. There were Jewish homes, Nathan, maybe the family in the apartment upstairs, in which the love for learning was not directed toward the American university but rather to the yeshiva, and there were many Jews who continued to pray long after their bar mitzvahs and grew up to join synagogues or till the soil on kibbutzim in the Galilee and others even in their affluence and success had no desire to mingle their semen with the most goyishe girl or boy they could find. In Ozzie's classroom only Ozzie made a scene about the possibility of the Virgin Birth, but he wasn't alone, hardly.

There is another paradox in this flight, this pell-mell headlong American meltdown in the pot we once thought of as a delicious and desirable stew. The child was not only free in this big country but was simultaneously kept on a leash. The leash could easily be yanked and yanked hard. The Holocaust was just such a pull on the neck. The facts of the Holocaust reminded Jewish children in America that they survived by luck, that their interests lay with their group, that they could stray but they could be rounded up and exterminated. Moreover it cast the others, the strangers, as killers, as haters, as immoral bystanders indifferent to the fate of the Jews. The result was a bonding, a welding of soul to identity, a shock that kept on shocking.

So when Nathan in *The Ghost Writer* imagines that the girl student the writer Lonoff (Malamud, believe me I know) is housing and bedding is in fact Anne Frank and that he might woo her himself and bring her home to his folks to prove his Jewish bona fides, to erase any scandal he may have created in his first stories, we have not only a wonderful grim joke but a brilliant recognition of the truth: the Holocaust, what we know of the Holocaust, makes us Jewish. Escape plans be damned, we are one with the dead and lose some of our otherwise robust appetite to dine with the American commonality. Anne Frank, a writer like Nathan, is the most kosher of Jewish girls, the anti-shiksa of all time.

Nathan who expresses his loyalties and troubles through his romantic entanglements can sleep with whomever he pleases and he does and yet he remains the Jewish son, the Jewish comedian, the Jewish identity pushing him around even when its God focus is absolutely gone missing, even when or especially when he is accused by some rabbis at a yeshiva event on minority writers of treason.

It's all very well to speak of freedom to invent yourself in America, and that is true enough as far as it goes but there is guilt that follows. There is the son's guilt at gaining an education that leaves the father behind in the dust. There is the guilt of leaving the people and embracing the stranger. From the first moments of conscious thought, the Jewish child is instructed in a we–them, in a history of what has been done to and what injustice has prevailed and this is not a myth that can be shaken off and walked away from. It is all true. After the very first steps up the mystical ladder of Jewish history, there is no way to back down. To betray, to expose to harm, to commit treason against this historical winding, this pilgrimage to something that will make a point, religious or secular, someday in some generation, is unforgivable. Guilt, terrible guilt, follows this accusation.

I know. It happened to me once and I really thought I deserved death. I wrote something in the newspaper about being a secular Jew. A Holocaust survivor called the house and accused me of betraying the dead. Distinguished rabbis wrote letters of outrage to the paper. What are you, you empty, traditionless airhead, historyless soul without color or memory? I could not go on as I had been, not because someone was mad at me but because the indictment was so astonishingly wounding. Why I cared, why Nathan cared, what is the tissue meld of Jew to the Jewish story is hard to explain rationally, but it burns and burns within me still. I understand how Nathan Zuckerman on reading Judge Waptor's letter attacking him for his short stories and accusing him of drawing Jewish blood felt he needed to bring home no less a figure than Anne Frank to redeem himself, to be publicly acquitted of this terrible charge.

The glue that keeps a Jewish child Jewish is a crazy glue indeed but effective. When Nathan in *The Anatomy Lesson*, suffering from acute back pain, addicted to Percodan and other painkillers, goes to Chicago to fulfill every Jewish mother's dream and turn himself belatedly into a doctor, he attacks an old man in a cemetery because the old man complaining about his drug-addicted adopted grandson has implied that the boy has no brains because he isn't Jewish by blood. This old man's prejudice, this clannishness, this assumed racial superiority so infuriates Nathan that he goes berserk—Percodan berserk to be sure—and ends up breaking his own jaw, puncturing his tongue, and knocking out his own teeth. As he chases Mr. Freytag he rails against "our genes, our sacred little packet of Jewish sugars." Zuckerman doesn't believe in Jewish genes and yet he does. If he didn't he wouldn't be so outraged. Caught between his belief in the universal and his unwilling attachment to the particular, Nathan howls and tries to strangle his friend's mourning father.

What makes Nathan so angry is not simply the old man's clan loyalty and somewhat simple-minded superiority to others; it is the attempt once again to make Nathan a co-conspirator in this Jewish separation from humanity. The result of Nathan's fury is only to harm himself, and in the mouth no less, which in his case is both his means of escape and the offending organ. Remember how Seymour Glass with a gun in his mouth killed himself. Nathan doesn't think God has it in for him for his blasphemy. He just punishes himself for his failed run out, for his lack of group loyalty, for his American-nurtured yearning to be himself and not his ancestors..

Religious belief may have been diluted to the disappearing point, but a harsh unforgiving guilt-provoked unease continues to assault Nathan in book after book. The wiring of Zuckerman's jaw, the painful back, the whole array of physical and psychological pains that fall on Nathan's head, are punishment for sure, a punishment for his success, a punishment for his betrayal of his family in books, a punishment for his ridicule of the Jewish community. Certainly Nathan knows how to torture himself, pay himself back. He is his own scapegoat—judge, jury and prisoner wrapped up in one package.

Nathan becomes a tragic guilt-ridden clown. Here is the heart of the problem.

I know this problem in my bones. As a girl wearing my first garter belt, I seethed when my mother would look for the Jewish names in the obituary column as if the dead were more worthy if they were one of us. I hated it when my brother would identify the names of Jewish athletes and Jewish judges and Jewish politicians as if their Jewishness were the significant marker of their days. I too, like Nathan, wanted to be just an American. I too discovered that it can't be done. The fictitious hypothetical unhyphenated is without a shape, a color, emptied of past and flat as a sheet, a winding sheet at that. It leads one's children to don orange robes and beg for change at airports.

This tie to the group, even if it has boiled down to a mere sentimental gesture, only a secular tie, an ethnic joke, seems almost magical—an idea, an attitude, a politics, a loyalty that drives one quite mad with its unwillingness to fade, with its intrusion on the better impulses toward universal humanity. So we are condemned to race and clan and origins. No matter the color or stripe or religion of whomever we may marry or befriend, the Jewish connection follows us around like our shadows. (Peter Pan may have been the only character in all of time to have been severed from his shadow, and he had to have it sewn back on.)

. . . .

Nathan Zuckerman and I meet at long last. Where else but in Miami? We are old but not altogether out of it. We are on the patio of the Fontainebleau, the warm breeze is sweet. At each of the cocktail tables a coconut lies split open and planted in its flesh a pink candle flickers. The centerpiece is surrounded by red hibiscus, stamen and pollen throbbing in the night air. I am alone and widowed, and he is with a woman much younger than he is, a Dominican woman with long neck, short cropped hair, she wears golden sandals and a diamond on the side of her nose. She is a poet who has won prizes, whose smooth beige skin deepens in color as she shifts positions at the table we share and her teeth are so white, I wonder if they are real. Mine are the color of a wedding dress kept in a trunk for generations. Also for the record my hair is white and I am plump, matronly, motherly perhaps, thick and slow. I listen to the music from the band and wish I could still dance. My dancing days are over except in certain dreams when I am dancing nude on a platform suspended above a football field that usually collapses, waking me up in a fine sweat.

We are in Miami, staying at the Fontainebleau at a writers' conference on the future of the Jewish writer. It's been almost sixty years since Nathan Zuckerman published his first stories, and we are still discussing the future of the Jewish writer. The future has come and gone several times over but here we are, a junket in winter, an adventure at a time of life when adventures are more likely to end up in emergency rooms than at dinner tables by the turquoise sea. I am a journalist still. Nathan Zuckerman is a famous man and very private. His shoulders are hunched as if someone even in this warm place might be throwing an icy snowball at his back and he glares around the patio with a wry bitter twist to his smile. He glows hot like a skinny piece of coal down at the bottom of the fire. His left hand shakes as he reaches for his wine glass. Nathan is in his eighties and I am approaching mine. We are geriatric and cranky. I can see that in him as he absentmindedly pulls on the strapless back of the poet's dress, exposing more of her fine straight spine to the open air, to the touch of his wandering fingers. Damn him. Across the table I feel his energy, as if a tornado had plunked itself in a chair opposite me and was spinning in place, daring me to invite it closer. Damn him. I resist the urge to point out that the blonde fair-skinned women who once represented American beauty to him and an escape from familiarity, from the nostalgically beloved but nevertheless-to-be-avoided Newark of his childhood, those women had wrinkled early, gotten skin cancers on the bridges of their perfect unbumped noses, and here I was, knowing well that Nathan Zuckerman, prizes and all, suffers from a paranoid need for attention and a simultaneous fear of his fans, an addiction to being famous that makes him want to kick the lesser souls who seek him out.

If, by my age, I give Nathan Zuckerman (even in my imagination) the time of day, I'm living proof that life is wasted on the elderly. Of course his lack of staying power, his sudden veering toward independence or freedom, toward discovering boredom in the bosom of the lady he had just a moment before found dazzling, this quality doesn't matter anymore—at our point in the life cycle. I raise my glass to him,

"To Nathan who has proved that fiction is truth and truth is only odoriferous laundry gathering in a hamper in the basement of the mind." He looks at me, offended but not entirely, interested but wary. He is not averse to a compliment, but were my words mocking or sincere? I have him off balance. His eyes glitter. The torches at the edge of the patio throw a red light on the top of his head where the scalp has been liberated of hair. He is hard, tender toward himself naturally, but protected against strangers, even fellow writers, perhaps especially fellow writers who might want a favor, a quote, an introduction to an editor or an agent. Even now, when most of the chips have been played, he's not looking to be a Good Samaritan. The protective shell, the you-can-go-so-far-but-no-further-with-me aura that he throws off, the antinurturing, I-don't-feed-baby-birds-with-eye-droppers look is simultaneously repellent and attractive. I know better but it always charms me. I can tell a man who will take all the covers, keep his accounts separate, tally all your defects and hold them against you, from a mile away, never mind across the table. Such men are not puppies to take home but mastiffs sniffing around the garbage cans, with hard muscular legs, drooling jaws, and a propensity to bite the hand that feeds them. Why that makes them attractive to the average female including me is a mystery still in search of a good detective.

At the panel discussion in the afternoon, a young man had risen to ask Nathan if there were any Jewish writers of the younger generation he admired. "No," he had answered. Did he see a future then for the role of the Jew in American literature? "No," he had said. There was silence in the room, the answer was not the one the assembled wanted to hear. Just no, nothing else? said the questioner. "Why do you believe that?" the questioner persisted. "What would it be for?" Nathan had shrugged. "Who needs it?" he added. Old men always think that everything dies with them, I thought. But Nathan was right, the glorious burst, the Malamud-Bellow-Roth comet in the sky has descended. Let us have a moment of silence. But at a writers' meeting there are no moments of silence. The blue room in the Fontainebleau's second floor with its gold-leafed chairs and its glass windows that overlook the bathers on the beach erupts in disagreement.

At the table I ask Nathan's Dominican poet if she feels a kinship with the Jewish experience. She looks at me as if I were dotty. That was not the right question. I am trying to think up a better one when I notice a commotion at the hors d'oeuvre table. The musicians have stopped playing. There is the sound of firecrackers behind me. I look back and see five masked figures in black jeans and T-shirts holding rifles feet apart standing guard while another of their group is engaged in extinguishing the decorative torches around the patio's edge. Darkness creeps toward us. There is a nervous laugh from the table next to ours. A woman in a short red dress and high spiky heels gets up casually as if she is going to the ladies' room to powder her nose. A masked figure approaches her and pushes her back into her seat. "Nobody move," a shout from the figure. Nobody moves. A waiter picks up a tray with water glasses on it. Drop it, the voice says, and the waiter drops the tray and there is a sound of breaking glass across the floor and ice cubes scatter and one hits my foot. Nathan looks frightened. It makes me sad to see that nervous twitch at the corner of his mouth. "Don't worry," I whisper to him, "inside the hotel they will call the police. We'll be rescued soon." Nathan glares at me; he doesn't like it that I saw his fear. The Dominican poet has gone stony-faced. She is sinking down in her chair so as not to seem so tall, so imperious, so conspicuous. All around us are masked men, maybe twenty maybe more. Over on the path leading to the water I see more men carrying guns. On top of the lifeguard's perch there is another with a huge gun that looks at this distance like an octopus. Tentacles of bullets writhe above the sand. Who are they? What do they want? I take a sip of my wine. Nathan says, "I didn't want to come to Florida. I knew this conference would work like flypaper for fucking maniacs." We talk under our breaths, murmuring really. The masked men have us caught in a circle now. The door to the kitchen opens on the side of the main building. I see the chefs in their white aprons, I see a long line of chrome pots, I see the flame burning low on a restaurant stove, and I see the masked men, flashing their guns, running up and down the aisles of the kitchen. The musicians are on the ground face down, the waiters are on the ground face down.

The Irish-American short story writer is trying to show one of the masked men the pictures of his children. I saw those pictures at breakfast, tow-headed boys and a little girl blowing bubbles. The masked man takes his pictures and rips them up, letting the pieces fall into the wine glass. So much for his family values. "Who are they?" I ask Nathan. "Critics," he says. "Readers," I answer. "Rabbi critics," he says. "Muslims," I offer. The Dominican poet lashes out at me. "Racist," she hisses. Was it racist of me to think of Arabs under the circumstances?

"Right-wing Cubans," I say. Nathan says, "Colombian drug dealers demanding funding for their literary journal." We wait. The man who seemed to be in charge steps up to the microphone, the very one that moments before was held by the singer who was urging us to macarena, although only a few of the conferees had accepted the offer to step onto the dance floor.

. . . .

Nathan has been stung by the claim that he is a narcissist. And while he may protest too much I am basically on his side on this one. Only boors use the DSM diagnosis as a name-throwing resource. To do so trivializes the wounds of the heart and mocks the science that would heal them. Then too the fact that Nathan uses his own experience, mulls it, repeats it in several books does not mean that Nathan himself is incapable of feeling someone else's grief, that he treads on the souls that fall before him, that his love affairs are no more than experiments in self-love.

Nathan says in *The Counterlife*, "Being Zuckerman is one long performance and the very opposite of what is thought of as being oneself." On the other hand this is a little coy. Zuckerman is not just a mirror of human nature. He is very particularly Zuckerman. He says, "I certainly have no self independent of my posturing artistic efforts to have one. Nor would I want one. I am a theater and nothing more than a theater."

Nathan uses Nathan's ills ironically, comically, and histrionically. He does not cast his critical eye only on others. He asks himself all the right questions; he takes responsibility for his catastrophes. When Roth writes what is intended as a real version of his life, Nathan calls him on all the omissions, elisions, posturing fakeness that always appear when we tell each other the "real" story. Again and again Roth speaks of his grateful and loyal ties to parents, the same parents he has parodied and bloodied in *Carnovsky,* a.k.a. *Portnoy's Complaint.* Nathan is the one who points this out to us, his readers. He lets himself get away with nothing. "If you hang onto yourself any longer you'll disappear right up your asshole," he says. He knows he appears like a narcissist. "Had he kept a pain diary, the only entry would have been one word: myself."

But narcissism isn't his only problem. He's also a flasher.

What was Ozzie doing on the roof but opening his raincoat? If he wasn't, if he was reserved and dignified and didn't want you to look at him, his balls balling away, what fun would we have, what more would we understand about ourselves? Writers are exhibitionistic if you must put a clinical label on it, thank God for it.

On the other hand there is this odd passage in *Patrimony,* a nonfiction book about his father's death by Nathan's alter ego Roth. Roth wakes from a quintuple bypass in the intensive care unit. He has learned that his heart prior to the emergency operation has been functioning on only 20 percent of the needed oxygen. He thinks of his newly opened arteries and he feels exhilarated by the free flow of blood and he "whispered to that baby (his heart), just under my breath, suck, yes, suck, suck away, it's yours, all yours, for you. . . . and never in my life had I been happier. The thought that I was giving suck to my own newborn heart provided hours of most intense pleasure—partaking of the most delirious maternal joy."

What we are hearing is a grown man frightened of death, in the intensive care unit, soothing himself with a fantasy of being his own mother, of nurturing his own heart. His mother is dead. His father is dying. His life is threatened. This is a man who has not had a child of his own (which is another part of the story) and who must find mother love within himself. Oddly touching, even wondrous, that the human imagination can leap into the chasm and hold us secure in the darkest of times. Look how fiercely men want a mother, to what ends of imagination they will go to find one.

What ails Nathan, who remembers so fondly as a small child curling up in his mother's seal coat, her little marsupial, protected from the world? I think it's the extraordinary ferocity of his bind to Mrs. Portnoy, Mrs. Zuckerman, that makes him long so desperately for the loving saving hand of the smooching mother. This awful awesome neediness in turn ignites a rage against this woman who has evoked such love that might prevent a child from growing up and becoming a man. (This is the wild analyst in me speaking. A wild analyst has had no training and just tramples the flowers in other people's gardens— ought not to be allowed.)

Now is it mere accident that Ozzie on the rooftop demands an admission of the possibility of the immaculate conception? He might have chosen any other Christian miracle—the Resurrection would do. But he, little Ozzie, makes his stand on the birth of the son having occurred, miracle of miracles without the messy, annoying, rivalrous father ever having touched or done anything else dirty to the beloved Mary mother. There are no accidents in fiction any more than in dreams. All fiction is an extended Freudian slip. What Nathan longs for and never finds is the immaculate mother love of childhood, untainted by father, holy and pure, and what that love did for Nathan is make him angry, need to fight it off, and that anger fuels his books, turns the wheels with its heat, makes it hard for him to stay with women, pushes him to choose wounded types who will cling or bite or bore him. Guilt and anger, not narcissism, are Nathan's closest companions and so much the better for the rest of us who can go along for the ride, our own guilts and angers and affections, natural and unnatural, echoing on each page.

Nathan Zuckerman knows all this about himself and tells us so. He is the master of self-analysis. The question is what good does it do, what has it brought him? Not happiness or peace or rest. All criticisms, all insights, all possible remarks are anticipated in Nathan's own mind. He has created a fulsome self-portrait but don't hang it on the museum wall, not yet. There is a mystery still, there is the odd fact that knowing Zuckerman one still doesn't know Zuckerman, not really, not exactly. All that bouncing around and altering through acts of imagination the facts of one's life produces a kind of shimmer, the kind that comes off the pavement on a hot day, distorting, exhausting us, a moment in which the magician can disappear, saw a lady in half, stuff a rabbit into his top hat. Zuckerman shows us the way his mind works just as certain contemporary designers let you see the plumbing through the transparent plastic of the sink or toilet seat. This is just another act, another version of the real thing that is not itself the real thing. He keeps telling us that, and since no one quite believes it, he has to tell us again.

Oh, Nathan if you were my son I would take you back under my coat, warm and safe, I would hold you there. I would stave off all muscle aches and depressions. I would wave my arms and chase away all breakdowns. My great love for you, my endless admiration, would surround you with comfort and you would hate me for it, I suppose, and write a nasty book about me for sure, and then write sugary things ever after to cover up what you really felt. What a mess we are. What a mess we are in. I just want you to know that if you were my son instead of my contemporary, I would always hope that one day you would return to my coat and snuggle in for a long stay. Never mind that I don't wear my seal coat anymore because some virtuous person threw red paint on it. It hangs in my closet waiting for you.

Zuckerman to Roth: "The whole point about your fiction (and in America, not only yours) is that the imagination is always in transit between the good boy and the bad boy—that's the tension that leads to revelation." These words are from the nonfiction book *The Facts*, in which Roth is setting the record straight, sort of. This good boy has no nasty thoughts and would never ask Sharon Shatsky to put a zucchini in her cunt. The bad boy can't stay put, has sexual thoughts running through his head like subtitles to a foreign film, nonstop. The good boy is full of guilt. The bad boy is too but acts anyway or writes anyway. It is true that this tension is the crucible of art. Maybe for those who are not writers the wrestling match between the good and bad self just creates bad dreams and fears of flying or turning out the lights. But Nathan has it right: bad boys are sexy, sex obsessed, daring egomaniacs, and good boys are dull as dishwater. Every real boy is a little bit of both and every good novel has a bad boy pulling the strings. So be it.

This is equally true of true nonfiction—that is to say nonfiction that goes down past the platitudes into the real grimy stuff. Nathan wrote *Patrimony* under his Roth alias and a lot of it does sound like a real writer making public amends to a father he may have offended in fiction. It also reads as if the author had come to respect and admire his bossy but beloved father, speaking with great tenderness and grief about the last years of his life. But there is one big slip.

The father with a brain tumor, recovering from an operation, is visiting Roth in his Connecticut home and goes upstairs to the bathroom, the scene of other transgressive, impolite, wild Portnoy acts. Here the father, as he says, "beshat himself," loses control and shit is smeared all over the bathroom, the towels, the floor, the shower curtains. Roth describes himself cleaning up his father's mess, on his hands and knees, scrubbing the tiles. He speaks of becoming father to his father, his father becoming child to his child. The father is humiliated by this event. The writer son tells the world of his father's most intimate dreadful loss of control. This is not the Good Son writing. This is the wild Nathan who knows where the paydirt in the story lies. The father would surely have preferred his bowels left out of the tale. The son under the guise of love vanquishes once and for all the father, no longer the bossy man, no longer the rival for the mother's love, now an infant who needs someone else to clean up the shit he has spread about. The episode looks like love but the very telling of it reveals the opposite. Here is Roth being the good son for all the world's approval, and all the world did approve, but behind the curtain Nathan, Alex, Peter, have tipped the fact that they still have their hands on the strings.

The tension and the poignancy of this scene are increased by Nathan's childlessness. This came about not entirely by accident or fate. His care of his father is the nurturing of the past. It leads backward not forward. It leads toward a book about his father's death rather than an actual human being who would impose his or her erupting life on the author. It is part of the bad boy in the writer, who gives away as little as possible, who is ill suited to PTA meetings and reruns of *Barney*, whose id is still howling for exclusive attention and who hasn't loved as real fathers may love: wagered, lost, made mistakes, soul burnished, dented or polished, grieved, expectant, shaped through their child's peril, triumph, failure, illness, nightmare or simply learning to ride a bike or walk out the door. If books are your children, you remain in control of the product. If children are your children, then you are fortune's hostage ever after.

I do not find it particularly attractive in Nathan that his so smart DNA will not—not 50 percent of it, not any of it—be replicated. But the bad boy, the angry boy, the one we glimpse even when he is trying hard to be very good as in *Patrimony*, is no Dagwood Bumstead, no Robin Williams in drag turncoat he. Would I marry Nathan if he were the last man on earth? I would mate with anyone who was the last man on earth, so the question tells me nothing. But I suspect that my own good girl–bad girl problem would make me putty in Nathan's hands. How fortunate I am that he would not be interested in molding my clay.

. . . .

In front of the Fontainebleau, the trompe l'oeil, a painted archway leading to the ocean's edge, which is actually a flat wall, is illuminated at night by a series of bulbs on top of the structure. A faint glow from the lights extends into the patio area. We hear shots, more breaking glass, the glow is gone. The apparent leader of our captors stands in the middle of the dance floor. His men are on all sides. There is no talk of macarena. Nathan turns to me. "Am I imagining this?" I'm not sure if he is joking or if he is confused. "You might have," I say, "but you didn't." The terrorist raises a megaphone to his lips. It seems to be the same one that I saw the lifeguard use in the afternoon when he wanted someone to swim closer to the shore. In an accent, Middle Eastern, or perhaps from the Caucasus, or maybe from Peru, or possibly Pakistan, the words come blaring forth: "Writers who are not Jewish may leave the hotel. The Jews must stay. The Jews will stay. The circumcised men will stay unless they can prove Christianity." "We're going to have a debate?" Nathan whispers.

The Dominican poet gets up. "I'm going," she says. She bends to kiss Nathan on the top of his head. "You were good last night," she said. "If they shoot you, you'll die with my smell on your skin." As she leaves I say to Nathan, "She's not such a good poet you know. I hear she copies her stuff from her students." The Romanian essayist on my right gets up and drops his pants and pulls from beneath his boxer shorts his organ. One of the terrorists examines the exposed pale and very withdrawn penis. In order to see clearly he has to pick it up and pull it forward. The Romanian does not look unhappy. He is humming during the examination. He offers his name and adds that he too doesn't like Jews. He is allowed to pull up his pants and leave. The young Jewish writer who has brought her baby to the conference is white faced and grim. She holds her baby so hard he begins to cry. The terrorist takes the baby from her and for a moment we all freeze in horror, but the man simply puts the baby over his shoulder and pats him 'til the sobbing subsides. He then returns the child to its shaking mother. What can this mean, this act of paternal kindness on the part of a man with an Uzi, four hand grenades strapped to his waist, and a cowlick of black hair that sticks straight up from the brow of his mask? Could this terrorist know the latest wisdom—that paternal men are sexy? I look into his eyes hoping to see a motive, a future, a demand that can easily be met. I see brown eyes with a fleck of yellow in the center. I see pools of alarm, which I don't believe is a good sign.

We hear sirens, police cars zooming in. We hear commands to police. Is there a SWAT team outside? Bull Connor, where are you now that I need you? Nathan turns to me. "Am I making this up?" "No," I say. "I already told you. It's real." "I'm sorry," he says. "I always repeat everything. Not just in my dotage, I always have. It's my style." "I know," I say. I feel bad, my impatience must have showed. "There must be a good side to this," he says. "What do you think it is?" (He has learned over the years to ask a woman for her opinion.) "You'll not only be a famous Jewish writer," I say. "You'll be a famous Jewish martyr." "That'll make Irving Howe spin in his grave, that'll show those rabbis once and for all." I'm not listening to him. I'm trying to make eye contact with the man behind the mask who holds the microphone. There are only four of us left at the table.

· · · ·

Nathan, I agree with you mostly that truth is less interesting than fiction. This is one of your mantras. It serves you well, although you go to great lengths to prove it in your autobiography, *The Facts*. You let Nathan give it to Roth who has written a pallid basically boring version, a kind of public relations manual about his life. You point out all the ways that fiction would have let Roth say it the way it was, full of the boils and blood, the frogs and plagues that his life really contained. You point out that Roth is positioning himself as a sainted soul, a passerby in the more calamitous events of his life when in fact his crooked heart engineered many of the crashes and applauded some of the others.

Why are you so obsessed with this subject, so bent on proving to us that you have invented, that you are an artist not a journalist, not a mere cartographer of contemporary Jewish boys trying their best in a wicked wicked world? Some of the answer lies in the particular historical moment of your passage into adulthood. I was there too, a little behind you but there. God was dead for us. The Enlightenment seemed to have finished him off and his last gasp was surely at Auschwitz. The universe was empty of moral order but it had to have moral order or it would explode or we would explode—what to do? The shadow of destruction, A-bombs and H-bombs and stick-your-head-under-the-desk all lay just a button push away. Perhaps it was all over, the pathetic attempt at civilized life. A pox on all politics, we thought, we smart-asses with real valves already thickening our young arteries.

Communism was a gulag horror. Democracy was Jim Crow and better, just barely, than the rest. Fascism was the nightmare at the end of the socialist tunnel. Who cared anymore? Not us. We turned instead to art as our salvation. The artist became the priest of the new world order, one that even if it didn't provide salvation would at least explain us to ourselves. A whiff, a breeze from Paris brought us Sartre and Camus and the existentialist. Everything is dead out there, but the words to say it, describe it, still stand. Art is everything. For Nathan his education at the hands of a kindly English professor spinster was the boat back across the River Styx; on the life side of the shore he could make it as an artist.

Now I still believe most of this, but without the seriousness, the holiness, such an idea once carried. Nathan too fell for it. He just managed to keep his vernacular and his sense of humor dry during the crossing. Most of us fell in and drowned. But if you claim all he did was report well, that stings Nathan. It drives him crazy when you reduce him, strip him of the title, make a mere journalist out of a creative artist. So the question of what is art and what is simple truth haunts him. He has a big stake in your getting the right answer.

Maybe you had to be there to understand how important this matter of Art was to us. Today it may seem like much ado about nothing. Then it was everything, something like money seems right now.

Nathan says, "Dad informed me that it was a human impossibility for one person to pee in another's pants. Little did he know about the power of art." Nice earthy statement that. But don't be fooled by the bathroom talk. Nathan isn't just peeing. He's making that stream into a golden flow, a comet in the sky of the soul, a magic carpet to take us to ourselves, to make us laugh along the way, to guide us toward insight, self-awareness, maybe even a kind of damp urinary salvation.

Nathan said, "No, one's story isn't a skin to be shed. It's inescapable, one's body and blood. You go on pumping it out until you die, the story veined with the themes of your life, the ever recurring story that's at once your invention and the invention of you."

Now Nathan, there are salacious gritty details in your books that tell us that we are creatures who have raw needs. We fart and shit and masturbate and drool in our sleep. These are things you can talk about in your fiction but don't really want associated with you, your real person, and you get uncomfortable when someone reads your books as if they were literal reports of your life. You say in one of your disguises, "I happen to be no more immune to shame or built for public exposure than the next burgher with shades on his bedroom window and a latch on the bathroom door.—I am sensitive to nothing in the world as I am to my moral reputation."

Nathan Zuckerman is not a man who wants to go out to dinner and have everyone think about what he may have done with a liver in his hormone-besotted youth. What he is is a writer who wants us to appreciate his wit and keen observation and humor that brought us the hard-breathing boy and the meat and the atmosphere—most certainly accurate because we recognize it—of awkward desire and suffocating home filled with demands to cover up, bury deep down the baser instincts.

When Nathan is feeling less than cocky, no pun intended, he assesses his position in the world and says, "It wasn't literary fame. It was sexual fame and sexual fame stinks." What he means is that it embarrasses him. It makes him ashamed to have strangers leering at him. Well it's hard for an author to separate himself out from his character and the attempt is doomed to fail because everyone knows the author is absolutely not the character and absolutely the character at the same time. So Nathan just be proud of the scalawag you are and always were. Let the readers confuse what they will confuse. No one can make you ashamed unless you let them.

Of course Nathan grows weary halfway up the mountain. The Jews built a golden calf while Moses was talking to God. He says, "I can't take any more of my inner life, subjectivity is the subject and I've had it." He says, "Starving myself of experience and eating only words. It brings out the drudge in me." He says, "The burden isn't that everything has to be a book. It's that everything can be a book and doesn't count as life until it is." So sometimes Nathan turns against himself and his profession as do we all. Enough. Time for a change. Sometimes Nathan wishes he could stop "forcing the world to pay attention to my moan." But this fear of having nothing more to say, this post–*Portnoy's Complaint* pre–*The Ghost Writer* fear that Nathan was washed up, washed out, jaw wired, shut up, turned out to be a false alarm. Nathan went on, regained his strength, had more love affairs to mine and other books to write in which Nathan now often becomes the narrator not the subject, or so the illusion is cast. Again and again a new clown comes out of the little car and the audience applauds. Good for him.

What Nathan does want is for us to honor him, number one guerrilla fighter against the many armed forces of repressive civilization. He is doing battle for our vital juices, our life energy, our true feelings even when they are not so nice, especially when they are not so nice. He says, "Story telling is the form of resistance taken against the powers that be." Thank you very much Nathan for your brave soldiering on my behalf.

Actually Nathan I need you. Everyone needs you. Your story contains the nut of the resistance, the price for putting up that resistance—pain, depression, loneliness, breakdown. It does seem a little churlish, a little drawn out for you to be so concerned about what I think of you, whether I confuse you with the other you, the more fictional, therefore more free to tell the truth you or I don't. I know you hate it when you're denied privacy and dignity and everyone feels entitled to take as fact things that are not fact, just fictional truths. But perhaps you could chill out on this because the confusion between reality and realer reality is just an artist's sleight of hand, as you have demonstrated over and over again. So what if you sacrifice your right to seem to the public like a banker or a broker or the guy in the seat on the commuter train who is sleeping behind his copy of *Time* magazine? You shouldn't care if someone thinks you are really Portnoy or Tarnopol or Roth. Let them.

In *The Ghost Writer*, Zuckerman who has come to visit the older esteemed writer Lonoff learns from Lonoff that the writer's life is nothing more than his writing, as if it had been transformed from the ordinary slippery stuff nonwriters endure into pages and print, books. Lonoff claims to have lived only for his art but this is somewhat disingenuous. He has an affair going with a student and he has a marriage that itself is an Ibsen play and a half. Zuckerman has betrayed his ballet dancer girlfriend and come to a writers' retreat (Quahsay) to work on a book. This endless fooling around with what belongs to the writer's life in real time and what is art is not just a joke with mirrors. *It's real but it's not, it's a tease, but not just a tease* involves us in the whole conundrum of Nathan's endless self-justification.

What Nathan is telling us is: I use and I transform what I use into something funny, useful to you my reader, so stop blaming me or shaming me or pushing me around. Notice how hard I work at making the dross of dailiness into a comedy of manners, look at how I twist and turn for you my reader. This is Ozzie again hectoring us from his perch, I am right, you are wrong, art is superior to all else, and art is the only theology worth jumping off the roof for and you better believe it.

Well I do believe it—not as much as I used to. Now that I have children and my children have broken hearts and had disappointments of their own and now that I have seen real disease and loss not the *Magic Mountain* kind and now that I know that certain mountains will never be scaled by me at least, I find raw life, life without art, more tolerable, more interesting, than the plummeted, picked-over, shaped version a writer will offer as a present and then stand there waiting for a huge thank-you just as if your telephone weren't ringing, your bills weren't due, and you hadn't your own sex life to manage before the last morning comes.

Now about women. Nathan Zuckerman has been accused of being a misogynist and that's a crock. In one book he has one of his women say to him, "Zuckerman you don't know how to relieve the thing that aches and prods, to soothe the longing, to find the tender gesture so you say fuck and fuck some more and in your anger at what is missing and remains missing you scream fuck again. It's so sad. I could weep. It's not that you dislike, despise or deplore women, it's that you can't find your way toward them, you're always locked outside a door and through the keyhole you scream, fuck." This is Zuckerman telling himself what's up. This is not a man who uses or abuses women. More often in fact they seem to abuse him, with his participation of course.

The gender wars we have recently endured have left their scars. It gets so easy to see the man as a predator and the female as a victim. Nathan's fateful encounter with Lydia, Josie, Maureen, was with a woman so wounded by a destructive father and a shabby family that she became a tiger, a savage beast sinking her teeth into fresh meat Nathan, Peppy. She lied to him about being pregnant. She set up a situation in which he could never be good enough, loving enough, and was engaged in a sadomasochistic duel of recrimination, accusation, hostile and clinging love. It didn't last for that long. But the horror of it left a scar. It made Nathan think he wanted freedom when he wanted affection, connection, which itself alarmed him so he ran away when it became possible and he chose wounded birds, angry sometimes mute wounded songbirds to spend his time with. He went for surface instead of substance, and when he had substance he grew restless, afraid of normalcy, of the hot breath of ordinary time passing. This man is no misogynist, he is a lover, an idealist, a dreamer, as well as a man who needs to have his soup on the table when he comes in from the cold. Any man this funny is also this angry and the anger isn't going to behave properly, be turned only against political injustice, a critic or two here or there, it will in fact besiege the bedroom, knock over the wine glass, leap under the sheets and cause havoc, sweat, and tears.

All right. I'm thinking that if he had only known me, taken me home with him, all would be different. Why, on what grounds, do I think such a thing? He had many women far more beautiful than I. He had intelligent literary women. He had famous women. He had dutiful, respectful, and loving women and they all disappointed, wore out their welcome. Why would I have been different? Truth: I wouldn't. Truth: I'm not sure I even like him. Truth: just because a man can make you laugh, you shouldn't picture a life of happily ever after with him; in fact comedians may be better off left in the wild, you can't tame them any more than you can teach a faun to read or potty-train a hippopotamus.

. . . .

The red lights of Miami's police cars reflect in the sky, giving the stars—it will be a sunny day tomorrow for those who live to see it—a pink sparkle. The palm trees by the side of the patio shake their fronds in the evening breeze. The leader of the group is counting heads. Ten Jewish writers in all—six women and four men. Malamud has died, Bellow is home with the latest newborn baby, Heller has died. Miller and Mailer don't like to be thought of as Jewish and wouldn't show up. Podhoretz in his dotage is home flogging yet again another dead horse. Since he is now the last cold warrior alive, he's afraid that a warm place would be harmful for his icy heart or so he hinted to the conference organizers. There is a group of Poles who have immigrated to America who claim they are Jewish writers but most of their claims proved to be false, names taken off cemeteries and adopted as grandparents—that sort of thing. There are two German writers who converted to Judaism out of sympathy with the victims who were covering the conference for ACHTUNG, the German cultural Internet connection, but they left with the first dismissed group of hostages. You can carry identification just so far. I understand that.

The younger crop of Jewish writers, Nathan Englander, Allegra Goodman, the hopefuls who are not from the secular squeeze generation but refugees from the ultraorthodox world of the outer boroughs—they want their turn at fame and money. They haven't had a chance to write about much more than their adolescence. This is their first grown-up material. They are truly afraid not only of dying and being dumped into the grave of the unknown Jewish writer but of not using the event as fantastically brilliantly as the person sitting next to them.

Cynthia Ozick sits Ganesh-like at the other table. Her gray Mamie Eisenhower bangs look brave on her wide forehead. She is schoolgirlish, long skirted, a nun in street clothes. Her only concession to Florida is her cherry pink socks that keep her maryjanes from rubbing blisters on her feet. Her lips are pinched tightly together. She always knew they would get her, she always knew that as Jew she would die a violent death. Her enemies have called her an ideologue, a fanatic, an uncompromising hater just because she fought against peace in Israel until it was a done deal and the Iraqi prince married Miss Israel in a wedding celebrated at what had once been Saddam Hussein's palace. However, she was correct: the Jews will always be the first to go, and this night, the attack on the Fontainebleau's minority writer conference, justifies her lifelong fears. She is not displeased. You can see it in the set of her body, in the mist on her glasses. It was always going to come to this. She will give these terrorists a piece of her mind before they shoot her, she will. She will invoke Henry James and George Eliot to show them what barbarians they are at the gate or here it should be called the port, or the marina of the decent moral world.

I am bored. What is happening? Why is a real crisis so slow, not like the movies at all? Is Bruce Willis right now sliding down a banister or riding the top of the elevator cab? I begin to count the freckles, the age spots on Nathan's hands and forearms. Hold still, I want to tell him as I keep losing my place.

The leader of the group comes to our table. Zuckerman, he says in a loud voice. Nathan Zuckerman. Nathan turns. I can see he is angry, more angry than scared. "Don't shout," he says. "I can hear you. I have a state-of-the-art hearing aid. You want to see it?" He puts his forefinger into his ear and digs around. The terrorist shakes his head. He doesn't want to see it. The terrorist sits down at the table, laying his huge gun over the turquoise cloth, knocking over the coconut centerpiece, sending the candle spluttering. With his bare fingers, the terrorist pinches the wick, extinguishing our little light. I have tears in my eyes. I wanted to be there for my youngest grandchild's graduation from nursery school. I can see I won't make it. There must always be some celebration you don't make. I try for philosophical calm. "What I want, what my demand is," says the terrorist, "is that you Jewish writers come to our little island in the South Pacific and write about our problem with the occupiers of our homeland. You know how to get the whole world worried about you, how to be the center of political attention. We have no press. The counterinsurgents killed our public relations officer six months ago. No one knows or cares about us. We are the Jews of the atolls. We need novelists and storytellers and you're the ones we have decided on. Jewish writers know how to get the job done. I want to take you back with me, helicopters are waiting on the beach. I will put you up in my very own quarters in the jungle. You will write and then you will publish and as a result we will be saved."

I say, "We could consider that." Cynthia Ozick says from her table, "Never will I write for them. They are anti-Semites pure and simple." "Not so simple," I say. One of the young Jewish writers says she has to go find a phone, her mother is expecting her to call. The terrorist offers her his own cell phone. We hear her dial. She says, "Mom, it's great down here, I haven't met anyone yet but there's a big dance tomorrow." The terrorist shrugs. "Why," he asks me, "is it so hard for a Jewish girl to find a Jewish boy?" "It's a long story," I say. "Ask him." I point to Nathan. Nathan laughs, not an entirely kind laugh. "How shall this evening end?" I ask him. "As usual—dead Jews," he says.

"I'll go with you," I say, "but leave the others. I'm seventy-six years old and in fine health. I had a polio booster a few years ago. I'm happy to serve your cause. It would be my pleasure." "Good," says the terrorist. "But I want Nathan Zuckerman and Cynthia Ozick too."

Nathan stands up. His legs are not as good as when he played baseball for Weequahic High so many years ago, but they still do their job.

He is wearing a blue blazer and looks like a member of the Century Club as well as the Academy of Arts and Letters, or the Union Club or the University Club, the real McCoy who is now the real McCohen. He takes my arm. "Come," he says, "we'll go."

"Who exactly is oppressing you?" Cynthia asks as we leave the patio and walk past the stone lions that guard, not so effectively, the path to the cabanas at the beach. "Goyim," says the terrorists. "Cossacks," he adds for good luck. Cynthia nods. She understands. "You must be firm," she says. "Don't give an inch, never sympathize with the enemy or you're lost. Kill those in your own ranks who would compromise or backtrack or talk nice to terrorists." "But we're terrorists," says the man who is now poking me in the rib with his rifle. "Nonsense," says Cynthia. "You're not terrorists, you're patriots." She is the first one of us to develop Stockholm syndrome.

Huddled together in the back seat of the helicopter, too noisy for conversation, I remember I left my blood pressure pills in the cosmetic bag in my hotel room. Cynthia Ozick is sitting on the seat facing us. She is explaining to the terrorist that she cannot eat any meat on their island and must have a vegetarian diet. The terrorist has promised to get her kosher cereal flown in from Israel. "We have connections there," he tells her. Nathan has his hand on my knee, or is it higher up than that? He is leaning his head down onto my shoulder as we rise above the Atlantic. I feel his tongue wiggling against my collarbone. The thought comes to me, Will he want me for my mind or my body? That old question, it never goes away.

The English-speaking terrorist removes his mask. He looks eighteen years old. From a satchel under his seat he pulls a well-thumbed copy of *Goodbye, Columbus*. "Will you sign it for me?" he asks. Nathan reaches out for the book.

As he pulls his pen out of his pocket, he says to me, "This is my material. I hope you agree it's my story to tell." He is not smiling. "All right," I agree. I smile sweetly. I am lying. Writers are liars. He holds his pen in midair. He says to the young terrorist, "I think you might want to push her out of the plane." He is shoving me, his old man's hip pushing against mine. He is shoving me toward the door.

· · · ·

6

Frank
...... Bascombe ....

Frank Bascombe

Richard Ford's
Independence Day

Cat on a Hot Tar Highway.

F *r a n k* Bascombe: what a wobbly, sad, half-drowned, almost domesticated tabby you are.

And what exactly is this need of mine to sweep you up in a towel and dry your fur, stroke it 'til it shines again, let you stare glassy eyed into my face, you, tom cat, night cat, alley cat, sportswriter, short story writer, walking wounded? I can tell you've been in a fight, your fur is matted, one ear is bleeding. I have a feeling your opposition doesn't look so good either. How did you get so bedraggled, and what's that proud shake of the tail and that indifferent turn of the head? Don't you want my lap, my hands, a little bit of Neosporin ointment on those wounds? Why do I, and I know better, think you would be the perfect man, the proudest and the most loving, the sweetest and the strongest of men if only—and "if only" is the story, isn't it? "If only" certain events, particularly American events, didn't grind the will out of us, making love and marriage, sex and marriage, children and marriage, into chronic sorrow. If only something, our optimism, our vows to each other, our innocence, our trust, had not broken, split, dashed. If only we could prevent the resulting retreat from our truest bluest dearest selves. If only we didn't have to enter, as you call it, "the existence period."

Frank Bascombe I hear you outside my door and I know I can't coax you in.

My cat analogy is actually not so good. On second thought I see its flaw. Cats have pea brains, and yours is sharp, brilliant, witty, ironic, sweet, underneath it all sweet, but perceptive like a genius, words used like blades to cut the self, to cut others, to draw a picture, to make a design, to make me feel what I am reluctant to feel, to see what I would prefer not to see, to wish for you more happiness than you would dare to wish for yourself. The cat analogy reduces the part of you that is words, advanced cortex, to a mere purr and lick, and that is wrong. You are a man of lyric mind, a mind caught in a maze, but mind nevertheless. There were moments reading *The Sportswriter* and *Independence Day* when I thought you were Virginia Woolf in drag or a smarter, better, more dazzling Raymond Carver or a Faulkner domesticated—a T. S. Eliot who had somehow discovered himself selling real estate split levels in Haddam, New Jersey. Sometimes at a line here or there, my face flushed, my pulse suspended in an unhealthy God-sighting pause. You sure know how to give a reader the payoff, the perfect image, the parry and thrust of the sword in just the right organ.

Your paragraphs are not the bearers of glad tidings, except that a man has written them. Like a dog a human being can mark his place (with words instead of pee) and that itself is good news in a sad second-best-to-a-joyful-life sort of way.

The facts. *The Sportswriter* and *Independence Day* are together really one novel—too long to be called a novel, but something like a long sea journey, *Moby Dick* perhaps. You, Frank Bascombe, are the narrator, the point of view, the mind we travel in, and *travel* is just the right word—up and down routes and highways and off ramps and exits and turnpikes. The route numbers are exact, 27, Nine, One, 87, 287, 684. The car's path weaves back and forth, locally, interstate, north and south, and you travel on commuter train and airplane as well. "Up the ink-dark seaboard Garden State, past Matawan, Raritan, past the toll plaza, the cooling vats of Elizabeth, toward exit 16W." Here is the essence of the American experience, motion, highway, tunnel, bridge, car: some coming and a lot of going. You crisscross New Jersey and Connecticut and New York like a spider spinning a web, a plot to catch a reader in, weaving a snare for a wandering soul, tattooing out a metaphor for our unrootedness, our pacing around the country, anxiety our constant companion, motels, hotels, for beds and transient flesh joined to transient minds.

The story is simple enough. Frank Bascombe in his twenties wrote a well-regarded book of short stories. Then his inspiration dried or his courage faltered or he just lost interest. He married a woman he loved named Ann, a golfer, an athlete, a good-spirited easygoing beauty, and he had three children, a boy named Ralph and another boy named Paul and a little girl named Clarissa. He worked as a sportswriter and lived with normal restrained contentment in a house in Haddam, which seems very much like Princeton, New Jersey. (It has a theological institute instead of a university.) Then all unexpectedly Ralph dies of Reye's disease, a fatal response to aspirin in children. And in the muted mourning that followed, husband and wife lost each other. Frank went to bed with other women and stopped holding his beloved as close and as firmly as a man must. He began to have sex the way a tongueless man has sounds, without grace or intention. When Ann discovers one evening while he is burning leaves on the lawn that he is writing aimless chatty letters to another woman, she burns the contents of her hope chest and lets the marriage go up in metaphorical and literal smoke. Ann moves to a new house in Haddam but Frank comes by on insomniac nights to sleep on her couch. Frank tries to love again, other women. He cannot. He has sex but he does not have love.

Theoretically, or so conventional wisdom would have it, these gropings should bother females and not matter to testosterone-bedeviled males but Frank is either a lemon model of his gender or we've all been sold a bill of goods. Frank minds, minds the acts of the body that exclude the soul, not that he can tell himself this clearly, but his lovelessness, his sleepless nights, his driving up and down roads, reveal a man in search not of girls, not of sexual release, but of the big

thing, the thing of the soul, the hardest thing of all, the thing he seems
to have irreparably lost, a little true mating.

The long slow decline into a shadow self begins with the loss of the
child. Frank doesn't tell us very much directly about this death. We
see him and his ex-wife at their annual visit to the cemetery. Each
brings a poem to read. Each recognizes the other's grief but is not
quite able to address it, to cut through barriers old and new. Frank behaves as if a rock had slammed into him, disconnecting emotion from
thought, miswiring the mind-body so that a near zombie seems to be
narrating the story. He describes the evening light, the church bells
ringing, the gas station attendant, the personality failures of his irritating real estate clients, the ins and outs of selling a house but can't
explain, can't say, has trouble like the rest of us with death.

What has been broken, the child who has been lost, the marriage
that has cracked, this does not simply haunt Frank as it might any man
but it transforms him, knocks him out, chases him first to a small college to teach English, where he tries meaningless, frequently sexual
attempts at the pretense of living and then goes back again to his
empty house, his long nights.

By the time *Independence Day* begins, Frank has abandoned sports
writing for real estate. He rents out apartments in two buildings he
owns and he works for an agency in town. He has learned the business
well. He knows how to manipulate, to cajole, to console, and to woo
his clients. He has had an affair with a black woman in his office
who throws him over for a more suitable suitor and is then killed
in a random murder. He grieves for her in a quiet stiff-upper-lip, a
drowning-man-releasing-bubbles-in-the-tide sort of way. His wife
has remarried, one Charley O'Dell, and lives in Connecticut in a
Waspy enclave of wealthy boating and tennis-playing types. His children live with her. He still thinks perhaps she will return to him. The
weekend of July 4 he is taking his angry fifteen-year-old son to the
Baseball Hall of Fame. He wants to find out why the boy has been acting up, barking like a dog and making strange noises and getting himself hurt, not to mention tossing an oarlock at his stepfather's face.
Independence Day is the story of this trip. It is about how Frank might
be able to pass through this long dark period of his life toward some-

thing better, from an "existence period" into a "permanence period," perhaps or perhaps not.

Each of his two books takes place over a holiday weekend. *The Sportswriter* takes us through Easter weekend and *Independence Day* covers the Fourth of July. Rebirth and renewal, political and religious, are certainly the subject here, strange only in that the events seem so embedded in our daily suburban, most ordinary realities: banking, plane tickets, sex, a fishing trip with the Divorced Men's Club, a job, a daughter with a red hair ribbon. Frank Bascombe may be an ordinary fellow, hit with the death of a child, separation from a wife he still feels bound to, whose body still means home to him, a man whose original ambitions have settled rather admirably into no more than he could expect to have, who seems on the surface to have come to terms with the details of his life, and yet the reader feels as with Walker Percy that the hand of God is everywhere, even or most especially in its absence.

Which brings me to Edward Hopper. Yes, the decade is all wrong. Frank lives in the late eighties, while Edward Hopper's famous painting of a nighttime diner counter in New York City is most distinctly a work of the depression, the thirties. However, the lady in a green hat and the people seated too far from each other for conversation and the strange, harsh, cruelly clear electric light and the dark structures of the city visible just beyond the plate glass window that is our viewpoint onto the canvas kept leaping into my mind as Frank was reporting his journey outward and inward. Political freedom (Frank brings Emerson for his son to read, also the Declaration of Independence) may make us free, but misery, the plight of the soul, is more related to human connection and lack of it than are politics and freedom. John Adams and America's glory story offer an ironic landscape, a kind of leering Disney World that hangs over our private memories, our gray failures.

Redemption of the human condition (a man who made a failed pass at Frank dies on Easter eve) may or may not have come, the risen Jesus may or may not be doing his job in heaven, but the byways around Haddam look a lot like purgatory. (So does Edward Hopper's diner.)

However, redemption and freedom are good enough ideas that serve at their best as a light beckoning across the moors. Commercial tinkling does not change the fact; redemption, God's hand, may in fact have come. I think Frank believes in God's hovering presence. But maybe not, not so neatly anyway. Most of us looking in through the window at Edward Hopper's diner imagine ourselves walking on, finding another place to get a cup of coffee, or maybe we just hurry and go home. Frank Bascombe (his home is such a shambles) would go right in, take his place in the frozen tableau, sit under the light that casts a green shadow across human skin, and wait.

There was in my lifetime a great snapping of marriage that came like a countrywide ice storm causing branches to fall. I too have an ex-husband and I too had a child who finally had a stepfather and half-siblings. And I too remember nights when I couldn't sleep in my bed and I thought though I was only twenty-nine years old that I would sleep alone for the rest of my days. I remember hearing the sound of cars on the avenue, of voices in the hall. I remember how men would look at me at parties, and how hopefully I would smile at others in restaurants, in bars, in airports. There seemed to be a twoness to the world, a natural mating, a Noah's ark flowing by me, and I was standing singly hip deep in the floodwaters.

One night I went to dinner at a college friend's. She was married to an English professor and they had just had a baby, and I went into the sleeping newborn's room to watch him as he sucked his wrinkled miraculous thumb in his elephant pajamas. I leaned over the crib, and suddenly hands grabbed me from behind and held me firmly so I couldn't turn, and a man's rough cheek was pressed against mine and his fingers were groping for my nipples. It was my friend's husband. He wanted to meet me in his office. He wanted to play doctor with me. He did not want his wife to find out. And I stood there over his son's crib and I tried to tell myself that all this was natural, physical, and the disorder was not personal. Lust was as natural as breathing. I was afraid of the hardening of my heart, the shrinking of my trust.

This divorce, mine, was not a normal life passage. It was a destruction of the holy, and I knew it. It was necessary for my survival (that's

what every divorcee says) even as it was a betrayal of my child. If only
I had met Frank, then we could have consoled each other, not very
well of course, but we might have tried.

Frank's collection of short stories called *Blue Autumn* was probably
very like a collection called *Rock Springs* by Richard Ford. Here are
stories where one Montana boy, around fifteen or sixteen years old,
one after another endures the snap apart of his life as his parents—a
loved mother, a loved father—break under the pressure of things, take
lovers, move away, leave behind a child with a single parent, a lonely
child in the wreckage of the marriage, in the wipe-out of the home. A
father goes to jail or moves to a remote place without television. But
the son loves the father and the ache for him or his substitute is the
yeast of the tales, the alive writhing frothing factor. Some terrible
ache this is, some awful wound is covered there, some terrible understanding of boy need and man need, lies there. I wish I couldn't imagine what he's talking about. I can. The thing that is broken in these
stories is the marriage, and that is what Frank cannot endure, what has
driven him into his "existence period," that and the capricious loss of
his son in a coma, in a hospital, with a wife whom he could no longer
speak to, not because it was her fault but because it wasn't. She was,
however, there, witness to his helplessness, to the unmanning of a
man before the power of death. Maybe that or some other reason
like it.

The abandonment of children, too soon forced into adulthood,
witnesses of murders, adulteries, drinking bouts along the long-off
roads of the empty plains, the tiny towns with grain towers and bars
and car dealerships, towns that trains pass through and hardly bother
to blow their whistles: this desertion by the adults, this brokenness is
Frank's subject long after he stopped writing stories.

His man's voice is really the voice of the child who could not recover from the absence of a parent and perhaps he shouldn't have. It
drives him on. It makes him search for a new place, a new bed, a love
that might last. Frank's search is sadder, richer in its sadness than any
other in the American collection of hard times and bitter pills to swallow because, as with the face of God, he cannot look at it directly and

can only report the shadows at the edges, the fragments of light he sees. This oblique glance intensifies the heat, the radiating soreness.

Oh Frank, I agree—what should have held together has come apart and there is nothing to do about it but get a new job, move on, try again. What has cracked apart has cracked apart. Knowing that is the deep secret of your one novel told in two parts and it is important. Very.

The thing is that Frank and most of the other divorced men of Haddam who went on fishing trips with him were not interested in women like me, readers of short stories, war protesters, mothers against nuclear drip in their children's milk. The women Frank pursues rather hopefully are a registered nurse, Vicki Arcenault, of callow coarse soul but sensual body; an intern at a magazine, much younger and on a different life path, Cathy Flaherty; and last and perhaps more seriously a woman, Sally Caldwell, who organizes theater trips for elderly groups, good sorts, good sports, healthy limbs and ready to play. Women who have themselves been damaged by deserting men, abusers, drinkers, but women who are plucky and have good breasts and fine legs.

The problem is that Frank has trouble loving again perhaps because he is a one-woman man, not in sex but in love. There are dogs like that who howl after their masters and never become attached again no matter how good the feed or gentle the replacement hand. Geese it is said by Richard Ford himself mate only once and for life. On a city street over by the park under a bench I saw a dead pigeon lying, feathers flat, on the cobblestone and its mate pacing frantically around the body and then around the body again, wings fluttering, head shaking, with such grief, such absolute grief and bird brain confusion that I myself hated the universe for a while, until my mood changed.

What Frank does still love, in his own low-key painfully muffled way, is his children. By "low-key" I don't mean a little or barely or with a small sound. I mean deep, constant, uncertain now after the divorce, attentive but aware of failure, afraid of being cut off, forgotten, unneeded, extra. Low-key because, as he says, he promised himself he'd "never complain about how things hoped out." It's as if King Lear, holding Cordelia's body in his arms, was constrained by a sort of Protestant ethic that enforced a stiff upper lip, a going on even when the point is lost, a thin sort of human sound, filled with Presbyterian orderliness, decency, restraint.

At the opening of *Independence Day* Ralph is in the ground in the cemetery behind his old house and Frank's son Paul has been arrested for stealing condoms and fighting with the arresting officer. The boy is seeing a psychiatrist in New Haven. He has taken to barking and making a sound like "eech" at random moments. He has stolen his stepfather's car. He is in trouble. Frank wants to help. He says, "The worst of being a parent, my fate, having to stand like a lamppost with its lamp lit, hoping my child will see the glow and venture close for the illumination and warmth it mutely offers." Here is the helplessness, the hope against hope, the hands tied—in this case if you're a lamppost no hands at all. It is the sweet hope of the lamppost that makes Frank, yes passive, slow, reactive, stumped Frank, the father he is. The one that would do for any of us well enough.

He hurtles through the night making phone calls to Sally whom he has left as if he were leaving her forever though he didn't mean it and wants to take his icy departure back. He says that his son needs what he can supply, even if he can't really supply it. He promises himself to try his utmost to imagine himself into his son's mind. Frank never, not in the worst emergency and some emergencies lie ahead on this weekend trip, loses his sense of ironic double take: what seems true only seems true and the best of emotions are only attempts at exact feelings. Still what's a man to do but act on his better impulses, pretend he knows what to do and then do it?

This uncertainty, this ambivalence, this detachment and persistence in the face of detachment is what makes Frank a modern hero, my hero at least.

Bravery is not much of an asset for a modern hero if the book is not a war story. Brave acts in civilian characters tend to make us suspicious or wary. I'm ready to call a mental health professional at the first sign of altruistic sacrifice. Modern literary heroes that are capable of holding our attention are too cautious, too self-aware to go plunging into raging rivers to save drowning babies, not in real books anyway. War hero bravery, bullets flying, a dash to save a comrade lying wounded a thousand yards beyond the trench, that bravery has its counterpart when Frank says, "Though if it weren't that tears had just sprung stinging to my eyes I'd accept my loss with dignity since after all I am the man who counsels abandonment of those precious things you remember but can no longer make hopeful use of."

What is brave is to allow the emotions to come seeping up through the defensive armor, to prick and wound and make you sad. This Frank does again and again. "I love you," he says to his son who has put himself right in the way of a machine-pitched baseball and stands to lose his eye. "I love his fair delicate scalp," he tells us. And in admitting this love he risks loss and he knows it. He admits that he is angry, and getting directly angry is not an easy thing for Frank who would rather tell you about real estate deals than admit to the pain in his gut. He says, "I come toward him suddenly pity and murder and love each crying out for a time at bat." Frank has his own kind of courage. It is this that has sent him off on his trip with his most annoying, unbeautiful, awkward, anguished son in some vague hope of helping, reaching, holding his child once more.

Perhaps Paul is barking because the family dog, Toby, back when the Bascombes were a family, had been hit by a car and died in his arms. Paul is barking in order to both express and avoid his mourning for his brother and his home. Frank knows this but doesn't know what to do about it. The bravery here: Frank's helplessness does not result in movement away from his son. He hangs in there. He tells us, "Any time spent with your child is partly a damn sad time, the sadness of life, a going bright, vivid, each time a last. A loss, a glimpse into what it could have been." Paul, jokester, quipster, ironist, is in a fury. His Yale psychiatrist has asked him if his father abused him. This he tells his father. The assault and the pain of that question ride in the car with the father and son. The father who loves his child takes the question as a body blow. He continues to love his son and hope their trip will be a blessing not a further curse on them both.

There is something brave about the way he holds his wounds close and can even afford a wry ironic pass at the pain. Here he says, "It's never easy to see why your ex-wife marries the man she marries if it isn't you again." This desertion of Ann, as if a train car had been disconnected from the engine and drifted off by rail, and her remarriage to the odious security-providing older Charley is the latest bloodletting he has had to endure. He can't reclaim the wife he wants and needs. All gestures in that direction fly back in his face. He knows that time, the time to grab back his wife, has come and gone. He has hopes but he knows his hopes are odds on headed for disappointment. Here is a hero, contemporary, a hero without illusions.

Religion, the soul: what has become of it in Haddam, New Jersey, in the midst of the commerce, the flat soreness of American suburbia which has little to inspire, no rose windows of Chartres, no ancient temple walls as in Jerusalem, no single-spired, dignified churches tucked into the evergreens, perched high on sloping hills above the rivers of New England or set bravely against the fields of Biloxi, Mississippi? The churches of Haddam are near police, train, and gas stations, near card shoppes and cleaners and supermarkets. The mystery of things persists, there are cemeteries as well as banks but the resurrection, the holiness of things, the God who might speak in a whirlwind or who appears in wafer and wine, seems pale, distant, like a fresco on a wall washed nearly away by time, human breath, hot and cold climate, dust. The vigor of the line is still there but you have to peer close to see it.

Which is why Frank goes to see a palmist who reads the tarot cards just out of town. She doesn't inform him of any truth. She is an ordinary woman with a list of clichés as long as Rapunzel's hair, and Frank can't climb them anywhere but he continues to go, to be reassured by the sessions, by the unused crystal ball, by the voice of the palmist. What is this—a joke?

There is an Institute of Religion in Haddam. Frank has taken an African roommate from Gabon, a prince of a tribe, who is attending the institute and will be ordained as a proper minister after his studies. This institute is not the same as religion itself or perhaps it is religion boxed in, walled up, passion down, mystery lacking. Frank is not looking for anything that can be packaged in an institution. The real thing must be wilder, freer, more reeking with raw power. His dependence on the palm reader who lays claim to be on good terms with the supernatural and operates out of a tacky home just off the road to town is a token gesture, a taking of an aspirin when serious chemotherapy is in order.

Frank attends Easter service at the end of *The Sportswriter* and he tries to feel the renewal, the touch of Christ on his heart. But the respectability, the dutifulness of it, the social orderliness of it, do not answer the rage of his heart. His son has died. He allowed and created the conditions in which his wife has left him. The break has seared him. His other son is lying in a hospital with his eye badly damaged and his soul battered from a fury he cannot contain in his jokes or his sounds. He says, "We just have to be smart enough to quit asking places for what they can't provide." This is a sad sort of wisdom. Frank I wish you such a Christ as Gerard Manley Hopkins would provide, a winged bird plunging, a wild speckled dappled thing on morning's mignons bright colors across a wondrous sky. I don't want pathetic resignation from you or sorry consultations with fortune-tellers, clowns, con artists, forgeries, who mock the genuine Fates who step on us as they will and let no one in on their plans.

You know this. You report the language of the scriptures and it rings in your head as it does in mine—a magnificent miracle, a wonder of God, thinned out in Haddam but still there. It is to your enormous credit Frank that you accept no pap, wait for something, hope for a miracle, are soul struggling still, not mere decaying meat.

It is to your enormous credit that you move among the basketball players, the football players, the baseball players, among the housing units of developing Haddam, the advantages of kitchens with hallways and those without, and you never lose the hope of a burning bush, a voice in the wilderness, a walk on water, a baptism that will bring the spirit home. You speak of the fellow churchgoers on Easter morning as either "bored or else full of longing for something they can't quite name." You are in the latter group. You speak of "the far flung longing for conviction among the convictionless." This applies to you, to all of suburbia, and to me. That's exactly it. I admire your saying it. I love you for it. You talk of the moment "to rise from transitory things toward heaven." The religious hook is baited. It remains baited, no real takers, not in Haddam, not really.

I know this God matter isn't the only issue in your life, more of a chorus, a theme that plays gently in the background. It is good, though, this thwarted, aborted religious impulse. It deepens and marks who you are.

And while we're on the subject of religion I have a small complaint. It's small in the scheme of things but it's not so small to me. The word *Jew* is not a neutral word. After the history of this century if you make a character a Jew and you call that character a Jew that choice has meaning and resonances. It is not the same as a hair color or a city of origin, like Spokane or Albany, like Frenchman or Costa Rican. Frank—that your mother may have married a Jew from Skokie, Illinois, and that you had a Jewish stepfather and a Jewish stepbrother is not a random fact, as if you had a stepfather from New Orleans and a stepbrother who was on the wrestling team. In your description of your stepbrother Irv Ornstein who comes upon you at Cooperstown and drives you to the hospital and keeps you company as you wait for the arrival of your wife after your son, in a moment of adolescent fury, has stepped into a batting cage and deliberately invited the ball to hit him in the head, you keep saying you like Irv, that he's a decent fellow, that you always liked him, but then you describe him, you let us listen to him talk to you. There is something vulgar in his language, something too loud, too close-up, too broad in his feelings that disturbs us. He seems very much the wrong companion for the fraught hours that end this entered-into-so-hopefully trip with your son. He is dressed wrong. He is too big and clumsy. He pretends to an intimacy with you that you do not feel or really want. He intrudes on you just like those few who do not grasp our social agreement on how far away they should stand from the person they are talking to, who invade our space and make us back up and back up again.

Irv is in the simulator business as an engineer. The word *simulator* is the important one here. I know that he is simulating a real life with real human connections in the way that you feel you are too, you in your endless existence period. But you've given him the role of the all-too-eager kid in the class who will never make real friends, who is destined to outsider status and a certain pathetic simulation of belonging. Is it really an accident that this fellow is a Jew? Were you really content to have his father marry your mother, not a twinge, not a stab, not a resentment anywhere? Are you by chance echoing T. S. Eliot's Jews rubbing their hands as the paint peels off civilization's holy walls? I know you didn't say that. But something here.

There are no coincidences, no accidents in fiction. Are Jews the half-brothers of Christians? Is this a statement for brotherhood or some subtle needling of the traditional outsider? I'm not asking for political correctness here. I suspect all the nice things you say about Irv are bones tossed in that direction—a sort of ecumenical blessing at a conference of Christians and Jews that takes place in your head.

It made me anxious, reading this. And this anxiety was intensified by finding another Jew in what I assume to be one of your stories, "The Womanizer." In this story the Jew is the ex-husband of the Frenchwoman pursued by Martin, an American who has left his wife to pursue a sexual and romantic fantasy. The Jew, Bernard, is described as a "bulbous faced, dark skinned Jew with a thick black mustache that made him look like an Armenian." Bernard has written a terrible book about his ex-wife. Our hero suspects him of having a bullying nature. Why does he have to be Jewish? When you use the word you mean something, something more than if he were Swiss or Thai. Of course there are Jews who are bulbous and bullying and I wouldn't want them to come to dinner either but in a novel or a story one has to wonder, Aren't you using the word *Jew* here as in *barbarian at the gate*, as in *moneychanger*, as in *victim*, outcast like the Armenians?

Bernard is described laughing using a racial epithet about a toy pickaninny eating a watermelon. Why the need to have a Jew be the bigot, the one that we must more legitimately place on the American southerner's conscience? You were born in Biloxi, right? Why place the guilt of racial cruelty on a Jew when it more properly belongs with the ancestors of the author of the story? Is this a way of reducing Christian guilt for the crematoria? Perhaps I read too much into the character of Bernard and the scene with him in the store, but perhaps not. Perhaps you are actually exposing the midwestern smugness of your character Martin by giving him these perceptions—but I doubt it. You know that standing in the store Martin was just a few blocks away from the train station where 100,000 Jewish children, some with French citizenship, were contained behind barriers by the French police until they could be carried off to their deaths in the camps. Not your subject I know. Not your problem here I know. But mine.

But then I wonder why in another story, "The Occidentals," that has an alter ego character for Frank, here called Charley, and an ex-wife like Ann and a girlfriend who has cancer and will kill herself on a weekend trip to Paris, you have Charley look out the dreary hotel window and observe a Jewish funeral, yarmulkas and all, in the cemetery next door. The funeral foreshadows the suicide to come. The cemetery announces the death in the story, but Jews, why? Is it because of the Jewish death that hangs over Europe? Is it because you wanted your American writer to feel doubly alienated surrounded by Frenchmen and Jews, or is it more simply that you cannot go about your business without bringing Jews into it—perhaps a tic of a southern writer who knows his competition this half-century has been the Jewish writer, the Jewish intellectual. Is it Saul Bellow you were burying in that grave? Have Jews become for the Christian mind like vultures whose circling in the sky signifies a coming death?

Something here, since all the choices of religious identity are yours, makes me queasy. Your Jewish references make the whiffs of Christian salvation that float through *Independence Day* seem suddenly alien, cold, and potentially dangerous to the health of me and mine. Well, I am your loyal reader anyway. I know how to keep this in perspective, to shrug it off. How could I read if I weren't capable of sometimes ignoring a slap in the face? But I just want you to know, I noticed this and I wish I hadn't.

On the other hand the Divorced Men's Club is just about the saddest sorriest thing I've ever come across. Since the early seventies we've had novels by irate, deceived, betrayed, belittled, bemused, impoverished, innocence lost, divorced women by the shredderful. I even wrote one myself (mine naturally was entirely justified). There was a time when you couldn't turn on your television without seeing some woman bright eyed, straight backed, a survivor of some horrible tale of male perfidy ready to talk to us, report from the battlefront. In the subsequent flood of female grief I sometimes overlooked the fact that men are lonely too, clumsy at social exchanges, eager for a pat on the back, a road map that will tell them how to reconnect, to love again.

Early in *Independence Day*, on page 34, you say, "A good sense of decorum can make life bearable when otherwise you might be tempted to blow your brains out." The Divorced Men's Club is a decorum prop, a little like a hat you wear to church or the dog you walk each evening past the neighbor's fence.

The Divorced Men's Club is not really a club. It's a group of men, an odd assortment without much in common, from Haddam whose wives have left or who have left their wives and who get together once a month or so and have dinner or go to a bar or best of all go down to the shore and charter a fishing boat for a number of hours. They drink beer, they tell jokes. The middle-aged guys, successful enough at what they do, ordinary suburbanites with houses and obligations, gain some comfort from the nearbyness of each other. They do not as women would do discuss the details of their romantic failures, their lawsuits, their children. They mostly talk about sports or fish or the weather or where they should eat or drink. The gatherings do not as they would with women create lifelong attachments, someone to call at midnight and say you're having heart pains or delirium tremens or going bankrupt. Their concept of mutual support lies in the continuity of their meetings and that they do meet.

The fishing trips on a charter boat provide comradeship but don't provide a reason for living. Frank goes along because it is one of the things that now mark his place, part of his existence program of just getting through, making it from day to day without a fuss, without a crack-up.

The sadness, bleakness of it is in sharp contrast to the female vision of divorced men making their way gaily through a sexual field of beautiful young women who drop grapes into their open mouths. It calls up short the female vision of male indifference and callous childishness. In fact the men in this group are among the walking wounded, hiding their wounds of course in the usual male-muffled stiff-upper-lip-way, but wounds they have—far more than the average female consciousness-raising group would ever have imagined.

I didn't want Frank to be in the company of these men. I wanted him to wake up—catch his fish, find his way back to his wife and children, come alive, write stories again, bleed if he must but don't die, not slowly, soul stifled, deadened in the heart, not like this, not as a member of the Divorced Men's Club or at the local Y's meeting for single men. Mourn Ralph with a loud scream at the deity and then let him go.

Never more than when he is fishing with the Divorced Men's Club does this decent, sweet, more-hurt-than-hurting man evoke such love in this reader. I could barely stand it that I could not go to him, hold him, play with him, kiss him as his mother would, as his wife or girlfriend should, a life-giving kiss. Of course he's just a character in a book, and we, he and I, are permanently separated by my unshakable three dimensions and his condition as a mere figment of imagination imprisoned within the pages of the book.

. . . .

I am fishing in the Poconos. It is trout season. I am not an expert fly-fisherwoman. I do know how to do it. One, two, three snaps of the wrist, loose and easy, eye on the spot I want to reach. I am persistent. I can get my line into the water within a three-foot radius of where I aim. The problem is that I still can't see the fish moving in the current. The shadows change, the leaves float, bugs dip and rise, flashes of sunlight turn the water silver. I can make out rocks, branches, soggy moss, what I seem unable to find is the fish. But that's all right, I like it on the bank, the heat soaking through my back, the water seeping into my sneakers. My wrist flicks back and forth. I feel like the amateur I am, the pretender I am, but I also feel comfortable, as if the stream and I have known each other a long time. This is not true but that doesn't matter. I am content to fish, to let the afternoon pass without conversation, without a thought about the future, with no concern for the happiness of my children, the future income of the family, the meaning of life. The fish is swimming stealthily beneath the moving water, feeding on insects or not feeding as his mood suits. I am watching the thin black thread of my line as it rises into the rays of sun when I hear footsteps on the other side of the stream. I look up just as I feel a pull, a beautiful firm pull on my line. I have found a fish. I know not to panic, not to reel in too fast. I hold my rod up to put tension on the line, I take a step backward. The figure across the stream, only about ten feet away, does the same. He seems to be imitating me. I don't look at him, I concentrate. My trout is sinking down toward the bottom, running to the deeper part of the stream, I let him go for a moment. That is the right thing to do. Then I begin slowly winding. My arms are tired from all that casting. I feel a pain between my shoulder blades. The fish is not coming closer to my side of the shore. I call out to the man across the water, "You have one too?" He nods. "A big one," he says.

After a few minutes he says, "Something's wrong." Something is wrong with my fish too. The man yells at me, "Don't wind up." I stop. He continues. I am being pulled into the water. I follow my fish, I follow my line. I am standing in the water. It is now up to my knees. It is now up to my chest. I still have the fish. The man says, "You have my fish." "I don't," I say. "Oh yes you do." He wades into the water and pulling out a net scoops up the fish. It is not so big. It does have two hooks in its mouth. A greedy fish, a stupid fish, a fish without guile or cunning, it had taken both our flies at once. "You can have it," the man says. "You take it," I say. He walks across the stream toward me. A long linear angled man with a gray cast to his face. Hard eyes, very hard eyes, but a gentleness when he smiles. "Frank Bascombe," he says.

He shows me his day's catch. He has five trout. I have none. I watch as he hits my trout over the head with a stick. The fish shivers for an instant and then lies still. He slits its throat, letting the blood seep into the pebbles at the edge of the stream. The blood is very red, I always forget that real blood is dark and stains the ground.

"If you catch the same fish as another person are you bound to that person?" I ask. "No," he says, "there are no rules like that I've ever heard of." "If you catch the same fish as another person are you entitled to a prize?" "No," he says, "no prize." "So then," I say, "you just go off back upstream, take your car, and go home." "No," he says. "I'll stay here and catch you another fish."

"What can I do for you?" I say.

"Nothing," he says. "I can take care of myself."

"Too bad," I say and gather my things, my fish, and go back to the lot at the edge of the road where I have parked my car. On the way home the radio host encourages callers to resist the building of a Gap store on the far side of the mountain. My neck hurts from straining forward trying to haul in the fish. I pass a sign that says "Jesus Saves." I wonder if two people catching the same fish is a kind of miracle, a symbol that we were meant to be together but won't be.

. . . . .

A new man, Walter, joins the Divorced Men's Club. His wife has run off to Bimini. Frank has a beer with him in a bar on the dock after one of the trips. Walter tells Frank that a few days before he has had sex with a man he's gone home with. Walter is disturbed. What does this mean? Frank is not ready for this subject. His thoughts are elsewhere. Walker goes with Frank back to his house in Haddam and there kisses Frank and abruptly leaves. Frank is not pleased. But he is not judgmental. He seems more like a drowning man who encounters another bobbing figure in the sea. He has his own drowning to attend to. He is helpless to help and while a decent enough person, decent enough to feel a pressure, a passing cloud of another's muted anguish, he has little but the hollow forms of friendship to offer. Then Walter kills himself and leaves a note for Frank so Frank is called by the police to identify the body, becomes involved in this virtual stranger's death.

Walter can't live with the shame of his own sexual desire. What is this but yet another appearance of *Civilization and Its Discontents*? We set up a structure to contain our impulses, to ensure that the species continues, and then we make harsh laws and our policemen are specialists in shame and guilt and our policemen are inside us, beating us up with billy clubs, with Mace on the heart. They can kill you, these representatives of the social order. They killed Walter. Frank would never have hurt Walter or revealed his secret but he couldn't help him either. Men fail each other in subtle ways, ways they hadn't intended. The thing that is the worst shame of all, that little boys get guns and kill in high school corridors because they've been called this faggot thing, is just a social rottenness that makes the night more dangerous than it need be. Remember Holden's English teacher making a pass in the dead of night at the almost sleeping boy. This fear of homosexuality, this discomfort in its presence, is a fact about the male, an awful fact.

This plotline is not offered to suggest that Frank is latently or any other way homosexual. It is hooked into Bascombe's social discomfort, lighting up the space between who we are and what we think we must be. Walter's death is a sharp kick in the ribs to Frank, illustrating the explosive violence that lurks just beneath our most innocent routines, our fishing trips, our business lunches, our churchgoing, and our daily commute. Frank too thinks at the most peripheral corners of his mind of killing himself. He doesn't do it because he has locked himself down, kept self-destruction at bay, put on his own straitjacket, developed coping systems that involve not seeing and not feeling. His soul has created its own white noise. Walter is the suicide. Frank is merely his brother in despair and how little they have helped each other.

The orderliness of Haddam—its neighborhoods, its well-kept lawns, its Institute of Religion—is placed right on top of a metaphoric toxic dump, a ready-to-explode (or implode) minefield of blood and death.

I know something about this. How easy it is to become an actor on the stage of your own life. That I recognize too well. I know what it costs to seek social approval, which only means social invisibility, to hide the truth and live by a mirror trick. I think of my mother afraid of the scandal, unable to divorce a man who betrayed her. I think of my father unable to divorce a woman he could not abide because he needed the accessories of acceptability she provided: a good address, membership in an athletic club, social prestige in a small circle. You can say, sometimes I do, Well, it served him right that he was lonely, angry, shouted at people for fear that he was invisible. But I remember when I loved him and he would come home from his office, slam the front door, ask me to fix him a drink, and sit in a chair in our turquoise-walled living room on a French sixteenth-century chair beneath a decorator-chosen Chinese wall hanging and there was a look in his eyes, a blankness, a tightness, and he would look around. What am I doing? his look seemed to say. Why am I in this room? I too was in the room but it was not me he was waiting for. It was not my mother. He was lonely and there was no way to ease his condition. The men in the Divorced Men's Club are far kinder than my father but just as clumsy when it comes to touching other people, to putting their heads in someone's lap, to holding a hand, to looking into other people's souls. My father used to refer to divorced women with children as women with baggage. He himself would have traveled light and alone. But he didn't.

I think of my brother hiding the cause of his final illness for fear of other people's curiosity, disapproval, dislike. He was cut off from his friends and his colleagues for a long time. He kept his secrets but they made him lonely. The loneliness underlined the many ways in which God had betrayed him. The loneliness mixed with the acid odors of strange medicines. He watched the tennis matches in Forest Hills and I came into the room and I saw him cadaverously thin on the couch, the bones on his face making one instantly think of skulls in the ground. The room was lit by the blue flickering light of the television. I was there but I couldn't stop him from being lonely, alone.

I think of pretending men and pretending women, friends and relatives, frozen in sexual places they would not choose to be if they were free to choose, could choose without shame, and I know that I have felt ashamed when my first marriage broke, when my child was clearly having trouble, clear to any passerby. I know that I have felt ashamed at secrets large and small and so does everybody and we don't all live in Haddam, just Haddams of our own selection.

Frank is a gentle man. His language does not contain as my father's did many references to smashing someone's teeth in, to knocking sense into someone's head, to ripping out the guts or beating into the dust. He most tentatively imagines vanquishing his wife's self-satisfied new husband whom he hates but not enough to actually physically harm. He grows irritated with his most irritating clients but does not imagine planting a car bomb. But around him in Haddam there is violence. Clair, his short-lived black girlfriend, has been murdered. He has himself been mugged. His partner in a root beer stand on the road carries a gun because of threatening Mexicans riding by. There is exterior violence and interior violence. There is a murder in a motel in a room near Frank's when he stops for the night on the way to pick up his son in Connecticut. There are police sirens and lights and crime scene tapes. When he goes to interview a paralyzed football player, the man instead of mouthing inspirational words as the magazine would have wished tells Frank a story of a dream in which he kills three blind women.

And worst of all there is the violence that Frank's son Paul does to his own face when he deliberately, out of self-hatred, out of rage at targets he cannot find, steps into the batting cage and lets the machine's fast ball knock him senseless. Then come ambulances and helicopters and all the usual companions of blood and gore. True—a story can always use a little action. Something external to the thoughts of the character should happen eventually, otherwise we readers become bored and lose focus. But the violent acts that Frank encounters are multiple, strangely multiple for a single non-mob-connected man. First is the random violence like the murder of the man in the motel room or Clair's murder in an empty condominium. There was the Easter weekend violence of Walter's hanging himself after leaving Frank's house. There is Paul's violence against Charley O'Dell; he hits him with a hurled oarlock. Then there is God's violence, equally random but far more personal, afflicting Ralph and leaving him buried in a grave near the grave sites of three of the writers of the Declaration of Independence. Then there is the less literal violence of the separation from Ann and the subsequent chronic weight of loss that erodes the soul and casts the mind into its own pit of tortures. Then there is Frank's need to get out of Manhattan, "before the whole city reached out and clutched me like the pale hand of a dead limo driver." Frank survives the city unharmed but the threat is there in his head.

I have known the violence of sickness. My mother died of a brain tumor that caused convulsions and paralysis. My brother, a scientist, cut himself in his lab and died of AIDS. I too have feared the violence of robbers, thugs, muggers, rapists, although I have seen none of these up close. I have feared nuclear bombs and I have seen in movies and photographs lynch mobs and soldiers of all races lying dead or mutilated in killing fields the earth over. I know about gulags and Babi Yar, Manchurian massacres and gifts of smallpox-infected blankets. My very first real grief, one that can still bring a lump to my throat, was caused by a hunter who killed Babar's mother. My second great grief was caused by another hunter, who killed the mother of Bambi.

This raw inchoate menace—the reality that man can be so easily crushed by metal, by bacteria, by grief—makes it so urgent that Frank be protected from the evils that are riding up and down the east coast with him, behind his back, waiting ahead. It drives me mad that I can't protect him and I can't protect my own either.

Paul, Frank's fifteen-year-old son, already in trouble with the law, is one angry not-so-little boy. He is angry that his home has broken, that his brother has died, that his mother has remarried and moved to a place where he has no roots, no friends. He is not impressed that his housing has been upgraded. He has most likely cruelly killed a bird, which bothers Frank a lot. He has definitely cut himself. He has stolen his stepfather's car. He has punched out a policeman trying to arrest him for shoplifting. Once he had been a sweet ten-year-old boy trying to send a pigeon to Cape May where the family had vacationed as a message for his dead brother. Now he is a smelly surly hard-to-talk-to boy who drifts in and out of contact, needy and remote at the same time.

I wish I couldn't really imagine this child. I wish I hadn't made my own trips to psychiatrists, "Help my child. Tell me what's wrong." I wish I couldn't imagine how Frank feels. He never tells us directly or clearly about his child. But I know. Frank is superbly sensitive to his son's every gesture, word, body language. He understands the child near him the way our guardian angel might (if angels existed) understand us, hovering over the shoulder, prevented by some law of the universe from actually intervening, even from letting us know by the slightest lifting of wings that he is there.

I know what that's like. A beautiful child may turn awkward, grow fat or thin, leave cigarette ash over the sheets, pile up laundry, and suddenly fail subjects or stay out all night; control is lost. Watching this is hard, fear is constant, love becomes mingled with its opposite. Sometimes it's just the way we Americans do our growing up (a giant Boston tea party in which everything of value is tossed into the sea), become independent; a few years later things look better. Sometimes not.

How to explain the ache all that causes—the constant pain on the amputated part that was once a Perfect Child. How I love Frank for his caring, his trying, the intensity of his fatherly love: his own failure to express, to mourn, to win back his wife, to make his life whole— making it just that much harder to haul in his spinning graceless son and make him safe.

I have been on journeys with a child, to the psychiatrist, to a new school that might do what the last one couldn't. I have been on planes to distant cities after car wrecks, after trouble, what should I have done? How better, just better. I too have thumbed through *Time* magazine and eaten meals in Pizza Huts and drunk Coke from vending machines in the green-glow vestibules of motel hallways in pursuit of a child.

Frank is a father who although he himself may be damaged goods is still there, still intending to be his child's right arm, his stout friend, his leader to a peaceful country. This makes Frank a hero not just in a modern ironic sense but in the original ready-to-risk-your-life-for-the-life-of-another meaning. He deserves to have his son move back to Haddam with him. He deserves better than what he has. It isn't always true (a father loves his child), but when it is true it comes like joyous tidings, it comes like a reprieve, it makes us glad and seems like rescue. It says to us, the choppers are coming in.

There are things about you Frank that drive me crazy. You are too slow in responding to insult. You are so dreamy with your pain that you can't act. You responded to the death of Ralph with such withdrawal, such anesthesia that of course your wife withered and turned away from you. You failed a big test. Then when you realized you failed, you couldn't do anything about it. I suggest you might have pursued her harder, talked to her more, insisted that she reunite with you, promise her anything, take her into your confidence, let her see how you felt about her, not played a dance of After you, Alphonse, risked rejection, acknowledged need, come pounding on her bedroom door. You didn't have to let her get away. Your fault.

Second and here I know I am on shaky ground, perhaps self-interest motivates me but the way I see it is that you have always, consistently been after the wrong women, desired them for the wrong reasons, and this wrongness is the explanation for the lonely pit you find yourself in. I know you think that at the end of *Independence Day* by actually moving toward Sally Caldwell, marriage is in the air, you will enter a new period of life and all will be if not well, better. I think this is a mistake and here is why.

The women you have been involved in are all tall healthy types. They look good. They have some wit and capability. Even Vicki is probably a good cheerful nurse and you needed nursing no doubt, but you are a man with a particular kind of poetry in your soul. You think that the stories you wrote were unimportant in your life but I doubt it. I think writing it down, putting it into words, is right there at the top of the list of things that matter, matter to you. A woman like Sally who has made a life out of getting tickets to Broadway musicals for old folks, a cheerful type who lives on the beach, is a good soul, but you look at her and say you don't love her, and you think this thought came to you out of the stuckness of your life, that you didn't mean it, but I think you did. I think you need a woman with a stench of poetry, with a sounding of the ocean depths closer to your own, a woman who is lighter and shivers more with the winds that blow. You need someone who is strong yes, but not strong like a piece of lumber, but strong like the willow.

The self-interest here: maybe I'm proposing myself. Maybe I just want you to love a writer, not a golf player, and that's not fair. What I really want is for you to find a soulmate. Emily Dickinson would do. So would Jane Austen or Virginia Woolf. I grant you these ladies would have been sexually less experienced than the ones you did choose, but perhaps under your tutelage they would have blossomed in that department. I grant you that they might not have selected you but it's a risk worth taking.

Your choices in women seem ordinary, flat, and you are not a flat man. I know it's a sign of your gray mood that you could listen to Vicki chat with the airline stewardess about nail polish and still think she might be a lifetime companion but really—

I know that some of Frank Bascombe's literary admirers have called him a fine example of an alienated man—as if Camus's *étranger* had dropped down into a suburban community in New Jersey. It may be no accident that Frank has named his current time of life "an existence period." This may be a nod to Jean-Paul and Paris. But Frank's period is not quite like Picasso's blue period and is a lot more like the Dark Ages, during which time certain monks guarded the manuscripts from ancient Greece while others painted flowers on the margins of prayer books and literacy itself was nearly extinguished.

In fact *alienation* is not the right word at all. Frank is just plain old-fashioned worn out and sad, the way we were before we became creatures of the pharmaceutical companies and so many were given labels to wear with their sorrows. Frank is running down. Not like an economy on the skids but like a man in a funk, a man in a blue period, a man who has lost his joy but is holding on, who has occasional thoughts of suicide and murder but who holds himself still, sidelined from action, depressed, under a cloud, sad. No pick-me-ups in bars, no lays in the hay, no Prozac will cure his depression. He is waving at us while drowning and there is the philosophical quandary. The wave itself, the book we are reading, is a sign of life, an effective antidepressant. The depression we see is in the process of evaporating because we can see it.

The tawdry town Fourth of July celebration, which has its sentimental sweetness about it, its marshals in costume, its parade watchers, its bunting on the poles, its burghers wearing tricornered hats, its red-white-and-blue waving, might be causing our old sourpuss to smile, to dance a little. The combination of business and idealism that is America is not so bad after all. Frank can find his way out of his foggy swamp if he tries just a little harder. Independence is not what he needs. A hug is what he needs, a folding into the other is what he needs, his child in his home is what he needs, a woman who will admire and cherish him is what he needs.

He thinks he might be entering a permanence period but that's silly. Nothing is permanent, everything changes, one just needs to be light-footed, quick-fingered enough to change with the changes as long as breath lasts. Frank I know you can make it—I know you can do it. Go back to writing it down, go back to telling a story. For some of us that's the only way to keep our heads afloat.

Will God rock you in his arms? Not likely. Will you sell real estate for the rest of your life? Not likely. I am hopeful for you, not for the reasons you gave me but for the things I know about you, the way the love in you and the sex in you refuse to fizzle out no matter how damp the conditions.

Also I think you should move away from Haddam (suburbs are in themselves depressing), maybe north where the snow is deep and the trees are tall and evergreen and small wood creatures leave tracks in the dirt and the birds fly high above, black winged and beady eyed. Perhaps you would like the shore where the seals bask on rocks, their newborn by their side, spring after spring. Maybe you would like the cold morning air in August and the Northern Lights tilting up toward Orion's belt, disappearing somewhere over Canada.

• • • •

I would be an old lady and I should go down South instead of up North but I can't. I need the crispness. I need to feel the ice age still receding or is it coming? I will have a small house. As an unexpected but pleasant surprise you will be my neighbor. There you are, the man I met on the stream fishing one afternoon years ago. I don't fish anymore. My ankles are unreliable, my arms not so strong. But I walk by the river. Early in the morning I can often find you there. This is good. You are older now. Your body moves lightly as if some irritation has been lifted. Was that the meaning of our mutual fish—we would be neighbors?

Perhaps you will bring your pages over for my comments. Or if you have given up writing you may have taken to building sailboats or making harpsichords or maybe you work for the state checking pollutants in the rivers and the potato fields. Perhaps I will not be senile and still have interesting things to say. I will be old and have hair on my chin and my teeth will be yellow. You will be my younger friend who brings me my mail when the road has not yet been plowed. I will bake treats for you and your wife and your children. Yes, you will have more children who will in their turn give you nightmares and cause your old ulcers to wake.

A man can have several families in a lifetime. Things that are broken are not always fixed but new things can be formed. We are capable of newness, renewal, change; men can go on having babies forever. This is not a recommendation, it's a fact, a biological fact having nothing to do with gender equality or ultimate justice, but there it is.

You can marry a painter or a violinist or a historian of the Middle Ages who teaches at a nearby college, a gentle woman grateful for the vein of affection you are always willing to open for her, a woman who leaves you alone at those times when the old blues return. She has no doubt that you will come back to her, flowers in hand, willing to go dance at the local hotel, or see the performance of *As You Like It* at the high school. The church spire will be visible from your house. The mosses on the tree outside your window will be deep green. You will own a black Lab with a soft pink drooly mouth and an ear half torn off by a quail defending her nest, a Lab who rides in the back of your pickup and smells of soil and rabbit and the apples that have tumbled to the earth, and one morning when you come to bring me some chopped wood, worrying that I might not have enough for a fire, you will find me gone and feel truly sad, not depressed, just sad the way a person should feel when an absence comes. Your children including Clarissa and Paul will be at my funeral. The thought makes me happy.

.   .   .   .

7

Max and
...... Mickey ......

Max and His Alter Ego, Twin Brother, or Earlier Self, Mickey

Maurice Sendak's
Where the Wild Things Are and
In the Night Kitchen

Puppy dogs' tails, snails, and other nongourmet items.

T h e r e is nothing obviously appealing about Max. He is not beautiful and sweet like Little Lord Fauntleroy. He is not gentle and well mannered and British and fond of walks in the forest with his cuddly friends, like that most adorable, perhaps too adorable, Christopher Robin who seems badly in need of a Christmas gift of Power Rangers. He is not a lover of a single red rose like Saint-Exupéry's Little Prince. He is not a servant of Christ (in the form of a Lion) like the good brothers and sisters in C. S. Lewis's chronicle about witches and wardrobes. He has no bag of magic tricks like the current darling of the Western world, Harry Potter. He is just a not very well-behaved little American boy who dresses up in his wolf costume and chases the terrified dog with a fork and hangs his teddy bear by the neck and informs his mother he will eat her up when she calls him, not (any reasonable person would admit) without justification, "a Wild Thing."

The expression on his face is hardly winning. This is a kid who couldn't sell you soup, Jell-O, or jeans if his life depended on it. He's no glad-hander, social charmer like Dick Diver, or war hero like Robert Jordan. He scowls and he pouts and he is just about as friendly as an iguana and you wouldn't want to take him to tea, not in a public place anyway, not if you wanted to keep your temper. If he were in an orphanage and you'd come to take one home, you'd leave him there if he were the last child on the premises.

But Max is the true thing, a boy revealed, a boy with gender male written all over his discontented little face. Trouble, that's what he is. Full of it, racing and bouncing with it, a *no* to sitting still, a *no* to being gentle with the dog, a *no no* to whatever you want him to wear, and a loud *NO* to having his face washed or his weekly shampoo—a male ready to strike out into the rough terrain beyond the front steps, to go to war, to go out with the guys and get drunk as hell, to take the car up to ninety on the highway, to hunt buffalo or whales or IPOs, if only he weren't too small, not ready, not just yet.

So the thing is that a woman, a mother, his mother of course, but also a woman who is not his mother, or maybe anybody else's mother, has to see in him the maleness of the man to come, and hold him dear, dearest in fact. Here's why.

When Max is in his wolf suit, a costume that transforms him from good little boy to predatory beast, he dangles his teddy bear from a wire hanger and makes a tent out of his blanket. Both of these, teddy and blanket, are precious objects. Psychoanalysts call them transitional objects. They are endowed by the child with the magic, the odor, the essence of mother, the protective, caring, holding of mother. So when you see a kid in the stroller with some ratty smelly piece of cloth or clutching a stuffed toy that looks as if it's been on several tours of duty in Vietnam, you know that the child is holding on to its mother even if mother has gone out to work or is in the kitchen or just behind the kid at the supermarket checkout counter. This endowing of a doll or a blanket with special soothing saving power is perhaps the first act of human creativity that will bring us to the stained-glass rose window at Notre Dame, a Mozart concerto, a Picasso, *Hamlet*, and all the other stuff that invents, transforms, reflects the glory and the anguish of our days. We make a neutral inanimate object a symbol for something else and then we comfort ourselves with our own invention. And this in the first two years of our lives: marvelous creatures we.

When babies discover, as all of them must, that mother has a will of her own and is not connected to their bodies, not obligated to fulfill baby's every wish, might in fact abandon or neglect (like Rabbit's wife Janice who drowned her baby while in a drunken state), the child invents a mother substitute, a mother who can give comfort when the real one fails. So when Max strangles his teddy, turns his blanket into a tent, symbol of outdoor (out of home) adventure, something serious is up. He is mad. You can see it on his face. He's not mad at a friend or the unfortunate dog. He's mad at his mother. That's why he's acting like a monster.

In the first year a baby never ever shows random aggression. The hunger crying may get angry, the protest at a soaking diaper may have an irritable twinge, but anger, aggression for no reason—that comes a little later. At first the baby assumes that the mother is like a limb of itself, one that covers with a blanket when cold, brings food when hungry, and rocks when needed. Gradually the baby learns from bitter experience that the mother is a separate being, one who comes but perhaps not as soon as wanted, who supplies, but imperfectly, what is needed. When a baby of eight months or so turns its head away from a stranger and wails, we know that baby now understands that mother is not self and self is not mother and the perilous lonely journey toward personhood has begun. If mother can walk away baby can be abandoned and will not survive. This perception brings terror. And who is to blame for this terror but mother herself or her substitute?

As soon as a baby realizes that mother is not its creature but (bad news follows bad news) that the situation is exactly reversed, anger shows up for no reason at all, a pinch, a hair pull, a kick will come out of the blue. The sweetest of babies will take a sudden hard bite of maternal flesh. What was before a sweet cooing, a babble of happy sounds, now takes on a sour note at least from time to time. It is hard to be angry at the person you need most. Little boys in wolf suits arise out of our fear of being alone, being abandoned: aggression is born out of our rage provoked by our own helplessness. Evil is not a visitor from other parts. It is not a bad blow from a tropical storm. It is not a snake in our otherwise peaceful garden and never a Satan with a pitchfork and horns. It is born out of our fear of abandonment. It is born out of our fear of not being able to force those we need to take care of us. If you can't dominate your mother, she just might leave you, and that thought surely provokes a temper tantrum, maybe a thousand temper tantrums, maybe even a big bang (after all, the one-celled amoeba evolved into Jascha Heifetz).

I remember being afraid of a large giant that slumbered above the windows in my childhood room. In the semi-dark I could see his shape, a long arm hanging down, a body stretched out, maybe he would wake up and crush me in a large hand. In the day I could see that my giant was nothing more than the curtain valance. The piece of curtain that hung straight down formed his arm but night after night he reappeared, my giant. I stared in fright at his menacing hulk. In my closet there was a witch. In the daytime she wasn't there but at night I knew somewhere behind the coats and the hat boxes and the old blankets she was there and she meant no good and her green face and long fingers pressed themselves against the door no matter how firmly it was closed. I remember fear of Wild Things that seemed to make their homes under the carpet, slithery oozing, fishlike things that had sharp teeth and were ready to bite me. I couldn't like Max stare at them and not blink and shout at them to be still. I closed my eyes fiercely and held my breath and kept my body very still in hopes they wouldn't notice me. What were they and why were they there? Now I know. Little bits and pieces of my own anger had become transformed into creatures of the other world who would attack me. That's a sleight of brain the human child achieves all too easily. For most of us the giants and the witches disappear for good and we learn to be angry without attacking ourselves with demons in the bedroom, except in dreams which is another story.

Max in his wolf suit is mad at his mother (we don't know what she did to him but for sure she foiled his wish and reminded him that he is vulnerable and under her law not his own) and he says, "I will eat you up," meaning I will destroy you and also have you inside of me forever whenever I need you. Mother naturally (off stage) gets mad back and sends Max to his room without his supper.

Negotiating this problem of separation and reunion, being angry at someone you need to give you supper, is the crucible, the hot forge of the human personality. Males have a real hard time with their desire to curl up in mommy's lap and the counter pull to reject her, hurt her and move off into the world.

This is Max's story: In his room he sails away from mother through night and day and in and out of weeks and almost over a year to where the Wild Things are. He does not stop to ask directions.

The Wild Things have horns and tails and scales and bristling hairs and very very sharp teeth and claws, part bull, lion, and dragon. When Max first sees them they roar their terrible roars and gnash their terrible teeth. But Max tames them by yelling at them to "be still" (how many times has Max's mother yelled at him with the very same command?) and then Max conquers the beasts by staring into their eyes without blinking and the wild things respectfully call him the Most Wild Thing of all. He has stared at the others and made them his servants by overcoming his fear, not blinking, not flinching but holding his ground, a warrior he.

The Wild Things make him king and now besides his wolf suit he wears a golden crown and holds a scepter in his hand. They have a huge rumpus and a wild party, a kind of frat boys' shindig without girls, a sort of after-the-football-game celebration. Finally Max sends the Wild Things off to bed without their supper, doing to them what was done to him. Ah what satisfaction that role reversal brings. Then Max smells good things to eat and he gives up being the king of where the Wild Things are because "he is lonely and wanted to be where someone loved him best of all."

Would not Holden, and Rabbit, Nathan and Frank, understand that? Robert Jordan was briefly where someone loved him best of all (a sleeping bag outside a cave in the mountains of Spain, but then he had to sail a year and a day and blow up a bridge and die). Dick Diver went so far away he got permanently lost. Rabbit wanted to be home with his mother in her kitchen eating cookies and says so often. Nathan speaks of wishing he could curl up marsupial-like in the pocket of his mother's fur coat. At the same time the domestic scene is experienced as a restraint. Holden wants to flee to a cabin in the woods. Rabbit is forever and at just the worst times getting in his car and heading south or running about the neighborhood as if motion itself were a solution. Dick Diver goes to Europe, and once in Europe moves from one resort to another, from one country to another. Whenever things become difficult he changes locale. All of these characters (except Holden who isn't old enough yet) dally, betray, run off in one way or another with women other than their wives who serve as the boats that will sail them off for a year and a day. Frank is grieved and angered by his son's death and he sails away to a New England college, to bed with whoever will have him. Our novelists tell us again and again, in different plots with different characters, that closeness is hard, adventure beckons, staying in place threatens the self, leaving makes you intolerably lonely, domesticity makes you furious, there is much to lose if you stay home and everything to lose if you run away. The child wants his mother but will never have his manhood if he stays with her. The man never stops wanting to be loved no matter how oddly he is behaving. Alcohol, a vast quantity of it, is poured over the problem to dull the wit, to cut the pain, to ease the fright, to make it possible for these men to go out into the world. We are marvelous creatures but with drawbacks, kinks, blemishes.

The Wild Things cry, "Oh please don't go, we'll eat you up we love you so." But Max says no and goes back to his own room where he finds his supper waiting for him. In the last picture he is still wearing his wolf suit but now he is smiling, not exactly sweetly but smiling nevertheless. For now at least he's happy to be home.

The wolf suit is an important detail in this story. Wolves are central to every literate child's fantasy life. There are two main wolves and of course many others. The first is Little Red Riding Hood's wolf. The wolf eats up the grandmother and comes very close to devouring Little Red Riding Hood who is visiting her grandmother. The second devouring wolf is the one who huffs and puffs and blows the Little Pigs' homes down, except for the Little Pig that builds his house of bricks and saves everyone. At the door is the big-toothed wild-eyed beast of a wolf ready to have his dinner. Every child identifies with Little Red Riding Hood and with the Little Pigs. Only potential serial killers identify with the wolf (and I'm not so sure about that). So when Max puts on his wolf suit he is becoming his worst fear. He is now the thing he is afraid of. How clever a way not to be afraid, how clearly it tells us that he is afraid.

Yes, I love Max. Max is male to the core, male to the nth degree, male in trouble with the authorities, male who wants to subdue the others, dominate, be king, who must go away from home in order to exercise his power but soon enough gets hungry and wants to be where someone loves him best of all.

This description does sound like a model of a prefeminist man, a commuter off to do business in the city but who will return each night to his wife who will have his supper ready. In part yes. But this behavior is also male for all times, our times, for at least as far out as we can imagine, male who has the irrepressible energy, the desire to break the rules, to turn something upside down, to make mischief with the proper order of things, to become king, to dominate everything around, to sail away and find new lands and dare and dare again. That this male will also chase the dog with a fork, will sass his mother and sulk in his room, have affairs like Rabbit or Frank, complain like Nathan about ex-girlfriends, admit that he needs his sister when he can't admit he needs his mother like Holden, well so be it.

Women have their own adventures, little girls have their own ways of becoming adults. The point here is not that women must stay at home and make supper but that men, males, need us, grow lonely for us, want to be where someone loves them best of all. Little girls also struggle with the wild things within, the wild things without, the journey out and away from home. The illustrations that accompany their stories would just be somewhat different.

• • • •

Perhaps I had a play date with Max. We are in the same nursery school class and he likes to play with girls and I like to play with boys. Neither of us knows yet that such things can have dire consequences. Max's mother gives us lunch, peanut butter and jelly sandwiches, and accidentally reaching across the table to poke me in the chest Max spills the milk. His mother is not amused. The milk spills on my pink jeans. I hold back tears. Max's mother wipes me clean. Max does not like it that his mother is patting me with a wet cloth. On his way to putting his plate in the sink, he kicks me. I don't really mind. It's not a hard kick just a little one to tell me that his mother is his not mine. Then we go up to his room. Max has an idea. We go into his closet to play doctor. He is the doctor and I am the patient. I have a stomachache. He pulls up my shirt and says he has to see my belly. I pull down my pants. My underpants have little red roses on them. He says he can't tell what's wrong with me while I wear those pants. I take them off. I suddenly feel cold. I giggle. Max has a toy stethoscope. He puts it you know where. I wiggle. "Be still," he commands me. I want to be the doctor I say. He takes off his pants. Just then his mother opens the closet door. She has a very angry expression on her face. "Get dressed," she says. "Right now," she adds. "I'm going to call your mother," she says to me. Max and I are silent. We are worried.

Max says come with me to the land where the Wild Things are. I sail off with him in his boat. It takes a long time but when we get there, the Wild Things are on the shore breathing smoke and fire in our faces. Max takes my hand and we party. He is the king and I am the queen. Then the Wild Thing he is riding rears up and he falls off. He bumps his nose. His nose is red. There is a blood spot on his shirt. He begins to cry. I get off my Wild Thing, take off my queen crown, and put on my nurse's hat. I get water and wet a leaf and hold it to his nose. I pat his hand. He stops crying. I kiss his nose. "All better," I say. We sail back to his room. My mother has come to take me home. She says: "Why do you have that silly nurse's hat on? You could be a doctor if you want." "I know, I know," I say.

* * * *

It has a kind of charm, this Max on his little boat sailing a year and a day to a place where he can be free from his mother's restraint, where he can pretend for a while he doesn't need her so badly, where his male soul can be king. I have never loved a man in whom I could not see Max in his wolf costume peering through the overlay of adult concerns. It has to do with the source of energy, the flame of self-invention, the right stuff to get to the moon, the office, the bank, the university, to survive in the whole dangerous, noisy, interesting land where the Wild Things are real enough and there is a rumpus all the time.

The man I live with in his profession as a psychoanalyst spends every day staring at the Wild Things, not blinking. He also drives too fast, swears at other cars that dare to be traveling in our direction, share our road. He has a temper. He will not be still. His wolf suit has many rips in it by now, but it serves its purpose well enough. As Freud said, as Hobbes said, man has to give up satisfying all his instincts in order to live in a civilized society and be safe from Wild Things—or safer at least. A boy has to learn to put his wolf suit away in the closet and play by the rules. But a man who hasn't kept that wolf suit, maybe smelling a bit of mothballs, taken it along as he moved from childhood home to college dorm to a place of his own, isn't much of a man at all.

One of those Wild Things is grief. Rabbit feels grief and guilt for his baby daughter drowned by his wife when she becomes drunk because Rabbit has once again run off. Frank feels guilt and grief for his dead son who died of Reye's disease and whose death destroys the family in part because Frank turns away from his wife instead of toward her, as if the death were her fault. Dick Diver loses his children as certainly as if they had died because he has no worldly power, because he has let himself go to seed and drink. Nathan is undone and forced into marriage with a woman he cannot stand because she claims she is pregnant. In this case it is a false invented child, but nevertheless the idea of the child ruins him for a long while. Robert Jordan is furious about the death of his father who killed himself. He is grieving but in anger. And Holden, grief is his Wild Thing, the one that is riding him right out of school after school. Death is the thing he cannot accept.

Max when his time comes will also probably not be able to tame that Wild Thing, to grieve without destroying or trampling on much that is valuable. For now Max is all bravado and he can tame the Wild Things but when he grows up they will be harder to keep still, to keep on a distant island. Some of them will move right into the house, scales and horns and all. In children's books we hint at the truth, we foreshadow the reality of grown-up life, but we don't (what child could stand it?) tell them everything. At some point everybody learns that you can't leave the Wild Things behind on an island and go home. Max's turn for that discovery will come.

• •

Max has an alter ego or a younger brother in Mickey, Mickey of *In the Night Kitchen*. You can tell they are related if you look at their faces. Mickey is younger, more rounded in the cheeks, but they are really one and the same, boys on the same track, in the same dream.

Mickey trying to sleep in his bed (or is he dreaming?) hears a racket down below and shouts out, "Quiet down there." Then he falls through the dark and out of his pajamas and floats past his mama and papa's door into the light of the night kitchen, right into the batter where the bakers who bake 'til the dawn so we can have cake in the morn are stirring the batter and chanting, "Stir it, scrape it, make it, bake it." You can hear the echo of the mother and baby pat-a-cake rhyme, "We'll pat it and roll it and mark it with M and put it in the oven for Mickey and me." The bakers all three of them are apparently triplets of Laurel, from Laurel and Hardy, a tipoff that something funny and something nasty is about to happen.

The bakers are about to put Mickey in the batter into the oven. But at just the last minute Mickey pops out of the cake and says, "I'm not the milk and the milk's not me. I'm Mickey." What a grand assertion of self, right at the edge of being cooked and eaten. Mickey insists on his own identity. He jumps into bread dough waiting to rise and punches it into the shape of a propeller airplane that he can fly away in. This isn't easy as we can see by Mickey's slightly demonic grimaces and tugs and frowns as he works at making his airplane.

Mickey is up in the plane, a sort of cookie-made Sopwith Camel, when the bakers run up demanding milk for the morning cake. Mickey grabs the measuring cup and now becomes the rescuer, the save-the-dire-situation hero of the night kitchen. He flies over the Milky Way and lands in a huge bottle of milk and he dives down to the bottom singing, "I'm in the milk and the milk's in me, God bless milk and God bless me." In the milk bottle he loses his cookie clothes and is again floating naked. He swims up to the top of the bottle and pours milk from his cup into the batter below, and the happy bakers make their cake and naked Mickey pretends to be a rooster and slides back into bed carefree and dried, back in his pajamas. His last word as he falls asleep is "Yum." He's anticipating his breakfast no doubt.

A psychoanalyst, Dr. Ellen Handler Spitz, has pointed out that the sounds, bumps, and thumps Mickey first hears may be the primal scene: the kid listening at night and feeling excluded while his parents are doing something loud and a little frightening to each other. As Mickey floats down to the night kitchen, he is first on his stomach and then on his back taking the positions of both parents in the common image of a sexual act. "Ah" and "oh" he says—being both mama and papa at once. (Meg Ryan's Sally would have said, "Yes.")

What certainly is true is that being eaten and eating are very much on Mickey's mind. He breaks himself free of the batter and extricating himself from a pile of dough he builds his own escape vehicle and turns from victim of the joke to hero. He flies to the extraordinarily tall, statuesque bottle of milk, a mother turned into a bottle of milk, the most remarkable building of them all in the night kitchen. The bottle of course could be a breast towering above, the way an infant might conceive of it. The bottle could also be the entire mother, the way a child could see her, the source of nourishment, the large object necessary for all life, milk as the source of goodness. Mickey pours the milk out of the bottle himself. He is no longer the helpless baby who must wait for Mama but becomes the active hero, the pilot, the adventurer, the confident source of his own breakfast, the source of others' nourishment. Mickey turns from a potential piece of cake into the one who feeds, who brings back nourishment. How lucky we are to have Mickey.

Philip Roth has written a book that put most critics in a terrible pout when it first appeared called *The Breast.* In it the hero, David Kepesh, turns himself into a literal 155-pound breast, a mound of flesh with a sensitive nipple at the top, losing mobility, self, and becomes hospitalized, helpless, a male soul imprisoned in a large breast. This is a joke sort of, a play with Kafka's metamorphosis, but it is also a kind of grisly expression of a primordial fear. The female breast will take over and absorb the male who will lose autonomy, self, life itself. So while men may love to fondle, suck, look at female breasts, they also fear them. There is something about the breast, source of life-giving milk, that never becomes as neutral as a pinky or an ankle, remains a symbolic substitute for the whole mother. While Mickey floats in the bottle of milk, he does not become the milk (that's Roth's fantasy not Sendak's). But he plays with the same metaphor: the milk is mother and I am in mother not separate from her. This prompts Mickey to rise to the top, pour the milk, and become a helper in the kitchen. Otherwise he might drown.

If God made man from dirt why can't Mickey give birth to himself from bread dough? There is danger in the night kitchen: a child could be cooked and eaten. There is also triumph for the brave and the forceful and the determined. The message is clear: if your parents are too busy making noises in the next room to pay attention to you then you can take care of yourself if need be. While he floats in the bottle naked, Mickey might be the baby in utero drifting around without direction, but once he floats to the top and pours the milk down to the baker, well then he is no longer in Mama but himself the source of her power.

When my grandson was four I picked him up from nursery school and as we walked down West End Avenue to my house, we would play a game. He would say, "I am a boa constrictor and I am going to swallow you whole," and I would answer, "I will change into a hawk and I will snip your head off," and he would answer, "But I will change into a condor and catch you in my claws," and I would say, "I will become an archer and shoot you with an arrow," and he answers, "I will change into a panther and I will eat you up," and I would change into a tree that falls on the panther's head, then he would be an elephant and remove the tree with his trunk and step on me, and I would change into a mouse that would frighten the elephant who would run off a cliff, and so it would go until one of us gave up—usually me. The game was about power and about eating up the other one. It was a good game, horrid in its way but very satisfying to both of us. Max would understand.

This fear of being eaten is primitive. Perhaps it has survived from the days when wild beasts would dismember us to take home to their young for lunch, or perhaps it is a built-in mental error: I am what I eat, what I eat is me. Anthropologists are full of such tales, and totems prove them right. When Mickey says the milk's in me and I'm in the milk, perhaps he means because I drink milk I am milk. This is like a native on a far-off atoll wearing a mask of a fish head. Either way it makes women, in whom every male once resided like Mickey in the milk bottle, a potential consumer of the product, potentially overwhelming, dangerous as all hell. Max too insults his mother with the threat of eating her up and ignores the same threat by the Wild Things who wish to keep him.

All men are born of women and most need them ever after—as mothers, as mates, as companions or friends or colleagues or daughters or nurses or investment bankers. Sometimes all of the above at once. In the early days of the feminist movement we said that we females didn't want to be cows, not anymore, not like that. And we had a good point, long ago argued and long ago accepted in most parts of our American landscape. But biology has its own imperatives and a bit cowlike we are no matter how we try to get away from it, and Mickey has a hard time not viewing us either as the bottle that will recapture him, take away his free flight, or as the source of the thing he must have, the nourishment he needs.

Max didn't need to take his sister along on his sailboat to a place where the Wild Things made him king. Mickey had no female companion in his bottle. He managed to survive and help the cooks without any female advice or any Princess Leia swordplay. This maleness of men, a place within where we are not wanted, where when you ask "What are you thinking about?" and they say with an irritable shake of the head, "Nothing," is just there, like the moon waxing and waning whether we like it or not.

The guys need us, want us, require us, but don't want to get too stuck, devoured, chained. They need a place where they are the most beloved and they need and long for some end to loneliness and they can't help but view that very place as a threat to their free miles.

Max and Mickey are literary boys, not as complex as Tom Sawyer and Huck Finn but just as eager to get out into the world as any other hero in our large library. Rabbit and Frank and Nathan, Robert Jordan and Dick Diver, Holden of course, what are they, after all, but Max and Mickey writ large, grown older, each with the particularities of his time and place? What woman wouldn't welcome any of them home into her heart? What woman wouldn't shout at any of them, "Be still." Ah men, the sweetness and ferocity of them, the salty taste, the neediness, the difficulty of them, the tragicomedy of them. "The milk's in me and I'm in the milk." Well yes.